W9-DIM-762

SHAKESPEARE'S SPEECH-HEADINGS

SHAKESPEARE'S SPEECH-HEADINGS

Speaking the Speech in Shakespeare's Plays

The Papers of the Seminar in Textual Studies
Shakespeare Association of America, March 29, 1986
Montreal

Edited by

George Walton Williams

DELAWARE

Newark
University of Delaware Press
London: Associated University Presses

Associated University Presses
440 Forsgate Drive
Cranbury, NJ 08512

Associated University Presses
16 Barter Street
London WC1A 2AH, England

Associated University Presses
P.O. Box 338, Port Credit
Mississauga, Ontario
Canada L5G 4L8

The paper used in this publication meets the requirements of the American National Standard for Permanence of Paper for Printed Library Materials Z39.48–1984.

Library of Congress Cataloging-in-Publication Data

Seminar in Textual Studies (1986 : Montréal, Québec)
    Shakespeare's speech-headings : speaking the speech in Shakespeare's plays: the papers of the Seminar in Textual Studies, Shakespeare Association of America, March 29, 1986, Montreal / edited by George Walton Williams.
        (AMS studies in the Renaissance ; no. 25)
    Includes bibliographical references and index.
    ISBN 0-87413-637-7
    1. Shakespeare, William, 1564–1616—Criticism, Textual—Congresses. I. Williams, George Walton, 1922–
II. Shakespeare Association of America. III. Title. IV. Series.
PR3071.S45 1997
822.3'3—dc20   87-45811
                                                                   CIP

N.B.: There is no missing text between pages 130 and 133.

In memoriam

John Hazel Smith
(1928–1986)

Contents

Participants

A. R. Braunmuller, *University of California, Los Angeles*

Thomas Clayton, *University of Minnesota*

T. H. Howard-Hill, *University of South Carolina*

William B. Long, *Independent Scholar*

Charles B. Lower, *University of Georgia*

Randall McLeod, *University of Toronto (Erindale College)*

Richard Proudfoot, *University of California, Los Angeles, and University of London (King's College)*

John Hazel Smith, *Brandeis University*

Sidney Thomas, *Syracuse University*

Robert Kean Turner, *University of Wisconsin-Milwaukee*

Steven Urkowitz, *Hofstra University / City College of the City University of New York*

Michael Warren, *University of California, Santa Cruz (Cowell College)*

Paul Werstine, *University of Western Ontario (King's College)*

George Walton Williams, *Duke University* (Convener)

FOREWORD

The University of Delaware Press is proud to present this collection of essays on Shakespeare's speech headings written by a number of outstanding textual scholars in England and America, collected and introduced by Professor George Walton Williams.

The essays, written and ready for publication by 1990, fortunately require no substantial updating or amendments. Originally to be published by AMS Press, which prepared the camera-ready copy, the collection has not appeared until now, although its long delay has occurred through no fault of either the contributors or their editor. References to the forthcoming publication by AMS in such books as Laurie McGuire's *Shakespeare's Suspect Texts,* are now inevitably in error, again through no fault of the authors. Future references, we trust, will recognize the actual publisher.

Jay L. Halio, Chair
Board of Editors
University of Delaware Press

ACKNOWLEDGMENTS

I am particularly grateful to C. B. Lower and to R. K. Turner for their notes of the discussion at the Seminar in Montreal and to A. R. Braunmuller, William B. Long, and R. K. Turner for their willingness to read through the "Preface" and to suggest improvements.

I acknowledge also the kindness of the Trustees of Amherst College and the Folger Shakespeare Library for permission to reproduce prints of the First Folio and *The Two Noble Kinsmen* from items in their collections.

Acknowledgement is also made to W. W. Norton & Company for permission to reprint material from *The Norton Facsimile: The First Folio of Shakespeare,* edited by Charlton Hinman, © 1968 by W. W. Norton & Co.

The production of the volume has been assisted by Dr. Peter Batke, formerly Senior Research Associate, Humanities Computing Facilities, Duke University, and by Katherine Sabre, Henry Schwartz, and Rebecca Hyman. I am cognizant also of the help of Professor Frank Borchardt in matters of technical support.

This collection is dedicated to the memory of our good friend and learned colleague who, though he attended the Annual Meeting of the Association in 1986, did not join us at the Seminar table, preferring, while yet he could, to enjoy the beauty of the world of nature and to be "walking on the Workes" and seeing the Fortifications of the city of Montreal. He has done the state some service and they know it.

G. W. W.

Preface—by Way of a Prefix

George Walton Williams

This volume contains the papers presented at the Textual Seminar of the Shakespeare Association of America, held in Montreal, March 27–29, 1986, on the topic: "Speech-Headings: The Bibliographer, the Editor, and the Critic." They concentrate on speech prefixes in printed and manuscript plays of Shakespeare and his contemporaries, but they also cite illustrations from dramatists of later periods as well. They examine the evidence provided by these little designators as it applies to the nature of the text, the performance, the acting companies, and the audience; they consider also authorial, scribal, and compositorial variations in these forms as they may bear on our understanding of the text and its transmission. They treat editorial problems deriving from the absence of necessary prefixes. And they note the special effects of Prefixes that identify characters by simple number or by the names of the actors.

The "set text" for the seminar was R. B. McKerrow's influential paper "A Suggestion Regarding Shakespeare's Manuscripts,"printed in *The Review of English Studies*, XI (1935), 459–65. That "Suggestion" considered the fact that some printed texts of Shakespeare's plays exhibited irregularity in the designations of speakers' names and that some did not. McKerrow suggested that on the one hand a play exhibiting this kind of irregularity must have been set up from holograph in which the author's emphases on the various aspects of each character in relation to the business of the scene produced variant speech-headings, and that on the other hand a play exhibiting regularity in speakers' names must have been set up from a faircopy, one in which a scribe had regularized the names of the speakers, had imposed a "formal consistency" upon the irregularities of the author. He would have done so, presumably, in order to prepare the prompt book for the bookkeeper to use in performance. (Less frequently—and McKerrow was not sure of this point—he might have been preparing a clean copy for a patron.) The basic assumption supporting the "Suggestion" was that "in any case a copy intended for use in the theatre would surely, of necessity, be accurate and unambiguous in the matter of the character-names" (p. 464). The importance of McKerrow's "Suggestion," which was adopted by Greg (as Werstine notes), has been considerable.

The seminar tested the hypothesis in two of its aspects: (a) that prompt-books must have been regular, and (b) that irregularities in printed copies must derive from author's holograph. That the first aspect of the basic assumption is unwarranted, the papers by Clayton, Long, and McCleod clearly reveal. Many texts printed from prompt books have such variation. Strange as it may seem to editors in their studies, prompters in their theaters managed (and still do manage) to identify characters correctly even when they appear under different names; but Long very reasonably reminds us that for a spectator there is no problem: no matter what shape the speech prefixes may have taken in the manuscripts or printed copies used as prompt books, the actor in the flesh did not change.

As to the second point, Werstine has demonstrated in his paper that prefixes in at least one text, showing the kind of variation McKerrow assumed to have been authorial, were in fact altered by the censor and that other variations were copied or introduced by the scribe. Clayton notes one change in "Sir Thomas More" that is the work of the scribe. Had prints from these two manuscripts come under McKerrow's eye, he must have assumed that the irregularities were in both cases authorial.

What then shall be made of McKerrow's assumption that—to be specific—the varying prefixes in the authoritative quarto (Q2) of *Romeo and Juliet* (1599) demonstrate that the copy was authorial? We must conclude that on the basis of such evidence alone the thesis cannot be sustained. For that text, however, there is other evidence—that from the presence of Shakespeare's "first and second versions" for particular passages throughout the play. These argue persuasively that the manuscript underlying Q2 was holograph uncorrected by scribe or bookkeeper. On the basis of such evidence we may examine the varying prefixes in that quarto with confidence that we are indeed dealing with a print from hologragh.

The most striking example of the irregularity of prefixes in *Romeo and Juliet* (Q2) is the record for Capulet's Wife, and these prefixes have excited the most critical comment. In the ten scenes in Q2 in which Capulet's Wife appears, there are 45 prefixes for the character. Four of these (I. iii. 1, 7, 12, 15) are reprints of Q1 "*VVife*"; as these cannot reflect the manuscript underlying Q2, they are excluded from the following analysis.[1] The remaining 41 represent five different functions, appearing as some form or abbreviation of *Mother* (16); of *Lady* (13); of *Old Lady* (6); of *Wife* (4); of *Capulet's Wife* (2). Generally the forms *Mother, Lady, Old Lady* occur in the seven domestic scenes of the play where the character appears as Juliet's Mother, as manager of the housekeeping, and as Capulet's Wife; the forms *Wife* and *Capulet's Wife* generally occur in the three public or street scenes where the character appears as the wife of a citizen and a representative of the family. In each of five of the domestic scenes, one of the forms is used exclusively, and in each of two of the domestic scenes (III. v, I. iii), more than one form appears; in each of the public scenes, one of the forms is used exclusively.[2]

The character speaks under some abbreviation of *Mother* in IV. iii, in IV. v, and in IV. In IV. iii, entering as *Mother*, the night before Juliet's wedding, she speaks maternally to her daughter as *Mo.* (6, 12). In IV. v (no entry) she speaks the laments for her daughter's death as *Mo./M.* (though in the first two speeches she is not aware of the nature of the Nurse's "noise" and might as properly be the Lady of the house). In IV. ii, entering with *Father Capulet* as *Mother*, she speaks two speeches to her daughter and to her husband, prefixed *Mo.* (36, 38). (In lines 37, 39, Capulet's prefixes which have been *Capu.* are *Fa.*) (Though these prefixes might seem to reflect parental consideration, the parents' four speeches [ll. 36–39] have to do with domestic or housekeeping arrangements for the wedding; in these matters their daughter, of course, figures as an instrument of only secondary importance.)

Capulet's Wife is designated by some abbreviation of *Lady* in IV. iv and III. iv. In IV. iv, entering as *Lady of the House*, she acts primarily in her domestic capacity. Her speeches addressed

to Nurse and to Capulet deal with housekeeping; the prefixes are *La.*(1,11) (through an argument could be made at line
11 that she is more wifely then domestic). In III.iv, entering
with Capulet as *his Wife,* she speaks in a formal setting in her
capacity as Mother of the prospective bride with the prefix *La.*
(10).

In III. v and I. iii Prefixes vary within the scene. In III. v,
entering as *Mother* (and termed "Lady Mother" by Nurse and
Juliet), Capulet's Wife is *La.* in lines 64–88, *Mo./M.* in lines
104–25, *La.* in 140, 158, *Wi.* in line 176, and *Mo.* in line 204.
An argument can be advanced that in this scene we have
Shakespeare laboring to prove McKerrow right; he does not
entirely succeed. Capulet's Wife, speaking first of the family's
need to avenge Tybalt's death, is *La.* (64–88). When the topic
changes to Juliet's marriage (a matter just as political as the
other), she is *Mo./M.* (104–25). When, referring to her husband, she addresses him (139, 175) and Juliet (158), she is *La.*
(though her husband has addressed her as "Wife") (137, 141,
164). When she speaks to her husband, she is *Wi.*(176). When
she speaks to Juliet, she is again *Mo.* (204), though her tone
has the bitterness associated with her rejection of her daughter
where the prefixes are *La.* In I. iii (after the reprinted passage)
in the discussion about Juliet's Marriage, she is steadily *Old
La.* (lines 49–96); at the end of the scene, she addresses first
the Servant and then Juliet with the prefix *Mo.*

In the three public scenes of the play, the character's prefixes, reflecting her public or official position, take three forms
which, though variant in shape, are not variant in function:
Capu. Wi. and *Ca. Wi.* (III. i) or *Wife.* (I. i, V. iii) (though an
argument could be made at V. iii. 206 that she is more maternal than official). One would not wish to argue that the differences in prefix form bespeak a distinction between the central
scene III. i and the opening and closing scenes I. i and V. iii.[3]

In short, McKerrow's analysis of the prefix pattern does
not reveal constantly the straightforward linking between a
speaker's prefix and the aspect that we would suppose to have
been dominant in Shakespeare's mind as he wrote a particular
line. In spite of some glaring exceptions in the treatment of

Capulet's Wife—pointed out in the discussion by Thomas—
however, the thesis seems to be correct, though as Werstine
suggests, what was uppermost in Shakespeare's mind cannot
finally be known. Critical attention has focussed on this set of
prefixes, but comparable examples are to be found throughout
the canon. McLeod cites the change from *Countess* to *Old
Countess* in *All's Well*, and Braunmuller notes the curious
change from *Eleanor* to *Queen* to *Eleanor* in folio *King John*.

McKerrow was satisfied that variation in good texts was
attributable to the author,[4] changing as his view of his characters changed. It is arguable that McKerrow was thinking of the
rapid and consecutive writing of lines and scenes, but another
cause of such variation may have been stages of development.
In the discussion, Braunmuller warned against the unfounded
hypothesis that Shakespeare composed seriatim without turning back; he argued that McKerrow's thesis will not explain
the variations of the Queen's prefixes in *King John*, speculat-
ing that they may disclose later additions. One or two other
examples are suggested below. Still in *Romeo and Juliet* Q2, if
we think of the *(Capulet) Wife* prefixes as a first stage—the
writing of the public scenes—we will need to explain the single
Wife prefix in a domestic scene, III. v. If we think of the *(Old)
Lady* prefixes as a second stage—the writing of the scenes of
the Wife's domestic activity (I. iii, III. iv, v, Iv. iv) and of the *Mo.*
prefixes as a third stage—the lines of the most maternal concern in the play, we have to explain in I. iii the *Old Lady* as she
talks to Juliet about marriage to Paris (though she is *Mo.*
when the subject returns in III. v) and the *Mo.* prefixing a
speech divided in address first to the Servant and then to
Juliet. Thomas argues that some of eccentric prefixes in I. iii
are the work of an editor. It may be that the *Old Lady* form in
I. iii evidences Shakespeare's uncertainty in getting into the
part. *Mo.* in I. iii can be explained only by speculation or wild
surmise. It might have been supplied by the author after the
time of original composition, the form of the prefix selected at
random (almost certainly not by the compositor or—in the
opinion of the present writer—probably not by any kind of "editor"). Clearly, a single thesis that strata of composition will

explain the prefix variation is no more adequate than is the single thesis of authorial intention or attitude; some hypothesis, sensitive to many theses, is required before we can think to have solved this problem.

The general sense of the Seminar was that McKerrow's article may no longer be credited with the omniscience once accorded it which, as Werstine shows, became eventually pernicious; and the group turned from considerations of McKerrow to evidences of authorial variation, instances of uncertainty or error, and matters peculiar to the setting of prefixes.

Though variation that is demonstrably authorial may derive from the author's close response to the varying qualities of his characters, it may derive also from his attention to their changes of "political" status, as (to oversimplify) Hal changes his prefix in *2 Henry IV* in Quarto and Folio from *Prince* to *King* (in V. v, but not, interestingly, in V. ii).[5] It may derive from his indifference to the name. It is of concern to Shakespeare that Faulconbridge in *King John* is not called 'Bastard' before he accepts his illegitimacy, but thereafter his prefixes may be forms of *Philip* or *Bastard*, apparently without special significance, as McLeod has shown. Another source of authorial variation may be joint authorship; Proudfoot cites the example of dual authorship and the consequent prefix variation in *Two Noble Kinsmen*.

Such instances of authorial variation may or may not merit editorial intervention, but there are certain situations in texts that suggest actual authorial error and constitute a kind of variant that has misled the compositor and would mislead the actor or reader. There are no doubt many ways in which Shakespeare could have left the speech prefixes in his manuscripts so carelessly that they must have presented difficulties to a compositor and so have occasioned errors of judgment or misreading. Errors in printed texts can be traced to the compositor's failure to understand the proper lineation—an error deriving from the habit of folding the paper as Long has argued,[6] from a damaged left-hand margin as Long and Clayton propose, or from late additions to the text misunderstood as Proudfoot suggests. Perhaps the most prevalent source of error may be the habit of adding prefixes after the author has written out the dialogue fully. There is evidence that this method of composition was sometimes used, and a careless author could (a) impose special forms of character names, or (b) misassign speeches, or (c) add prefixes on the wrong line. Of these possibilities, the last would seem to be the most common.[7] Such mislining may be the cause of some of the individual errors in *Romeo and Juliet* noted by Thomas.

Though we argue here for the integrity of the compositor's work, we must admit that there are, no doubt, errors that are exclusively compositorial; but we must remember that though presumably working under pressure, the average compositor was a man concerned—even in setting play-books—to maintain high standards of workmanship (and so keep his job). Indeed, the argument that some of the primary editions reveal that Shakespeare did vary his prefixes on his own private and unpredictable schedule would seem to require the corollary that the compositors of those editions were following him with care.

In the discussion, Proudfoot and Werstine cited the record of compositorial fidelity in the succession of folios, and one such instance can be found in the transmission of the 45 variant prefixes for Capulet's Wife in Q3, Q4, and F1 (Q3 set from Q2; Q4 and F1 set (independently) from Q3). In the transmission of these 135 prefixes in the three editions by several compositors, though prefixes may vary in the length of the abbreviation, they do not vary in the function: the five different forms are transmitted without change in every instance but two,[8] thus providing a fidelity rate of more than 98%. The same kind of accuracy is found in the succession of the three later Folios. Putting the author's vagaries right would have been the work of but a moment in *Romeo and Juliet*; that work evidently was not done. And that it was not done suggests further that no one thought that it needed to be done. Though it is reasonable to suppose a higher degree of fidelity in reprints than in prints from manuscript, still in the record of historical transmission of these variants which, one may say, cry out for editorial normalizing, no such freedom is to be found. Indeed, there is evidence that some professional reworking took place in readying Q3 for the printing of Q4 and again, and separately, for the printing of F1.[9] Neither of the "editors" took any action to regularize the variant prefixes for Capulet's Wife. There seems to have been from 1609 to 1685 no interest in "formal consistency."

There is unlikely to be final certainty in the definition of the causes for variation and error, whether from authorial behavior or from compositorial misunderstanding or from editorial intrusion The answer must be that variation derived from all of these in varying degrees and at varying times. But the general sense of the seminar was, finally, that the variation that appears in printed copies derives in an overwhelming majority of cases from the condition of the manuscripts that the compositors had before them.

Errors can arise in the compositorial process that do not derive specifically from compositor failure: the process of setting by formes contributed to the error mentioned below by Proudfoot in *Edward III* and to the faulty Q4 *Mer.* for Q3 *M.* cited in footnote 8; and the alternating stints of compositors as they work their way through a text can produce disparity and disagreement.

There are several particularities of these little forms that distinguish them from all other parts of a play-text or that set them off as unique in the work of a compositor.

One such particularity is the habit of using numbers, either as single digits or as terms used before Soldier, Watchman, Citizen, or whom not, to distinguish among speakers. Because such speakers are representative, sometimes no more than ciphers in the great account, it is not surprising to find that Shakespeare is occasionally careless of their designations. In *Julius Caesar*, after the murder, Brutus divides the citizens, some to hear him, some to hear Cassius: "*I. Ple.*" says he will stay with Brutus; "2." says he will go with Cassius (TLN 1539); yet the prefix "2." is still in the scene (TLN 1580), taking part in the dialogue after that speaker has presumably left. The copy for this play is thought to have been the prompt book. (Only A. R. Humphreys [Oxford, 1984] and the new Oxford

Shakespeare [1986] have adjusted this error. Riverside notes "consistently clear speech-prefixes."[10] Demonstrably, in this particular sequence the number has no consistent meaning: one voice is as good as another. Yet in the dialogue that follows the division of the citizens, even though he reveals his contempt for the mob, Shakespeare is attentive to the personalities of the speakers. Plebeians 1, 2, 3, and 4 are distinct: 1 is a practical man and an originator, 2 is a sympathetic reflector, 3 is good-natured and responsive, 4 is impatient, talkative, and suspicious.[11] Still, there is a sameness in Shakespeare's deploying of these four numbers. In the excited speeches of the citizens from TLN 1579 to 1648 (scenes ii and iii) in what we may call twelve (or so) sequences of rapid dialogue, on six occasions the four speak in numerical order. Personality, interest, or function breaks the routine—so "4" calls for the will—but the general pattern would seem to discourage individuality.

One should notice of these Roman citizens also that in the opening scene of the play, the only two citizens who speak are not numbered, but are distinguished by their trades—Carpenter and Cobbler—though 1 and 2 would have served equally well. Shakespeare here thinks of these two in terms not of their personalities but of their crafts.

But as we should expect, inattentiveness is not the norm in Shakespeare. Clear instances of attending exactly to personality are offered by Urkowitz as he discusses the numbered murderers in the *Contention* and in *Richard III*. In both texts of both plays (Q and F) Shakespeare and/or the director/producer of the plays have kept the two personalities distinct. We admire this attention in the author, but it can not surprise: in order to have some dramatic tension in even the smallest figures it is essential that they have separate observable characteristics that can, preferably, be represented in conflict, or, at least, opposition.[12]

Clayton addresses the problem of prefixes which seem to editors to run counter to their perceptions of the personalities of two numbered citizens in *Coriolanus*. The ambiguity that arises in assigning the speeches correctly in I.i derives, Clayton suggests, from Shakespeare's failure to specify what was clear enough to him or, perhaps, from his having forgotten temporarily which number he had assigned to which character. (Forgetfulness of this kind is not rare in the canon: we see it in *Julius Caesar* [1580 ff., as mentioned above] and in *Romeo and Juliet*, I.i. 64–65, where Shakespeare has forgotten either that Gregory is a Capulet, or that Benvolio is a Montague).

Another kind of numerical designation is that discussed by Clayton as "All" or "Omnes." Here there are many different methods of actual staging: "In general, '*All* must mean 'appropriate member(s) of cast in appropriate manner,' 'appropriate' to be interpreted . . . according to the composition of the company and the circumstances of performance." "*All*" must have stood in MS, intended so by Shakespeare, either because he had not . . . settled on final speakers . . . or because he had."[13]

Another oddity appears in those prefixes that designate characters by the names of the actors who are to play them. The most celebrated example is in *Much Ado About Nothing* (Q1) , where "*Kemp*" is the prefix for Dogberry and "*Cowley*" for Verges. But others occur: in *3 Henry VI* (F1), Sincklo and Humfrey are used as prefixes for Keepers. Werstine argues that it is no longer possible to consider the presence of these names as indicating foul papers.[14]

One characteristic of speech prefixes is that they appear almost always in abbreviated forms. And the normal custom of abbreviating can produce difficulty. Errors which can reasonably be traced jointly to the author and to the compositor will include the latter's misunderstanding of prefixes in spellings too much abbreviated by the former. Proudfoot has shown how steadily abbreviation can be practiced decrementally to various lengths, and he cites the situation in *Edward III*, when the prefix for Lodwike, reduced to MS *Lo.*, is expanded by the compositor erroneously to *Lor.*, the normal prefix for Lorraine, a character remembered from an earlier scene. So in *Coriolanus*: Clayton demonstrates that the MS prefixes for Coriolanus and for Cominius, normally, "*Cor*" or "*Com*", might have been reduced so far as to be no more than *C* or *Co* or *Cor* or *Cõ*— forms that would naturally give rise to confusion in the work of a compositor.[15]

As abbreviation sets prefixes apart from other kinds of evidence, so consideration of that peculiarity would seem to invite attention to the forms that are not abbreviated, that are fully spelled out, especially if the names are long. As Braunmuller says, such fully spelled out forms are "very rare." Two provoke comment in these papers: "Horatio" in *Romeo and Juliet* and "Hubert" in *King John*. The first of these, prefixing a speech in Mercutio's idiom (I. iv. 23), was emended and the speech assigned to Mercutio in Q4 and in Pope's edition (1723), following it, and is still so by all editors. They accept the emendation, supposing presumably that "Horatio" is a misreading for "Mercutio." Thomas, however, guesses that the speech prefix was here lacking in the MS and that an editor supplied a name he recalled from another play; because it was his own invention, he spelled it out fully.16

In *King John* appears "Hubert" which, though not a long name, is unusual in being nowhere else spelled out; Braunmuller speculates that Hubert was a "second thought, added to manuscript copy so emphatically that [the compositor] set the full name," even though the line was very full.17

The session considered the variations and errors in the prefixes found in printed texts as deriving from change of mind, misreading, mislining, misunderstanding; but whatever the cause of the error, the variations seemed to require editorial attention. Proudfoot acknowledged that though, like others, he had been brought up to believe that the goal of a definitive text was attainable, he had now come to accept that it is not and perhaps is not even desirable. The question of editing thus having been brought forward, Long pointed out that editing "distances the serious researcher from Shakespeare's text," and McLeod raised the question whether any editing is necessary or appropriate. The body of the session, however, composed chiefly of scholars actively engaged in the preparation of texts for one Shakespeare market or another, did not welcome the concept that a play in its raw state fulfilled all the requirements of modern study. The interests of these scholars lay in editing. Their papers and their discussion argued for the continuing of the discipline. To edit is human, they seemed to say.

Notes

1. It is not possible to sustain the argument that any other of her prefixes are also reprinted from Q1. In fact, the opposite argument would seem to be more plausible; the two texts vary independently.
2. In the discussion, Howard-Hill asked how a company scribe would know how to make up a part if the prefixes varied; Werstine theorized that a scribe could regularize as successfully as any modern editor. Braunmuller suggested that casting decisions might have been made at the time the play was read to the company (or the company read the play).
3. In fact, we find the reverse of what we should expect. Capulet's Wife takes a more prominent position in III. i(she speaks two speeches) than in the opening scene of the play(where she speaks one speech), but it is, we must suppose, as important in III. i as in I.i that she be distinct from the other "Wife" on stage at the time, Montague's (Montague's Wife does not speak in III. i and does not appear in V. iii)—indeed, more important that she be distinct in I. i, for there Montague's Wife speaks twice: at 77 "*M. Wife 2.*", 114 "*Wife*". Nevertheless, the prefix for Capulet's Wife at I. i. 83 is *Wife*.
4. Because he was concerned to reconstruct the underlying manuscript, McKerrow addressed chiefly texts from good copies. But we may briefly consider also texts from the bad quartos, even though—or perhaps because—McKerrow did not include them. Variations appear in bad quartos as well as in good. McKerrow indeed alludes to the bad quarto of *Romeo and Juliet*, but with a casualness indicating that he did not realize the vulnerability of his assumption, for if variation appears in texts printed from reported versions that cannot possibly have represented the holograph, then variation in texts printed from the holograph cannot have the unique value that McKerrow attributed to it. He notices the variation of *Wife/Mother* in the first quarto of the same play (Q1). (But as the change in these forms can be seen as coinciding with the change in printers of the quarto after sheet D, it is arguable, at least, that the cause of the change is to be found in the printing history, not in the scribal).
5. Perhaps it is worthy of note that Macbeth, though crowned at Scone, never enjoys the full kingship represented by the prefix

King; he is *Mac.* / *Macb.* throughout.

6. In the discussion, Howard-Hill explained the tradition followed by the scribes of four-column folding of the leaf as a means of separating their task into its separate calligraphic constituents, but he argued that this practice was not standard with authors.

7. The present editor is now persuaded that this kind of composition with its concomitant inexactness may have produced mislineation by the compositors and consequent misassignment of speeches over several lines as in *Henry V*, III. iv. 7–12, and *Richard III*, I.i. 134–44, tempering his earlier skepticism as to the validity of the thesis in the latter passage (*Shakespeare Survey*, 32 [1979], pp. 245–46.

8. (1.) The single anomalous *Wi.* at Q3 III. v. 176 becomes in F1 *La.*, so following the form immediately preceding in the scene. This change is very likely the result of editing, not composition, a control seen also in the changes for the prefixes of the Musicians in IV. v. These, varying in Q3—96 *Musi.*, 100 *Fid.*, 105 *Fidler.*, 110 *Minstrels*—appear uniformly in F1. changed to *Mu.* Thereafter the form *Min(strel)(s).* changes five times to *Mu.* And 3.*M.* becomes 3 *M.*; but 2.*M.* (123, 136) and *M.2.* (149) are reproduced.

   (2.) At III. v. 125, Q3 *M.* (Mother) becomes in Q4 *Mer.* (for Mercutio). This change is probably compositorial. The Q4 compositor, setting by formes (the outer first), as he set the top of H2ᵛ, came upon the Q3 *M.* Because this seemed an inadequate prefix, he proposed to improve it. Not having seen the *Mo.* forms on H1ᵛ, and H2, he remembered the last speaker whose name began with "M"—though he had died on F2, many pages before—and resurrected Mercutio to speak Juliet's Mother's speech. (This reconstruction supposes one compositor; if there were two, the compositor of H outer alternated with his fellow.)

9. The Cambridge Edition has shown the connection between Q3 and Q4; for the very interesting relationships between Q3 and F1, see S. W. Reid, "The Editing of Folio *Romeo and Juliet*," *Studies in Bibliography*, 35 (1982), 43–66, and "McKerrow, Greg, and Quarto Copy for Folio *Romeo and Juliet*," *The Library*, VI, 5 (1983), 118-125.

10. Werstine has noted a comparable error in *Romeo and Juliet* Q1 where "*1.*" refers to two different Watchmen—the copy was a scribal report. As our interest in the useful qualities of the bad quartos increases, so, Long notes, must our circumspection.

11. Variorum, p. 164.

12. In the discussion, the reliability of the numbers was questioned, and Warren said that he was becoming increasingly sensitive to 'out of character' moments and distrustful of the editorial standardizing in the Virgilia/ Volumnia assignment in *Coriolanus*, IV. ii.

13. Braunmuller noted *"All."* could reflect a corporate action, such as kneeling, with the line of dialogue coming from a single spokesperson.

14. In the discussion, Werstine asked why the name of Burbage, or of some other major actor, does not appear in the documents; Turner noted the distinction to be made between the company members and the hired men. Authors name major actors (presumably because the author is thinking of the regular member of the company when creating the role); prompters name minor actors (presumably as an aid to memory). (Kempe, of course, was a "major actor" and a shareholder.)

15. Variation in the length of prefixes can, however, be useful to the editor. In *Midsummer Night's Dream*, Q1 (1600), the progressive abbreviating of the prefix for Philostrate on G3 and G3v argues for seriatim composition. (The long form on G4 may have been adopted for justification in a full line.)

16. During the discussion, Urkowitz suggested that the aberrant prefix might have been authorial, and the present editor, grasping at straws, hypothesized that the name might have been that of one of the "other Maskers" whom Shakespeare intended to develop but never did. It could be argued in support of this hypothesis that Shakespeare had not fully conceived the character of Mercutio as he began this scene: Capell conjectured, for example, that the prefixes in lines 3 (*Ben.*) and 13 (*Mercu.*) should be reversed. If Capell is correct, Shakespeare was not yet certain as to the specific character type for Mercutio (though he should have been so for Benvolio). Shakespeare had this bit-character uppermost in his mind for this single miscellaneous line of dialogue.

17. In a paper presented at the annual meeting of the Association, Philadelphia, 1990, Professor Richard F. Kennedy suggested that by 1590 "a compositor was free to choose as a Speech Heading . . . a character's first name or last name, or generic name, or title, etc.. . . . Thus some time when scholars claim that variant [Headings] point to authorial foul papers, they do not: they signify a compositorial change, usually because of type shortage."

A Suggestion Regarding Shakespeare's Manuscripts*

R. B. McKerrow

Anyone who, in the attempt to prepare a new edition of the plays of Shakespeare, bases his work directly on the earliest printed texts or on those which appear to be most authentic, instead of working backwards from those of his editorial predecessors, will inevitably notice a great difference as regards the character-names in the various plays. In some the names appearing in stage directions and those of the speakers are, allowing perhaps for a few obvious misprints, identical throughout the play; in others the designations of certain characters, not generally the protagonists but persons of secondary importance, vary from time to time. Thus a character who is in one scene indicated by his personal name may in others be called "Father," "Servant," "Merchant," or what not, according [p.460] to the particular aspect of his personality which is at the moment prominent.

This is, of course, not a new observation, for in certain plays the variation in the names of the characters has been made the basis of arguments for composite authorship, or of theories of the transcription of the MS or the addition of stage directions, etc., by another hand than that of the author. It seems to me, however, that it may throw a light on the genesis of the MS. used by the printer as copy which has not been fully appreciated.[1]

As examples of the two groups of plays let us take *The Two Gentlemen of Verona* and *The Comedy of Errors*, both of which, so far as is known, made their first appearance in print in the

Folio of 1623. If we examine the stage directions and speakers' names of those two plays, we shall find that in the *Two Gentlemen* the names given to the various characters, major or minor, remain constant throughout the play. Thus, for example, Speed is always designated as "Speed,"[2] and Launce is always "Launce." They are never described by any periphrasis such as "Proteus' man," "Valentine's servant." Similarly, Antonio is always named; he is not called "Father" even when speaking to his son. To put the matter briefly, the names given to the characters are permanent labels, and are quite unaffected by the function of the character at the moment. This of course accords with the practice followed in printing plays nowadays, whether these are modern or ancient.

When, however, we turn to *The Comedy of Errors* we find a very different state of affairs. The names by which the characters are indicated, instead of being the same throughout, frequently depend, much as they do in a novel[3], on the progress of the story or on the [p. 461] person with whom the character is conversing. Thus the father of the two brothers Antipholus, whom we know from the text to be named Egeon, is in the opening stage-direction described as *"Merchant of Siracusa,"* and throughout the first scene is, as a speaker, simply *Merchant.* In the next scene, however, a different merchant (of Ephesus) appears, and later, in IV. i., another. Both these characters are called as speakers simply "Merchant" (*Mar., E. Mar., Mer.*). In V. i., however, while this last Merchant is on the stage Egeon enters and recognizes his sons. As his original designation of "Merchant" is now in use for someone else, Egeon becomes first "Merchant Father" (*Mar. Fat.*) and later simply "Father."

Similarly the goldsmith Angelo is called "Angelo" at his first entry in III. i. and again in III. ii. Later, however, his business as goldsmith being the chief point of his existence in the play, he is, as a speaker, simply "Goldsmith," and so for the rest of the play, his personal name Angelo being dropped.

More significant than either of these, but also more complicated, is the case of the brothers Antipholus and the two Dromios. The first of the four to appear is Antipholus of Syracuse, called at his entrance "*Antipholus Erotes*,"[4] whose name, as a speaker, is abbreviated simply to "*Ant.*," his servant Dromio being "*Dro.*" When, shortly after, the second Dromio enters, this latter is, in order to distinguish the two, called "*Dromio of Ephesus*," abbreviated to "*E. Dro.*"

There is now (II. ii.) a re-entry of Antipholus of Syracuse, who is still called "*Antipholus Erotes*," his second speech being marked "*E. Ant.*," the later ones simply "*Ant.*" as before; but the first Dromio, returning, is now "*Dromio Siracusia*" (*S. Dro.*). We thus have the confusing arrangement of the master being called "*E. Ant.*" or simply "*Ant.*," while his servant is "*S. Dro.*"

At the beginning of Act III. the other Antipholus enters for the first time. He is "*Antipholus of Ephesus*," abbreviated to "*E. Anti.*" or "*E. An.*" the distinctions of "*E. Dro.*" and "*S. Dro.*" being maintained. When in III. ii. Antipholus of Syracuse re-appears, the confusing "*Antipholus Erotes*" (*E. Ant.*) is dropped and his name is on the first occasion given as "*S. Anti.*" but for the rest of the scene merely "*Ant.*" or "*Anti.*" Similarly in IV. i. [462] his brother, who enters as "*Antipholus Ephes.*" appears in the speech-headings once as "*Eph. Ant.*" but elsewhere as "*Anti.*" or "*Ant.*" from this point onwards the four are consistently distinguished as *E. Ant., S. Ant., E. Dro.,* and *S. Dro.*

To put it briefly, the writer of the MS. evidently marked the distinctions between the two pairs of characters only as and when this became necessary. Further we can see that he had not considered in advance how he could best do this, for having determined to call Dromio of Ephesus "*E.Dro.*" he indicates Antipholus Erotes (the Syracusan), when he needs to distinguish him from his brother, by "*E. Ant.*" Later, however, it becomes obvious that the *E.* and *S.* of the Antopholi should correspond with the *E.* and *S.* of the Dromios, and he calls Antipholus Surreptus (of Ephesus) "*E. Ant.*" and Erotes "*S. Ant.*," dropping in fact the confusing "Surreptus" and "Erotes" altogether.

Having dealt with the *Comedy of Errors* at some length, we may glance at certain other plays in which a similar treatment of the character names is found.

1. *Romeo and Juliet.* Here in Q2, the earliest print of the accepted text, while there is no uncertainty in the names of the lovers, there is much as regards the other characters. Thus Capulet is at first called by his name,"*Cap.*," or when another Capulet is present "*1 Cap.*" When, however, he is engaged in talk with Juliet in III.v. he changes from "Capulet" to "Father," as he does again in the course of IV. v., becoming again "*Cap.*" in the final scene. Much more remarkable are the variations in the designation of Lady Capulet, who in I. iii. is "*Wife*" or "*Old La.*," in III. i.,151,181 "*Capu.Wi.*" or "*Ca.Wi.*," in III. iv. "*La.,*"in III. v., after "*Enter Mother,*" she is "*La.*" for a while, then "*Mo.*" or "*M.,*" and later, when Capulet comes in. "*La.*" again. In IV. iv., in a stage direction, she is "*Lady of the house,*" in IV. v. again "*Mo.,*" returning to "*Wife*" in the final scene. A similar uncertainty is found in IV.v. concerning the Musicians, the author apparently not having decided whether they are musicians or minstrels.[5]

2. *Midsummer Night's Dream.* We find here similar variations in the names. Theseus and Hippolyta are in V .i., during the performance of the play, called "*Duke*" and "*Duchess*" (*Du., Dut.*). Titania is sometimes called "*Queen.*" [p. 463]

Bottom is sometimes called "*Clowne.*" (The word seems to have been regularly applied to the principal "funny man," and is so used in other plays as an alternative to the personal name.) Puck is sometimes called "Robin Goodfellow" (*Rob.*)

3. *Love's Labour's Lost.* The King of Navarre is called "*Ferdinand,*" "*Nauar,*" or "*King.*"

The Princess of France is thus named at her first entry, but as a speaker first "*Queene,*" then "*Princess*" (*Prince., Prin.*), then later again (IV. i., etc.) "*Queen*" (*Quee.*).

Armado is sometimes "*Armado,*" at others "*Braggart.*"

Holophernes sometimes has his proper name, and sometimes is "the *Pedant*" (*Ped.*).

Nathaniel is alternatively "*the Curat.*"

Moth is alternatively "*Page,*" or "*Boy.*"

Costard is alternatively "*Clowne.*"

4. *All's Well that Ends Well.* The Countess of Rossillion is variously "Mother" (I. i.), "Lady" (II. ii., III. i.), "Countess," and "Old Countess."

Bertram, Count of Rossillion, is *"Ross."* (II. i., iii. 9, iv.), and *"Ber."* II. iii. 112–83.

Lafeu is "Old Lafeu" (*Ol. Laf.*) in II. iii. ("*Ol. Lord*" used once is probably a mistaken expansion of "*Ol. L.*").

The French Lords at III. ii. become Captains in III. vi.[6]

The "I Soldier" in IV.i. becomes "Interpreter" (*Inter., Int.*) as soon as he takes on the duties of one, and so remains.

5. *The Merchant of Venice.* There is comparatively little opportunity for variation of names in this play, but the following may be noticed:
Shylock is often called *"Iew."*
Launcelot is often *"Clowne."*

6. *Titus Andronicus.* Saturninus is called "Emperor" (I. i. 299) and "King" (IV. iv., V. iii.).
Aron is frequently *"Moore."*

Against these seven examples of plays in which the speakers' names vary we may set seven in which they do not, namely, *The Two Gentlemen of Verona, The Taming of the Shrew, Measure for Measure, Twelfth Night, King John,* and *Macbeth.*[7] [p. 464]

What, then, is the meaning of this difference between regularity and irregularity in the way in which the speakers' names are shown? Simply, I think, that a play in which the names are irregular was printed from the author's original MS.,[8] and that one in which they are regular and uniform is more likely to have been printed from some sort of fair copy, perhaps made by a professional scribe.

It is, I think, generally agreed that the *Two Gentlemen* was printed from such a fair copy. In fact the way in which in this play (and in the Folio *Merry Wives*) all the characters who are to appear in any scene are given at the head of the scene, irrespective of whether they are on the stage when this opens or not, seems to indicate that the copyist was one who was familiar with plays on the classical model, and who deliberately altered the arrangement which he would find in his copy in accordance with the practice in these.[9]

Whether in the case of a transcript of a play intended merely for the study a copyist would, as a matter of course, take pains to normalize the names of the characters, may perhaps be regarded as uncertain, though it seems to me that any competent scribe would probably look on this as part of his duty. But in any case a copy intended for use in the theatre would surely, of necessity, be accurate and unambiguous in the matter of the character-names. A prompter of a repertory theatre could hardly be expected to remember that Bertram was the same person as Rossillion, or Armado the same as Braggart. Such variations would be an intolerable nuisance to him when he suddenly needed to know what actors were on the stage in a particular scene, or to follow the action and be ready to prompt while thinking about something quite different, as one familiar with his job would probably do! It is difficult to imagine a theatrical scribe, at any rate, not attending to a point of this kind.

But on the other hand, consider the *writer*, who is perfectly familiar with his characters as characters, and who from moment to moment sees them in different aspects. Is it not natural that, in [p. 465] his first draft at any rate, he should at times follow the practice of the novelist rather than of the person writing a play for the Press, distinguishing his characters just as and when they needed to be distinguished (as in *The Comedy of Errors*), calling them by their functions (Goldsmith, not Angelo; Father, not Capulet) or their peculiarities (Braggart or Pedant, not Armado or Holophernes) just when those functions or peculiarities happened to be uppermost in his mind, knowing perfectly well that the most cursory indications were quite sufficient for his purpose and not troubling himself about any formal consistency? I cannot help thinking that even nowadays in the heat of composition a writer might easily do the like; and it must be remembered that we have cause to suspect that Shakespeare was not any too careful of minor details.

But if there is anything in this view, if we can with some confidence assert that a play showing, in the character names, irregularity of the kind which I have described, was printed directly from the author's MS., the fact seems to be of considerable importance, for such plays must necessarily be regarded for purposes of textual criticism very differently from those which we can suppose to derive from a fair copy made by someone else. In the one case we must allow for confused corrections and careless writing, but can take it for granted that the compositor had before him something which, though perhaps difficult to decipher, embodied the intention of the author, and that the text as we have it must represent fairly closely what the MS. *looked like* to the compositor. In the other case the compositor would presumably be working from a MS. which would in itself be easily legible, but the text of which might already have been tampered with by someone who had views as to what the author ought to have written, and who placed the construction of a readable text above the duty of following closely the *ductus litterarum* of his original. The kinds of error which we should expect to find in prints from MSS. of the two groups may evidently be very different.

Notes

*Reprinted from *The Review of English Studies,* Vol. XI, 1935 (No. 44, Oct.), pp. 459–65, by permission of Oxford University Press. Page numbers of the original article have been retained in brackets.

1. So far as I am aware, the point to which I have to call attention has not been appreciated *at all*; but it seems almost impossible to make any statement or put forward any theory about the work of Shakespeare which is not already, somewhere or other in print! It is in the hope of discovering whether my suggestion is a new one, and, if it is, of obtaining the opinion of others upon it, that I have put together this admittedly incomplete note.
2. I do not of course mean that there is no variation in the *spelling* of the names, or in the abbreviated forms of them. It is a matter of

indifference whether "Speed" appears in full or as "Sp.," "Spe.," etc. In what follows I ignore all such non-significant variations. Simple misprints or errors such as "Panthion" for "Panthino" have also, of course, no significance in this connection.

3. Thus in a novel concerning one John Smith, we might find "said John," "said Mr. Smith," "muttered the bearded stranger," " his father replied," " her husband protested," and so on, when in all cases the words quoted are those of the same John Smith. There is, of course, no ambiguity, for the reader is perfectly aware of the speaker's identity. The change of designation is merely in accordance with the function of the character at the time.

4. Actually he is here and in some other places called "Antipholis." I ignore these minor variations or misprints, as also "Errotis" in II. ii. for "Erotes."

5. It will be asked how this compares with Q1, in which, if the text is simply a "report" we should perhaps not expect to find any variation at all. Actually there is some, though much less than in Q2. Capulet, indeed, is "*Cap.*" as a speaker throughout, though we find him in stage directions described as "*Old Capulet*" and sometimes as "*Oldeman.*" Lady Capulet, however, after being "*Wife*" in Acts I and II and entering as "*Capolets wife*" in III. i., becomes as a speaker "Mother" (*M. or Mo.*) and so remains for the rest of the play.

6. The curious *E* and *G* added to their names—"*French E*" and "*French G*,","*Cap. E*" and "*Cap. G*"—as well as "*I Lord G*", "*2 Lord E*" earlier have been reasonably explained as indicative of the actors who were to take these parts.

7. I have chosen what seem to be straightforward and simple examples of the two groups. Others would require discussion or qualification. In some, such as the Roman plays, there is little, if any, scope for variation in the names. It may be noted that in *King John* the Bastard is in his earlier speeches "Robert" [i.e., Phillip], but as soon as his bastardy is established his name is altered. This has no significance in the present connection, but is parallel to those cases in which a character's style is *necessarily* changed, as when a pretender to the throne becomes "King."

8. Several of the plays in the "irregular" group are, of course, on other grounds, already generally regarded as printed from the author's MS.

9. The method is, for example, to be found in such Latin plays as *Hymenæus* and *Fucus Histriomastix*, and in certain English

plays on more or less classical lines, such as Brandon's *Vertuous Octavia* (III. i., IV. i.) and Daniel's *Queen's Arcadia* (II. ii.) and in translations such as Gascoigne's *Supposes* (III. i., iv.). In all these, characters are listed at the head of scenes though they do not appear until considerably later.

McKerrow's "Suggestion" and W. W. Greg*

Paul Werstine

The historical context of R. B. McKerrow's "Suggestion Regarding Shakespeare's Manuscripts" (1935) may be of some interest.[1] In 1931 W. W. Greg, who later became chiefly responsible for the wide influence that the "Suggestion" has enjoyed, had published his two-volume survey of extant dramatic manuscripts from the period ca. 1590 to ca. 1650.[2] Greg there had asked, "What treatment did the book-keeper mete out to the author's stage-directions?" and had answered "that as a rule he left them alone" (I, 213). The same is true of speech prefixes. "[T]he whole question," Greg went on, "badly needs studying in relation, not to *a priori* expectation, but to the actual evidence of the Books [dramatic manuscripts] themselves, and meanwhile the more we are able to suspend judgment perhaps the better" (I, 209).

But McKerrow, busy generating editorial theory to serve as a basis for his Oxford Shakespeare, neither suspended judgment nor studied the extant manuscripts when he made his two-fold "Suggestion" that variable naming of characters in the stage directions and speech prefixes of printed texts indicated that such texts had been set into type from Shakespeare's "original MS"; and that "a copy intended for use in the theatre would surely, of necessity, be accurate and unambiguous in the matter of the character-names" (p. 464). McKerrow's attention was focused exclusively upon Shakespeare the individual and upon presenting "Shakespeare's work as nearly in the form in which he left it as the evidence which we have permits, clearing it indeed as far as possible of the numerous errors with which the ignorance and carelessness of copyists and printers have disfigured it, but without superfluous comment or any attempt to improve upon the text as the author left it."[3] He needed a principle according to which he could categorize the early printings of the plays in relation to their author and select as the basis of his edition the versions that represent, as nearly as possible, the "author's original wording" (*Prolegomena*, p. 2).

And so McKerrow imagined the principle that he needed and articulated it by constructing a concept of Shakespeare the author through "projection, in more or less psychologizing terms, . . . the traits" that McKerrow established to be pertinent in some of the early printings.[4] He simply asserted that variations in the naming of characters in some of these printings emanated intelligibly from the operation of Shakespeare's "creative" powers:

> Is it not natural that, in his first draft at any rate, [Shakespeare] should at times follow the practice of the novelist rather than of the person writing a play for the Press, distinguishing his characters just as and when they needed to be distinguished . . . , calling them by their functions (Goldsmith, not Angelo [in *The Comedy of Errors*]; Father, not Capulet [in *Romeo and Juliet*]) or their peculiarities (Braggart or Pedant, not Armado or Holophernes [in *Love's Labor's Lost*]) just when those functions or peculiarities happened to be uppermost in his mind, knowing perfectly well that the most cursory indications were quite sufficient for his purpose and not troubling himself about any formal consistency? I cannot help thinking that even nowadays in the heat of composition a writer might easily do the like; and it must be remembered that we have cause to suspect that Shakespeare was not any too careful of minor details. ("Suggestion," pp. 464–65)

If Shakespeare varied his naming of the characters according to function or peculiarity, then one would assume that Armado, for example, should be designated Braggart when he is bragging and Armado when he is not. Such, of course, is not the case, since he is always called Armado in I. ii, even though he brags a good deal, referring to himself as "a man of great spirite," "a compleat man," and claiming that he excels Samson with a rapier just as Samson did him in "carying gates" (sigs. Bl^v–2^v; I. ii. 1, 44, 75). Then in the first part of III. i (before the entrance of Costard) he is called Braggart; yet he brags little except perhaps in the last speech prefixed "*Brag.*": "Most rude melancholie, Valour giues thee place" (sig. C4^v; III. i. 68). Such facts, however, are irrelevant to McKerrow's position, for he never argued that Shakespeare varied the naming of characters according to peculiarities evident in their speeches but, instead, according to the functions or peculiarities "uppermost in [Shakespeare's] mind" at the time that the dramatist was inscribing a name. Therefore the first part of McKerrow's "Suggestion" cannot be falsified by reference to play texts; but it cannot be verified either.

The second part of the "Suggestion" concerns the treatment allegedly handed out to Shakespeare's variations in naming by theatrical personnel. According to McKerrow's a priori expectation,

> A prompter of a repertory theatre could hardly be expected to remember that Bertram was the same person as Rosillion [in *All's Well*], or Armado the same as Braggart. Such variations would be an intolerable nuisance to him when he suddenly needed to know what actors were on the stage in a particular scene, or to follow the action and be ready to prompt while thinking about something quite different, as one familiar with his job would probably do! It is difficult to imagine a theatrical scribe, at any rate, not attending to a point of this kind.   ("Suggestion," p. 464)

Had McKerrow bothered to look, for example, at the manuscript of Henry Glapthorne's *The Lady Mother* (1635)—one of those that Greg had listed as an Elizabethan "promptbook"—then he could have repaired the failure of his imagination. According to Arthur Brown, editor of the Malone Society reprint, *The Lady Mother* is a scribal copy; the scribe was employed in the theatre, for he consistently supplied warnings for actors to be ready some twelve to twenty lines before their actual entrances—a purely theatrical concern.5 Did this scribe render character-names unambiguously, as McKerrow was sure a scribe must? No. One of Glapthorne's characters is the steward Alexander Lovell. The scribe usually designated him "Alexander" in stage directions but "Lov:" or simply "L:" in speech prefixes (with only one exception—lines 1276–77) until line 1919, after which the scribe used "Alex:" as the speech prefix. We cannot know if the scribe introduced such ambiguity or merely transcribed what he found in the no longer extant authorial copy. Yet we know that other ambiguities in character names were *introduced* in the process of the preparation of the scribal copy for the stage. As originally transcribed, the first scene of Act Five called for the entrance of a character called the "Recorder," whose speech prefix was always "Re:" ("Rec:," "Reco:," or "Recor:"). In censoring the play, Sir William Blagrave, Deputy to the Master of the Revels, altered "Recorder" to "Iudg" or to "Sr" in the stage direction and text, but left the "Re:" speech prefixes untouched. Then the theatrical scribe changed the first half-dozen "Re:" speech prefixes to "Sr Hu:" or to "He:" (for "Sir Hugh," the proper name provided by the scribe or the author to the Iudg-Recorder at this late stage) but left well over a dozen "Re:" speech prefixes standing. As a result this transcript by a theatrical scribe represents a character entering under the generic name "Iudg," but designated in the speech prefixes first by his proper name "Sr Hu:" and later by the official title "Re:". According to McKerrow's expectations, such variation in naming would have been intolerable in a theatrical manuscript like *The Lady Mother*; had the play ever seen print in such a form, McKerrow would have been forced by his theory to conclude that it had been printed directly from Glapthorne's own papers; in fact, such variation was produced collectively by theatrical censor and theatrical scribe—perhaps with the aid of the author, too, but long after original composition.

Although contradicted by historical documents, McKerrow's speculations were not rejected; instead they have been accepted by many, including Greg, the scholar of this century most familiar with dramatic manuscripts—but also McKerrow's close friend. Greg, at first, was cautious, but the further in time his writing became distanced from his study of the manuscripts, the more enthusiastic he became about McKerrow's hypothesis. The change can be seen in Greg's comments about *The Comedy of Errors*, the play that McKerrow discussed in greatest detail in the "Suggestion" and the one he was most convinced was set from Shakespeare's own papers. In 1942, in *The Editorial Problem in Shakespeare*, Greg refused to commit himself entirely to McKerrow's guess:

> The erratic speech prefixes point on McKerrow's theory direct to the act of composition . . . and in a carefully pre- pared prompt-book the abnormalities of the prefixes would presumably have been cleared away. . . . But the text is generally clean, and at this early date it is particularly dangerous to dogmatize. Perhaps a tolerably careful author's copy may have been made to serve on the stage with a minimum of editing.[6]

However, by the time Greg wrote *The Shakespeare First Folio* in 1955, he had come to embrace McKerrow's "Suggestion" much more fervently:

> In the case of an early play that must have come to the Chamberlain's men from some other company it is, of course, particularly dangerous to dogmatize, but the man- uscript behind F [the First Folio of 1623] *was clearly the author's,* and since it is difficult to believe that the confu- sion in the character names and prefixes would have been tolerated in a prompt-book, it would seem that the manu- script was *most likely foul papers.*[7]

Since Greg's *Shakespeare First Folio* has enjoyed almost scriptural status among Shakespearean editors and textual critics in the latter half of this century, McKerrow's "Sugges- tion" has lived on long after the editorial concerns from which it issued have changed.

Notes

*A longer version of this chapter entitled "McKerrow's 'Suggestion' and Twentieth-Century Shakespeare Textual Criticism" appeared in *Renaissance Drama* 19 (1989), 149–73.

1. *The Review of English Studies*, 11 (1935), 459–65.
2. *Dramatic Documents from the Elizabethan Playhouses: Stage Plots: Actor's Parts: Prompt Books*, 2 vols. (Oxford: Clarendon Press, 1931).
3. *Prolegomena for the Oxford Shakespeare* (Oxford: Clarendon Press, 1939), 1.
4. Words in quotations from Michel Foucault, "What Is an Author?" in *Textual Strategies*, ed. Josué Harari (Ithaca: Cornell University Press, 1979), 150.
5. Malone Society Reprint (London: Malone Society, 1958 [1959]), viii.
6. (Oxford: Clarendon Press, 1942), 140.
7. (Oxford: Clarendon Press, 1955), 201–2; italics mine.

McKerrow's Thesis Re-Examined

Sidney Thomas

Few scholarly arguments have won wider acceptance than R. B. McKerrow's modestly titled, "A Suggestion Regarding Shakespeare's Manuscripts."[1] McKerrow's thesis "that a play in which the names are irregular was printed from the author's original MS., and that one in which they are regular and uniform is more likely to have been printed from some sort of fair copy, perhaps made by a professional scribe,"[2] has not been seriously disputed by textual scholars since it was first put forward fifty years ago. I do not propose a rejection of this thesis, but rather what seems to me a necessary modification that takes into account some peculiar features of the so-called "good" quartos, in particular Q2 of *Romeo and Juliet*.

What McKerrow convincingly demonstrated, I believe, is that such a publication as Q2 of *RJ* could not have derived from a fair manuscript used as a prompt copy. The frequent shifts in the speech-prefix designations of Lady Capulet, for example, as McKerrow points out, would have thoroughly confused any prompter attempting to use the manuscript. That some, at least, of these variations are the work of Shakespeare himself, careless of consistency in his first draft and identifying his characters by their function in the particular scene, is also a reasonable assumption. What I would argue, however, is that some of the speech-prefixes in Q2 of *RJ* are so eccentric or obviously mistaken as to reveal the intervention of a printing-house editor, ignorant of the play to begin with and often relying on sheer guesswork.

Most telling as an indication of a meddling editor is the use of *Horatio* spelled out in full as a speech-prefix in place of

Mercutio at I. iv. 23.3 The mistake occurs in a passage of dialogue between Romeo and Mercutio in which two previous short speeches by Mercutio have been correctly assigned (to *Mercu.* and *Mer.*) and it immediately precedes another exchange between the two characters in which the correct prefix *Mer.* is again used. That Shakespeare could have carelessly written the name of a character who does not appear in the play, in place of the name of one of his leading characters, is hard to believe. Nor is it easy to accept the explanation that this is a compositorial misreading. Why should a compositor who has just correctly read two abbreviated forms of Mercutio have any difficulty with a third? And why, if he is misreading *Mer.* as *Hor.* should he bother to spell out the entire name? My guess is that there was a missing speech-prefix at this point in the copy, and that someone wrote in the first name that occurred to him, a name already familiar from *The Spanish Tragedy* and perhaps even (if I may speculate wildly) from a *Hamlet* newly on the boards in 1599.

Other mistaken speech-prefixes may also point to the presence of an editor. At II. ii. 187, *Iu.* is incorrectly used for *Rom.* At III. i. 173, *Capu.* is used for *Moun.* At III. ii. 73, *Nurse* is wrongly substituted for *Iuli.*, after having been omitted as a speech-prefix for the preceding line which then became part of a speech by Juliet. At III. v. 54, *Rom.* is used for *Iu.* Most curious and revelatory of all is the use of *Pet.* for *Balthasar* at V. iii. 21, following the identical error in the preceding stage-direction, *Enter Romeo and Peter.* It is hardly conceivable that Shakespeare should have confounded Peter and Balthasar at this point, particularly since Peter was, together with the nurse, the leading low-comedy character in the play and obviously intended for Will Kemp. I suspect that Shakespeare simply wrote *Man* in both the stage-direction and the speech-prefix, and that an editor attempting to make things clearer made them worse.

The most striking, and at first glance the most convincing, of McKerrow's examples are the series of changes rung upon Lady Capulet in the speech-prefixes of Q2 of *RJ*. She is, at different times, designated as *Wife, Old La., Capu. Wife, Mo.,* or

M., to mention only some of the variants. Most of these probably derive from Shakespeare himself, but I believe that *Old La.* in I. iii, if no other, can more plausibly be explained as the invention of an interfering editor. McKerrow's thesis rests upon the assumption that Shakespeare's speech-prefixes stress aspects of the character that are dominant in his mind at the particular moment. But in the scene in question, Lady Capulet, from the point at which she becomes *"Old La."* rather than *"Wife,"* is speaking above all as Juliet's mother ("tell me daughter Juliet"), not as some generalized old lady. It is interesting to note that the first use of *Old La.*, not only in this scene but in the play itself, comes at the exact point at which Q2 stops copying Q1 and begins relying on an independent manuscript,[4] presumably Shakespeare's own foul papers. I believe that here Shakespeare had simply written *La.* as a speech-prefix for Lady Capulet, and that an editor, confused by his first encounter with this prefix, expanded it to *Old La.*, after perhaps glancing further down the MS sheet and seeing the Nurse's words to Juliet ("A man young Lady, Lady such a man as all the world.")

I realize that everything I have said above rests upon the assumption that Shakespeare's speech-prefixes (and I believe this to be true also of his stage-directions) were often confusingly or inadequately supplied in the early draft that, in agreement with McKerrow, I think served as the basic copy for Q2 of *RJ*. Is there any evidence to support this assumption? There is, if we accept the Hand D additions to *Sir Thomas More* as Shakespeare's. W. W. Greg, after a thorough study of the More manuscript, concluded:

> The author wrote the text, at any rate of the first two pages, continuously, dividing the speeches by rules but without indicating the speakers. He then read it through, inserting the prefixes and at the same time making certain additions to the text.[5]

What this procedure produced, as might have been expected, was a MS. in which the speech-prefixes were sometimes negligently or ambiguously written, and at least once omitted altogether, so that another hand needed to correct or expand or supply the necessary prefix. That a similar procedure was followed in the copy for Q2 of *RJ*, with similar results, is a possibility, I believe, worth considering.

Notes

1. *The Review of English Studies*, 11 (1935), 459–65.
2. Ibid., p. 464.
3. All act, scene, line references are to the Kittredge-Ribner edition (Waltham, Mass.: Ginn and Co., 1971).
4. See my article, "The Bibliographical Links Between the First Two Quartos of *Romeo and Juliet*," *Review of English Studies*, 25 (1949), 110–14.
5. W. W. Greg, "Special Transcript of the Three Pages," in *Shakespeare's Hand in the Play of Sir Thomas More*, Cambridge: Cambridge University Press, 1923 (reprinted 1967), p. 229.

Perspective on Provenance: The Context of Varying Speech-heads

William B. Long

Although varying speech-heads in Elizabethan-Jacobean-Caroline playbooks are not rare, they usually are dismissed as being mistakes or curiosities needing to be regularized. In manuscripts prepared for presentation to private patrons and in some plays prepared for a printing meant to impress or as a tribute (such as Jonson's *Works* and Shakespeare's *First Folio*), there are easily demonstrable efforts to regularize varying labels for the same character; but in manuscripts prepared for use (presumably exclusively) in the theatre, there is seemingly no concern by the playwrights or by the theater personnel to "correct" or to regularize, that is, to clarify speech-heads for anyone reading the manuscript. Presumably theater people were concerned for their own needs and did not consider (or care) that plays might (someday, perhaps) have another life off the boards. Given the apparently very self-sufficient nature of the players on stage, the phenomenon of letting varying speech-heads stand in the playbooks should not be surprising; but for centuries it has confused, disappointed, irritated, and even angered editors and critics who believed that theatrical playbooks should not bear such "imprecise" and "confusing" inscriptions. The impediments to understanding the phenomenon lie in the common failure of scholars to view varying speech-heads in their proper theatrical contexts. This essay suggests some means for doing so.

R. B. McKerrow's "A Suggestion Regarding Shakespeare's

Manuscripts"[1] is both exhilarating and distressing: exhilarating because he attempts to ask intriguing and provocative questions, distressing because this article appeared over fifty years ago; and we sadly realize that the direction of study in the elapsed time generally did not follow the main thrust of McKerrow's inquiry but instead seems to have taken its inspiration from one descriptive word almost buried in his commentary. We can but lament that, for whatever reasons, scholarship did not follow McKerrow's promising suggestions. McKerrow was quite aware of the many differences between copy prepared to be acted and copy prepared to be read in the study. Unfortunately, instead of pursuing the ramifications of these differences, much scholarship has ignored the differences altogether and has been guided by vague generalizations and erroneous preconceptions about the need for regularization and "clean" copy which also are present in McKerrow's article, although in small measure.

The "buried" word is "uncertainty" which McKerrow uses in describing Shakespeare's attitude in using varying speech-heads in *Romeo and Juliet*, particularly the often cited ones of Lady Capulet.[2] However, "uncertain" can be in the eye of the beholder, in this case that of the modern scholar who finds that his observation does not match his expectation of what he assumed he would find. Therefore the playwright's actions are labelled "uncertain." But there is nothing uncertain about the use of most varying speech-heads by the playwrights. The labelling of the same character with different speech-heads in a theatrical manuscript is quite clear so long as those labels accurately identify the character by name, by title, or by function in that particular scene, as is the case in this play whether the speaker is labelled "Capulet's Wife," "Lady Capulet," "Lady," "Mother," or "Old Lady" (with varying abbreviations of all of these). It is intriguing to suppose that such discoveries allow us to peek into a small corner of Shakespeare's creative processes. We can believe that we see how he imagines a scene and the working of the characters—how he organizes the scene in his head in terms of the kinds of characters he is using at the moment. It is heady indeed to suppose that we see him in

the act of ringing in his multitudes of changes on stock characters and stock situations much as he does with his use of
proverbs and verse forms. This kind of working with the fabric
of drama is hardly surprising, but it is exciting to watch it hap-
pening. It is most tempting to believe that this supposition
accounts for the presence of most varying speech-heads, but it
is folly to subscribe to an essentially romantic fantasy. The present state of our knowledge is far too incomplete to bear that
kind of weight. What is certain is that these varying speech-
heads which editors seem bound to regularize exist in manuscripts and early printed editions because neither playwrights
nor theatrical personnel saw any reason not to have them
there. If such persons had been interested in regularizing
them, surely their manuscripts and more early printings would
bear witness at least to more efforts toward the "correcting"
and tidying that modern scholars expect of them.

Except for occasional confusions, Shakespeare and other
playwrights were not in any way "uncertain" about what figure
the speech-head indicated. Scholars who deem such matters
"uncertain" are forgetting basic differences in writing plays to
be acted by players—especially in a repertory company—and
in copying plays or in printing them for readers only. Regard-
less of the speech-head, the audience in the theater always
would see the same character; they would experience no confusion. We must remind ourselves of the obvious and then attempt to understand what that means.

The obvious and essential point here is that a play manuscript used in the playhouse presents words on paper meant to
undergo the mysterious transformation into theater. It hardly
need be said that the reading audience of a play is perforce at a
severe disadvantage and needs help that a theater audience
does not. The act of performance obliterates many problems
that can be most vexing in the study. It is salutary to remember that varying speech-heads would not be confusing to the
players because they would have studied their lines from parts
that contained no speech-heads, only cues.[3] Thus in acting the
scene, there would be no confusion on stage or in the audience.

At this point, the questions are both inevitable and off the mark: "But what about the 'prompter'? How could he not have become confused? Surely such a situation would make for confusion." I believe that scholars arrive at such positions by working backwards. I suggest that the plethora of surviving examples of varying speech-heads is strong evidence that the players and theatrical personnel did not find such things disturbing; if they had, they would have changed them. The expectation of confusion is a modern one; because we are confused, we assume that the players also were. Let us instead assume that they were not and see what might happen.

Since varying speech-heads are relatively common, is it not reasonable to assume that they are not mistakes or sloppiness and that the players did not find them particularly (if at all) troublesome? If persons holding book had found varying speech-heads a problem, surely they would have made some kinds of alterations which would have been visible in the surviving manuscript playbooks and, in turn, would have been reflected in the printed texts. Yet such changes do not exist. Playhouse attitudes toward such matters can be found in the practices of the bookkeepers as we find them in the surviving playbooks: they are not concerned with changing such matters. Our editorial needs which are for a readership patently were not theirs. One of the principal reasons for this is that Elizabethan-Jacobean-Caroline bookkeepers seem to have functioned much differently from modern "prompters." More recent practice is concerned with an intense watch on minutiae: word-for-word prompting and exact timing for entrances and exits as well as a seeming infinitude of other small details. The older bookkeepers were concerned chiefly with synchronizing backstage happenings with those onstage. Their principle concern seems to have been the proper timing of off-stage noises. Once a player is on stage, there seems to have been little worry that he could perform without assistance from backstage.[4] This situation is the outgrowth both of professionalism and of a repertory system where members of the company regularly worked with and depended upon each other.

There is another aspect that needs to be considered. Editorial concern for the reader often has had unfortunate consequences for theater historians. In rendering well-meaning assistance to readers, editors often destroy (or remove to textual notes) valuable evidence which may help to explain the phenomenon of how the plays were written and performed. Scholars studying the artifacts of the Elizabethan-Jacobean-Caroline theater should approach its few surviving manuscripts and early printings as if they were archeological remains— shards of a kind—that need to be respected and studied for what they are, not derogated as some sort of misshapen embarrassments. With a less supercilious approach, these fragments might be reconstructed into forms that would allow us to understand the early theater more fully and more accurately. For centuries scholars have regarded many aspects of the Elizabethan-Jacobean-Caroline theater with that kind of anti-theatricalism that views the stage and its representations as essentially crude—a vulgarization of the artist-playwright's works.

Because of such a history, scholars tend to look upon varying speech-heads as mistakes or at best as curious trivia. I suggest that new insights on the functioning of the theater might be had if we assume that, in most cases at least, varying speech-heads were not just tolerated by the players, but wanted. One of the many things that we do not know about the Elizabethan-Jacobean-Caroline playing companies is how they worked: how did they rehearse and hold in repertory the huge numbers, by modern standards and expectations, of plays? The problem is not just a matter of remembering lines—large numbers of them; it is also the staging, the blocking, the movements on stage in scene after almost countless scene. I suggest that one of the ways that these tasks were approached and organized (and simplified) is that actions often were regarded as occurring in generic or typological scenes with some general outlines for staging them; I believe that varying speech-heads may be a kind of vestigial remains of that planning, left by the playwright and used by the players. In such situations, certain kinds of scenes would have the same general blocking. Differences, of course, would be wrought, but players would not have had to reinvent the wheel for each play. They would have come equipped with a basic structure upon which they could elaborate. This is, of course, a variation of the playwrights' use of stock scenes such as: parents discussing a daughter's approaching marriage, a ruler and his consort being entertained at court, a governor haranguing a group of citizens, the storming of a wall, and on and on.

In other words, I suggest that far from being an uncertainty or an almost quaint bit of evidence of playwrights' compositorial technique, that varying speech-heads are integral parts of the skeleton of the construction of the plays which players found to be useful in creating performances. The players would know when to enter from their cues in their parts; the bookkeeper would see that this was a particular kind of scene or would know it from rehearsal; both players and bookkeepers would know the general outlines for staging such a scene; and within these parameters, it would not be confusing to the bookkeeper that characters had different names in their speech-heads (any more than it would bother him that they had different names in the dialogue) because such a fact would not be a part of his concern. We tend to look at plays as wholes because we see them as literary constructs. Certainly there is much validity in that view, but it need not be the only possible one. I suggest that the players saw things more in terms of presenting a succession of effective scenes. This approach would not necessarily change the interpretation of the play for the theater audience (and still less that of the reader), but it could have a very marked difference on the way playwrights and players approached the construction and presentation of a play.

The problem for scholarship in dealing with varying speech-heads as with so many other matters comes from those who pronounce upon what theatrical "prompters" would need and want. McKerrow leaps to seemingly sensible but, according to the evidence, totally unwarranted assumptions about what would have been done in the playhouse:

> a copy [of a play] intended for use in the theatre would surely, of course, be accurate and unambiguous in the matter of the character-names. A prompter of a repertory theatre could hardly be expected to remember that Bertram

was the same person as Rossillion, or Armado the same as Braggart. Such variations would be an intolerable nuisance to him when he suddenly needed to know what actors were on stage in a particular scene, or to follow the action and be ready to prompt while thinking about something quite different, as one familiar with his job would probably do! It is difficult to imagine a theatrical scribe, at any rate, not attending to a point of this kind.[5]

Such a perspective is indeed difficult to imagine if one comes with the outlook of most modern scholars. (McKerrow here, for instance, assumes that the "prompter" would have [and need and want] a complete dramatis personae at hand while "prompting.") However, I suggest that McKerrow has matters just turned around. His requirements for the stage much better fit alterations made for readers. The expectations of what a "prompter" would have needed are generally scholars' suppositions and gain no support from the surviving evidence. We certainly can understand McKerrow's wondering how players managed to avoid the seeming confusion of varying speech-heads, but the important point to remember is that, according to the extant manuscript playbooks, they did; it is the problem of modern scholarship to figure out how (and why) they did it, and why they were not confused by situations which we see as fraught with problems. What happened, or better, what did not happen in the playhouse is easily seen by examining the surviving playbooks. The players allowed all manner of speechhead irregularity to stand without regularizing or "correcting." Apparently the sixteenth- and early seventeenth-century bookkeepers were not bothered by "irregularities" and other "problems" as McKerrow and succeeding textual scholars have presumed that they would (or should) have been. That this original playhouse treatment of varying speech-heads is not generally known can be seen in Fredson Bowers's comments on McKerrow's article:

ever since McKerrow's pioneering study of the speech-prefixes of Q2 *Romeo and Juliet* explained the various forms as Wife, Mother, Lady, Lady Capulet for the same character as the result of setting from Shakespeare's own irregular papers, such a variety of prefixes (unknown in promptbooks and, so far as we can see from such examples as *Julius Caesar* and *1 Henry IV*, generally smoothed out in a scribal fair-copy transcript) have seemed very strong evidence for autograph printer's copy.[6]

Bowers presents a picture that would be very confusing to anyone who had not worked with the surviving playbooks. "Such variety of prefixes (unknown in promptbooks)" implies that variety itself rather than merely the variety of Lady Capulet's appellations is unknown in the "promptbooks" when it patently is not. Furthermore, by supposing a "scribal fair-copy transcript," Bowers assumes both that such a transcript existed at all and, yet more confusing for investigators, that this "transcription" (and the cleaning and regularizing that it implies) was done for the benefit of the players and not for the readers of the printed book. These are exactly the assumptions that misled McKerrow half a century ago.

Although none is Shakespearean, the surviving playbooks range from 1590 to 1635, are the products of a number of playwrights, were designed for various companies playing in different theaters, and are remarkably consistent in the kinds of alterations done to them and in demonstrating the many types of occasions in which theater personnel did not feel the urge to make changes.[7] The bookkeepers simply were not interested in working with books that are as minutely complete and "correct" as modern scholars assume, on no concrete evidence whatsoever, that they would have needed. Indeed, one of the cleanest and most orderly of the survivors, Massinger's holograph *Believe as You List*, a King's company play, contains some speech-heads uncorrected from a previous rendition of the play which Sir Henry Herbert had ordered changed.[8] If such totally foreign speech-heads did not bother the King's company's bookkeeper, we surely are leading ourselves astray by assuming that differing (but correct) names for a character such as McKerrow discusses necessarily would be "corrected" or regularized in the theater.

It also must be remembered that slight mis-linings of speech-heads (and of marginal stage-directions) occur frequently because of the almost universal writers' habit of folding the leaves of paper lengthwise into four equal columns before beginning to write. Nearly all of the surviving playbooks show definite signs of such creasing even after having been pressed flat for nearly four hundred years. Playtexts were written in the center two columns; the right usually was reserved for stage-directions, the left for speech-heads and some stage-directions. But for the purposes of considering varying speech-heads, the important factor is that copying (and often composition) was done by columns, not line for line across the entire page. Thus the speech-heads were entered after the text was inscribed. Although they thus are often out of exact alignment, such mislineation generally is as unconfusing as it is common. Copying a play by columns also deprives the copyist (playwright or otherwise) of the continuity needed to review who is speaking—even if he should wish to regularize. All this does not necessarily mean that all went letter-perfect in all performances of all plays. Such an assumption would betray an ignorance both of human fallibility and of what can happen on a stage. Many times mistakes can be made about which the audience will never know. This depends both upon the severity of the problem and upon the professionalism of the players to set things aright. Even such seemingly serious matters as missed cues, dropped lines, and speeches wrongly started, then correctly redone, usually pass unnoticed. The assumptions of many scholars often seem unrelated to the workings of the stage, ancient or modern. Then, too, one must remember that no contemporary audience could possibly have been as familiar with Shakespeare's texts as are modern scholars. Their expectations would not have been ours.

Let us return to McKerrow.

What, then, is the meaning of this difference between regularity and irregularity in the way in which the speakers' names are shown? Simply, I think, that a play in which the names are irregular was printed from the author's original MS., and that one in which they are regular and uniform is

29

> more likely to have been printed from some sort of fair
> copy, perhaps made by a professional scribe. (464)

This is rather too naive in light of much sophisticated compositorial investigation in the years since McKerrow; but if one does not expect regularity and universality, features conspicuous by their absence in surviving playbooks, there is more than a little sense here. As McKerrow points out (459-60), some plays have remarkably regular and unvarying speech-heads. It is not beyond the realm of reasoned conjecture to suggest that the explanation for this is that there was a certain amount of regularizing and "cleaning up" in preparation for First Folio publication—a printing of plays very much designed for readers who were away from the theater. That early seventeenth-century playwrights and theater personnel recognized the difference between copy prepared for the theater and copy sent to a printer for a "literary" volume can be seen in many of the revisions that Ben Jonson made in his plays for the 1616 *Works*. It is surely not inconceivable that Heminge and Condell (or someone delegated by them) or Jaggard and Blount (or someone delegated by them) revised the copy for some of the Folio plays with this difference in mind. A reader could well be confused by varying (let alone incorrect) speech-heads in ways that theater spectators (and bookkeepers) were not. That such alterations were not made on all sheets in all of the Folio plays is a matter far too complicated to explore here, but incomplete execution does not invalidate the concept.

However exciting in terms possibly of watching Shakespeare (and others) creating, however interesting in aiding attempts to reconstruct how theater companies operated, the most important thing to be learned from the existence of varying speech-heads is that they could and did appear in theatrical playbooks without causing confusion or consternation in the playhouse. This being the case, then the nature of the copy behind early printed versions of the plays needs to be reconsidered radically.

If scholarship is relieved of that burdensome notion (one entirely without substantiation in the surviving examples) that playhouse books had to be clean and correct according to modern (and even then, entirely unrealistic) expectations, then scholarship also is relieved of the responsibility of having to invent elaborate (and even ingenious) explanations of what constituted printer's copy. Because of the tacit assumption that playhouse bookkeepers demanded precisely correct minutiae such as regularized speech-heads (as McKerrow did), it is widely believed that printed plays containing such items as varying speech-heads cannot have been printed from a theatrical playbook. If a printed play bears such stigmata, goes the formulaic explanation, then it must have been set from the playwright's "foul" papers. If a printed text contains these "irregularities" in addition to some of those very markings which can with some considerable confidence be traced to the theater, then the play must have been set from a theatrical "promptbook" but the compositor also must have had recourse to the playwright's "foul" papers. (The amount of cross-referencing and cross-checking often glibly attributed to compositors easily stretches credibility.)

Manuscripts with any problems like speech-head irregularity almost always (again with no support from existing evidence) are judged to be "foul" since the (strangely elusive) "fair" copies by definition (not by example) would contain no such problems—or so the usual assumptions go. It is far more likely in many cases that playwrights' completed manuscripts, if reasonably legible (and one of the surviving theatrical playbooks, Heywood's *The Captives*, is not), went to the players without the bother and expense of having a "fair" copy made and that this manuscript with such alterations as the players would see fit to make to it (usually very few, on the testimony of the survivors) became the "promptbook." If a theater company bookkeeper merely added any new notations he felt to be needed to a legible book received from the playwright, one or more steps in many reconstructed histories of the transmission of playtexts can be eliminated.

There is another, less popular but nonetheless frequently assumed, notion for believing that the theater playbook could not usually serve as printer's copy: the belief that players would not lend a licensed book to a printer for fear of its being lost or mutilated. Bowers has capsulated and reinforced this position:

> in my private opinion no Shakespeare play was set directly from the promptbook, the last copy that would be permitted to leave the theater for ruination in the printer's shop, unless we may except one or two early works so long out of repertory that the promptbook had no value—but I do not know what plays these were.[9]

There is good sense to such an assumption, but that does not mean that setting from playbooks did not or could not occur unless a company deemed the play to be of value no longer. Manuscripts of non-dramatic works have survived the printing house complete with casting-off marks; not only have they not been mutilated, but also they still are in quite legible, even handsome, condition.[10] Unfortunately, like the manuscripts that have survived the playhouses, these printing house survivors are generally forgotten. Lending a licensed book to a printer might well have caused a company anxiety, but the process of composition by no means necessarily destroyed or even disfigured the manuscript. And considering the other kinds of extraneous markings which did not seem to bother playhouse bookkeepers, casting-off marks most likely would not have fazed them.

Given these options, let us look at the most influential examiner of the Folio, W. W. Greg. Of the thirty-five plays in the Folio, Greg found evidence of "foul" papers in no fewer than twenty-six. Greg stubbornly maintained that "prompt-books" had to be clean and without ambiguities—even in the face of radically conflicting evidence published in his own books. Thus, since his unsubstantiated opinions about what theatrical playbooks must have looked like had backed him into a corner, Greg had little room for considering other possibilities. In short, the evidence of the surviving playbooks strongly indicates that playwrights' manuscripts (Shakespeare's included) often stand much closer to early printed versions than is usually believed. But this possibility has been obscured by Greg's unwarranted assumptions about what "promptbooks" would and would not contain.

Let us look at some instances of how this works. Greg concluded that the 1600 quarto of *A Midsummer Night's Dream* was printed from Shakespeare's "foul" papers because of his tenacious beliefs about what cannot appear in a "prompt book." McKerrow's term "uncertainty" is brought into action. Once again the presumption is that varying labels for the same character represent authorial uncertainty; therefore a manuscript bearing such things is authorial but could go no further because a playhouse bookkeeper could not tolerate such things.

> There is some uncertainty in designating characters: Oberon is King of Fairies (or simply King) or Oberon indifferently; Titania is of course named in the text, but in directions appears only at II. ii. I. on her second entry, and may here be an addition; Bottom, on his most important appearance (IV. i. I) is merely 'Clowne'; Theseus and Hippolyta, after long appearing by name, become as a rule Duke and Duchess after the play begins in Act V; lastly Robin (Goodfellow) and the generic Puck alternate throughout, and since the names are used indifferently in the text and in the prefixes of a single scene (III. ii), we do not need to follow Fleay in the belief that they indicate different periods of composition rather than the habitual inconsistency of the author. . . . In view, however, of the absence of some necessary entrances and exits, and of the persistence of irregularities noted above, we are bound to conclude that the bookkeeper's notes, such as they are, were desultory jottings on the foul papers; for, in spite of the general cleanness of the text, we can hardly imagine that Q represents a finished prompt-book.[11]

In comparison with the way similar features were handled in the surviving playbooks, such conclusions are not supportable. It would seem that the printer's copy for Q very well could have been the "finished prompt-book."

Greg goes on to note that the 1619 quarto was printed from the 1600 quarto without significant variation and that the Folio was printed from Q2.

[Dover] Wilson is obviously right in assuming that the copy of Q2 used for F had either been compared rather closely with the prompt-book, or had else been itself annotated to serve as one. And naturally, since he sent the original prompt-book to press in 1600, he inclines to the second alternative. But this appears improbable in view of the many uncorrected abnormalities that remain, the clumsiness of the alterations themselves, and especially . . . the two fragments of dialogue 'Stand forth Demetrius' and 'Stand forth Lisander,' that Q1 printed as stage-directions at I. i. 14 and 16, and that still appear as such in F. It is difficult to believe either in a prompt-manuscript or in a prompt-quarto which allowed such an error like this to go uncorrected. Everything indeed points to Q having been printed from foul papers that had received some slight attention from the bookkeeper, and F from a copy of Q2 that had been compared with the prompt-book by a rather fussy but incompetent editor, meticulous in introducing manuscript readings whenever he noticed them, but liable to overlook as many as caught his attention.[12]

All this is possible, of course, but one wonders how likely it is. Greg has limited the possibilities of understanding the phenomena under investigation because he has prejudged opinions about what certain pieces of evidence can mean. Names used interchangeably or those differing in various parts of a play do not necessarily connote authorial "indifference." They very well might mean that the playwright had something else in mind from what the scholar supposes. Similarly, notations for entrances and exits that do not appear where twentieth-century expectations would have them do not necessarily betoken an error by late sixteenth-century playwrights or theatrical personnel. The surviving playbooks contain many anomalies such as Greg mentions (and many far more serious and even contradictory ones); yet the bookkeepers saw no reason to change or to "correct" them. One is led to wonder if, given the changes marked in it over the years, the same "promptbook" that served as copy for Q1 in 1600 could not have served in the same capacity in 1623. Here and in other plays, extra steps ("fair" copies, "producer's" copies, "foul" copies) seem to have been postulated needlessly.

Harold Brooks notes of Greg's commentary that "Though I have examined all the evidence independently, [I] am reassured to find my conclusions so largely the same as his."[13] What then occurs is not only typical of what has happened again and again in textual investigation but also has become almost formulaic: a possible explanation of a phenomenon seems to justify certain assumptions or predilections; this suggestion soon gets promoted to fact; and succeeding scholars shore their positions by quoting the original possibility as "proof." The entire process becomes pointlessly (and, depending upon the personalities involved, often viciously) circular. Scholarly articles and introductions proliferate, but the investigation of the texts of Shakespeare and others has stagnated badly. Existing evidence has been ignored regularly; knowledge of working theater avoided studiously; and we are little closer to understanding what happened with English Renaissance drama texts than we were half a century ago.[14] Brooks continues on *A Midsummer Night's Dream*.

> The First Quarto is of the very highest textual authority, since it bears many of the marks of having been printed from the author's 'foul papers': that is, his autograph draft (in this instance evidently in its final state; simply not a fair copy). Certainly it was not printed from the prompt-book which would be transcribed from the autograph.
>
> The stage-directions of the Q1 text would not have been satisfactory for regulating performance—the function of a prompt-book. The Q1 exits are some twenty short of those an editor finds essential. . . . There are ambiguities, too, which the bookholder (prompter) would have been obliged to resolve. Unless at III. i. 58 *Sn.* was the compositor's abbreviation of a fuller speech-prefix in the copy, a prompter would have wanted to know whether Snout or Snug was to speak. The generic titles sometimes given to characters in the Q1 text would not have sufficed him; especially not at the start of IV. ii, where 'and the rabble' does not reveal that only Snout and Starveling come on with Quince and Flute/Thisby—Snug as well as Bottom joining them later. . . . Variation in the designations of

characters, as with 'Clownes' and 'rabble' denoting in groups persons elsewhere individually named, has been recognized as indicating foul-paper copy ever since Mc-Kerrow pointed out how it would inconvenience a prompter, and how naturally it would come to a dramatist, thinking of his stage-people now in this way, now in that.[15]

Some of the assumptions here are so totally unproven that it should not be necessary to point out that they are based upon airy nothing. "The prompt-book . . . would be transcribed from the playwright's autograph." Such editorial certainty is almost breathcatching. On the basis of what evidence is such a statement made? The "evidence" is merely editorial presumption and/or wishful thinking. "The stage-directions of the Q1 text would not have been satisfactory for regulating performance. . . ." The obvious question to ask is "not satisfactory to whom?" Certainly they are not so to twentieth-century editors, but the question should be "how satisfactory were they to late sixteenth-century players?" What evidence do we have that the players did not find these directions satisfactory? If we can find none, then do we not have the obligation to accept, at least as a line of inquiry, that the players may have found them satisfactory and to consider what this might tell us about the crafting and performing of plays in the period? Do we really know what the players "required"? Are their "requirements" not just what modern editors believe that they needed?

"The Q1 exits are some twenty short of those an editor finds essential." No doubt, if one is thinking about readers. But to judge the provenance (let alone the theatrical effectiveness) of a sixteenth-century playbook by twentieth-century editorial "needs" is absurd. Brooks's comments about the ambiguities and generic titles yet further reveal one of the basic problems in the editing of English Renaissance plays in general and those of Shakespeare in particular: the editor does not perceive his task as an opportunity to explore a highly complex problem about which little is known, but rather (all too often) he chooses to "explain" in a dogmatic fashion based upon twentieth-century prejudices what "a prompter would have wanted to know" instead of using sixteenth-century playhouse documents to attempt to discover what the players needed to know and thus to try to discover how the players functioned.[16] Even then the answers may not be discoverable, but the directions in which more factually supported answers might lie can be suggested.

McKerrow's observation is an important pioneering moment even though he did not attempt to find out how "prompters" worked. Brooks's textual introduction combines McKerrow's weakest side with Greg's conclusions extended and expanded. The supports for Brooks's conclusions are Greg's statements. Greg's unsubstantiated assertions now are footnoted as "proof" to support Brooks's conclusions. Need I point out that what has been erected by McKerrow's successors is a very rickety house of cards? This is not to say that a number of things that both Greg and Brooks conclude are not in accord with the evidence of the surviving playbooks; but much is not, and no reader without prior knowledge of such material could possibly tell which conclusions are in accord with surviving evidence and which are not. As it stands, the Greg-Brooks textual explanation of *A Midsummer Night's Dream* is an unmarked path through a quicksand bog.

Against this treatment, let us compare that of *Henry VIII*. Greg judges the Folio copy to have been prepared "from foul papers carefully prepared for production (or a transcript of them)."[17] The speech-heads offer little variation; but then, there is little reason to expect that there would have been much because this play concentrates more on fewer characters than does *Dream*, and these characters are changed by historical circumstances both in relation to one another and to their status. When discussing speech-heads, Greg begins with a statement that is easily demonstrable as erroneous: "Nor is there ever any irregularity in the designation of characters."[18] He then proceeds to muddle the differences he finds:

> Wolsey is 'Cardinall Wolsey', seldom plain 'Wolsey' (once 'Woolsey'), or 'the Cardinal' (and always '*Car.*' or '*Card.*' as speaker). . . . Katherine is regularly 'Queene' til after the divorce, when (IV. ii. 1.) she becomes 'Katherine Dowager' (with the prefix 'Kath.')[19]

"Seldom" will not do. This vagueness tells us nothing about the context without which there is no hope of discovering explanations. Greg is wrong about Wolsey's '*Car.*' speech-heads—there is some alteration from Act II on, but he is chiefly "*Wol.*" after his fall. Thus Greg is partially right, partially wrong; in all cases, however, he fails to relate his findings to those observed in other plays; and most important, he usually fails to discriminate among the occurrences here: with Katherine he notes both when and why the speech-headings change (her change of status at different points)—a common Shakespearean instance; but the same phenomenon occurs with Wolsey, and Greg does not even record it.

In the Arden edition, R. A. Foakes is careful and, except for his assumptions about the "prompter," refreshingly free of preconceptions and unsupportable suppositions.

> Some regular variations in speech prefixes are due to the habits of the compositors who set up the text of *Henry VIII*, but several irregular variations were probably in the manuscript. In IV. ii. Katherine appears as *Kath.*, but elsewhere as *Que(en)* or *Qu.*; the *Old L(ady)* of II. iii. becomes simply *Lady* in V. i. . . . In addition certain pages contain what seems to be an indiscriminate use of *Wol(s).* and *Car(d).* as speech prefixes for *Wolsey*, which cannot all be accounted for by a shortage of italic capitals or transference from his name as it has just appeared in the text. This occurs notably in III. i, in which scene there are two cardinals on the stage, and the use of the prefix *Car(d).* here is in any case ambiguous. These differences in the speech-prefixes allowed to a character, which could easily lead to confusion in the theatre, again suggest the author's hand, rather than prompt copy, which needs to have clear and unambiguous speech-headings.[20]

That these variations are authorial seems indisputable, but the assumption of what the "prompter" needed simply does not accord with the evidence of the surviving manuscript play-books. There would not have been confusion in the theater unless the "prompter" were handling the players as if they were puppets. Surely Shakespeare (and/or Fletcher) knew that such labels would not cause confusion on stage. But confusion most assuredly can come in a reading edition, and (for his purposes) Foakes always correctly uses *Wol.* as Wolsey's speech-head. This eliminates confusion for the reader, but it necessarily distances the serious researcher from Shakespeare's text. That Foakes carefully records the Folio speech-heads in the textual notes follows the letter of accuracy but not the spirit of the Folio text; for that one must needs go to the Hinman facsimile. Simplification and even clarification cannot always be in the best interests of those seeking to understand the milieu of Shakespeare's texts. Such a predicament poses a serious problem for the creation of scholarly editions not just of Shakespeare, but of all English Renaissance playwrights. Shakespeare's use of varying speech-heads for individuals not unexpectedly can be found in his labeling of groups. *Coriolanus* ("from foul papers carefully prepared for production")[21] provides numerous examples. In an area entirely ignored by Greg ("There is no ambiguity in the designation of characters. . . ."),[22] Philip Brockbank speaks provocatively:

> Speech-headings present an abnormal number of difficulties, sometimes occasioned by apparent misreadings, sometimes by misrepresentations of alignment, and sometimes perhaps by lack of clarity in the playwright's intentions; errors could also arise from the compositor's anticipating the wrong speech-heading or by eye-skip in the margin of the copy. . . . There are occasional discontinuities between directions and prefixes, owing apparently to Shakespeare's inconsistent naming of the social groups and classes of Rome. In a dozen directions and twenty-five speech-headings the term *Citizen* or its contractions is used (in both stints and in the first four acts); four directions, however, speak of *Plebeians* (II, iii. 152, 253, III. i. 178, III. iii. 38), with one speech-heading *All Ple.* at III. i. 213. The anomaly is of interest, suggesting that Shakespeare thought of the Citizens collectively as *Plebeians* when they were making their presence felt as a political faction (*Enter a rabble of Plebeians* [III. i. 178]); it is therefore admitted into the present edition.[23]

This commentary is of considerable interest for two vital and encouraging reasons: it is free of the usual contentions unsupported by surviving evidence and draws its conclusions from the evidence of the text, and it (cautiously and partially) admits anomalies into its modernized readers' text. One is tempted to wonder if these promising developments are due only to the editor's perspicacity or whether his position as explorer of the text was enhanced (and encouraged) because Greg had not commented on these speech-heads.

This paper is a plea to editors and bibliographers to attempt to find the explanations to many problems in understanding facts of a theatrical tradition older than printing and by no means yet fully adjusted to it. Again and again editors attribute readers' problems to Shakespeare's being "careless" or "inattentive" or "forgetful" in situations where to have been "careful" or "attentive" or "remembering" would have been irrelevant, pointless, and a general waste of time and effort. This is not to say that Shakespeare (and his compositors) did not leave problems; it is merely to remind us that such excuses are too easily and far too frequently invoked by editors apparently unfamiliar with and unreceptive to theatrical habits and traditions. It is not the purpose of this paper (nor could it be possible in an essay) to consider all of the speech-head differences in all of the plays. I wish merely to establish some reasons for endorsing the claims of those who believe that the differences in speech-heads are important for examining the way Shakespeare (and others) worked, for determining the practice of handling varying labels in the theater, for investigating the possible meaning of such labels in the construction and performance of the plays, and for studying the very important evidence that varying speech-heads provide in tracing the provenance of the copy which lay behind printed texts.

Varying speech-heads need careful and thoughtful consideration on all of these fronts. We no longer can afford to dismiss them as errors or curiosities or playwrights' "uncertainties." Varying speech-heads are vital clues which significantly can aid research on very complicated problems. If scholarship wishes to be taken seriously, it cannot continue to base its conclusions on unsupported (and often unsupportable) suppositions. The careful exploration of the existence of varying speech-heads is one path out of the unfortunate tangle that exists in the study of English Renaissance dramatic texts.

Notes

1. *The Review of English Studies,* 11 (1935), 459–65.
2. Ibid., 462.
3. See Edward Alleyn's Orlando part from Greene's *Orlando Furioso* in W. W. Greg, *Dramatic Documents from the Elizabethan Playhouses: Stage Plots: Actors' Parts: Prompt Books,* 2 vols. (Oxford: Clarendon Press, 1931), I, 176–81 and II (unpaginated).
4. For an introductory survey of the use of evidence from the surviving playbooks, see William B. Long, "Stage-Directions: A Misunderstood Factor in Determining Textual Provenance," *TEXT: Transactions of the Society for Textual Scholarship,* 2 (1985), 121–37.
5. McKerrow, 464.
6. "Authority, Copy, and Transmission in Shakespeare's Texts," in *Shakespeare Study Today: The Horace Howard Furness Memorial Lectures,* ed. Georgianna Ziegler (New York: AMS Press, 1986), 22.
7. The sixteen surviving manuscript playbooks are, in chronological order: Anthony Munday, *John a Kent and John a Cumber,* 1590; Anthony Munday, et al., *Sir Thomas More,* 1592-93; Anon., *Thomas of Woodstock,* ca. 1594-95, and revivals ca. 1602-04 and ca. 1633; Anon., *Edmond Ironside,* 1590-1600; Anon., *Charlemagne,* ca. 1603-05; Anon., *The Second Maiden's Tragedy,* 1611; John Fletcher and Philip Massinger, *Sir John van Olden Barnavelt,* 1619; Anon., *The Two Noble Ladies,* 1619-23; Thomas Dekker, *The Welsh Embassador,* ca. 1623; Thomas Heywood, *The Captives,* 1624; Philip Massinger, *The Parliament of Love,* 1624; John Fletcher, *The Honest Man's Fortune,* 1625; John Clavell, *The Soddered Citizen,* ca. 1630; Philip Massinger, *Believe as You List,* 1631; Walter Mountfort, *The Launching of the Mary,* 1633; Henry Glapthorne, *The Lady Mother,* 1635.
8. Philip Massinger, *Believe as You List,* ed. Charles J. Sisson, Malone Society Reprints (London: Malone Society, 1927), f. 4ª,

32 and f. 21^b, 2199 (stage-direction).

9. Bowers, 25.

10. This phenomenon has been carefully documented by W. Speed Hill in "Casting Off Copy and the Composition of Hooker's Book V," *Studies in Bibliography,* 33 (1980), 144–62 and in his introductory discussion, "Use as Printer's Copy" (pages xxiv-xxviii and Illustrations 4–7) of Richard Hooker, *Of the Laws of Ecclesiastical Polity* Book V, *The Folger Library Edition of The Works of Richard Hooker,* Volume Two (Cambridge, Mass.: The Belknap Press of Harvard University Press, 1977). Randall McLeod also has identified printer's casting-off marks in the manuscript of Sir John Harington's *Orlando Furioso* and has discussed their significance in his work in progress "Or Words to that dEffect."

Of course, although Hill and McLeod recently have called attention to these manuscripts, their existence has been known for years. W. W. Greg discussed the *Orlando* manuscript in "An Elizabethan Printer and His Copy," *The Library,* Fourth Series, IV (1923), 102–18; rpr. *The Collected Papers of Sir Walter Greg,* ed. J. C. Maxwell (Oxford: Clarendon Press, 1966), 95–109. Greg noted:

> The fact that we possess copy which has actually passed through the hands of an Elizabethan printer does not appear to be generally known to bibliographers. In spite of Harington's manuscript having been for over seventy years in the British Museum, almost the only allusion to it I have seen is in a short contribution to *Notes and Queries* in 1910. Yet it is hardly necessary to insist on the importance of the information to be derived from such a source. (95–96)

While Greg does not make any direct connection with stage manuscripts, he certainly seems aware of implications that could be derived from this manuscript.

> Incidentally it may be observed that on the whole the manuscript is remarkably clean and shows little material sign of having passed through the printer's hands. There is no reason to suppose that all printers would handle their copy with equal care, but it is

clear that the present manuscript at least was treated with respect and perhaps returned to the author; and it may have been too readily assumed that any copy sent to an Elizabethan printer would in the nature of things be destroyed. After all, at a time when circulation in manuscript was still common and manifolding unknown, and when a carefully written copy of a work was more esteemed than one printed (as can, I think, be demonstrated), a printer must often have been called upon to deal with copy which the owner valued and would expect to receive again in good condition. (100–101)

Unfortunately for the discussion of playbooks, Greg then joined those who ignored or were innocent of the possibilities indicated here.

Percy Simpson in his *Proof-reading in the Sixteenth, Seventeenth and Eighteenth Centuries* (London: Oxford University Press, 1935; rpr. 1970) discussed both the Harington (71–75) and the Hooker (76–79) manuscripts and reproduced f. 296r of *Orlando*. Of the first of Greg's sentences quoted in this note, Simpson felt pleasantly confident enough to say of it: "A comment of Dr. Greg's [that] shows the advance in knowledge since that [1923] date" (p. 71); but Simpson, too, makes no connections between the printers' treatment of these two manuscripts and the possibilities of similar treatment for playhouse manuscripts. Reviewing Simpson's book in the very year as his speech-heads article (*The Library*, Fourth Series, XVI [1935], 347–32; rpr. in the "Foreword to the Reprint" in the 1970 edition of Simpson), McKerrow also draws no connections with playhouse manuscripts. Thus we sadly observe three of the finest as well as most knowledgeable minds in the field observing evidence and then abandoning it, a pattern followed by their successors.

11. W. W. Greg, *The Shakespeare First Folio: Its Bibliographical and Textual History* (Oxford: Clarendon Press, 1955), 241.

12. Ibid., 245–46.

13. William Shakespeare, *A Midsummer Night's Dream*, ed. Harold F. Brooks, The Arden Shakespeare (London: Methuen & Co., Ltd., 1979), xxii n. 1.

14. There are important exceptions to this picture, many of them being advanced by contributors to this volume. It is superfluous here to document these encouraging, even exciting, developments. There may indeed be hope, but the opposition is strong, entrenched, and often adamant.

15. Brooks, xxii, xxiii.
16. See, for example, Bernard Beckerman's incisive considerations of the evidence provided by the surviving stage-plots, "Theatrical Plots and Elizabethan Stage Practice," in *Shakespeare and Dramatic Tradition: Essays in Honor of S. F. Johnson,* ed. W. R. Elton and William B. Long (Newark, Del.: University of Delaware Press, 1989), 109–24.
17. Greg, *First Folio,* 427.
18. Ibid., 424.
19. Ibid., 424–25.
20. William Shakespeare, *King Henry VIII*, ed. R. A. Foakes, The Arden Shakespeare (London: Methuen & Co., Ltd., 1964), xvi–xvii.
21. Greg, *First Folio,* 427.
22. Ibid., 406.
23. William Shakespeare, *Coriolanus,* ed. Philip Brockbank, The Arden Shakespeare (London: Methuen & Co., Ltd., 1976), 20. It is to be noted that two years previously G. Blakemore Evans also admitted this Folio direction into his *Riverside Shakespeare* (Boston: Houghton Mifflin Co.).

Who is Hubert? Speech-headings in *King John,* Act II

A. R. Braunmuller

After almost two hundred lines of argument about who has sovereignty over Angers, the kings of France and England decide to ask the citizens "Whose title they admit" (*King John* II.i.200).[1] The Folio directs:

Trumpet founds.
Enter a Citizen vpon the walles.

(II.iii.200.1–2/TLN 504–5)

This actor speaks, and his four brief but intransigent speeches in the next ninety-odd lines are all headed *Cit.* After an inconclusive battle, first a French Herald enters *"to the gates"* and then an English one, each demanding some pledge of loyalty. The reply begins:

*Hubert.*Heralds, from off our towres we might behold

(II.i.325/TLN 636)

This speaker, like *Cit.*, resists the heralds' and, soon, their kings' demands for a decision; with the exception of a single error (*Fra.* at II. i. 368), this speaker's prefix is *Hub.* for the remainder of the scene, and *Cit.* never reappears. John Dover

Wilson suggested that *Cit.* and *Hubert* might be the same character,[2] and the play's three most recent editors (Ernst Honigmann, William Matchett, and Robert Smallwood) have merged the characters into a single "Hubert" who (re)appears in Act III, scene iii, in all three scenes of Act IV, in Act V, scenes iii and vi, and possibly in Act V, scene vii (at the end of Act V, scene vi, the Bastard says to Hubert, "Conduct me to the king," but Faulconbridge enters alone in scene vii, and Hubert has no lines in that scene).[3]

*

Before we consider the explanations proposed for F's evidence, we should note the following:

1. The line in which *Hubert* appears as a speech heading is full and justified: it is indented less than usual and no space was set between the stop following the speech heading and the first word of text.

2. In F *King John,* speech headings do not customarily give a full name upon a character's first speaking (with the usual exception of the play's very first speaker and these further exceptions: *Essex* at I. i. 44, *Lewis*—erroneously—at II. i. 1, and perhaps *Philip* at I. i. 50 and *Robert* at I. i. 56), and very rarely do so for a character's subsequent speeches (*Philip* at I. i. 59 and I. i. 92, *Elinor* at I. i. 148 and 155, *Lewis* at II. i. 18, *Arthur* at II. i. 163, *France* at II. i. 235, *Blanch* at III. i. 300). A spot check of three plays set before *John* suggests that no convention governed the setting of full names in speech headings and that full names are very rare.

3. *Hubert.* appears in the first page of the first forme of *King John* to be composed; Compositor B was working "outward" in the gathering and would therefore not have had the reader's sense that *Cit.* had changed to *Hubert* and *Hub.*[4] Rather, the compositor would find speeches assigned to *Hub.* in text following the point where he set the name for the first time and (if he thought about it) no assignments in text that preceded that first setting.

4. The Folio contains several apparent confusions of names in speech headings in Act II (or "Scaena Secunda" as F calls this division); one of these confusions involves a speaker from the walls of Angers (II. i. 368, where F's *Fra[nce]* may be explained as a graphic misreading of *Hub.*), and another (II. i. 149ff.) involves an apparent confusion among speeches by either Lewis the Dauphin or his father King Philip.[5] To them, we may add the following: John's mother is called *Queene* in the entry direction at II. i. 83.1 and *Queen, Qu. Mo., Qu.,* and *Que.* in the speech headings for all of Act II, but some variant of "Eleanor" or "Elinor" for all her other speeches in the play (that is, in Acts I and III). The only anomalous speech headings outside "Scaena Secunda" are two for Philip Faulconbridge; the heading for his speeches changes to *Bast.* at I. i. 151, but reverts to *Phil.* at III. i. 131 and 133, and then changes back to *Bast.* at III. i. 199 where it remains (with one *Ba.*) for the rest of the play.

5. "Hubert" does not occur in the dialogue until Act III, scene iii, when King John repeats the name eight times in 53 lines; Arthur also uses the name frequently two scenes later (Act IV, scene i).

6. Professional actors and producers might be expected to cope with discrepancies, but the audience is much less flexible and much more ignorant. It is therefore not surprising that the dialogue contains few confusions of names. Nor is it surprising that they all involve Philip Faulconbridge, knighted as "Sir Richard and Plantagenet" (I. i. 162). John addresses him as "Richard" (I. i. 178), and he immediately calls himself "Sir Richard" (I. i. 185); he soon rejects Gurney's "good Philip" (I. i. 231), only later to call himself "Philip" (III. ii. 4), by which name King John immediately addresses him (III. ii. 5). A Messenger calls him "Faulconbridge" (V. iii. 5, and then "Richard" at l. 12); Salisbury calls him "devil Faulconbridge" (V. iv. 4). In Act IV, scene iii, where the names appear as part of an increasingly angry conversation and are probably used as social obloquy, the Bastard is first addressed as "Sir, sir" (32), then "Sir Richard" (41), and then "Faulconbridge" (94, 101). Otherwise the dialogue emphasizes his bastardy (I. i. 246ff., II.

i. 65, II. i. 276, III. iv. 171), his new familial relation to the royal characters (John and Eleanor use "cousin," "kinsman," and "gentleman" when they require his assistance: III. iii. 6, III. iii. 17, IV. ii. 137, 159, 166, 177), or his anonymity ("One," "cracker," "villain," "ruffian," "Brave soldier," "sweet sir" at II. i. 135 and 147, III. i. 132, III. i. 200, V. vi. 13, and V. vi. 19, respectively).

7. Shakespeare seems to have had trouble keeping his characters and their historical names straight. "Cardinal Pandulph," for instance, combines two, perhaps three, historical figures, and the historical model for most of Pandulph's fictional acts was never a cardinal. This confusion is not bothersome, and it is theatrically effective: a cardinal's red robes would burn brightly on a Protestant stage. Similarly, the merging of Richard I's captor, the Duke of Austria, with the man, Viscount of Limoges, who commanded the castle where Richard received his mortal wound, causes no difficulty because the two historical events are themselves merged.[6] The way the speech-headings waver over who is King of France— Philip or Lewis—earlier in Act II and the suggestion that "Lewis" and "Dolphin" are two different characters (in the entry direction of Act II) are not encouraging, nor is the dialogue's uncertainty over the precise familial relation among Geoffrey, Richard, John, and Arthur (II. i. 6 and 13).

8. F's stage directions here, as elsewhere, do not provide all the information the contemplative reader might wish: after the entry for *a Citizen upon the walls,* there are no explicit exit directions for the subsequent actions, but instead only entries for the two heralds (*Here, after excursions, enter. . .*) and the two kings. The editorial addition of an exit when the kings depart to do battle is easy and obvious, but what about Citizen? The usual assumption (partly supported by the text: "from off our walls we might behold . . . the onset and retire / Of both your armies") seems to be that he remains *upon the walls,* although only Smallwood makes this assumption explicit in additional stage directions.

9. Before the battle, Citizen speaks in the plural, and the kings address a plural audience:

Who is Hubert?

Who is it that hath warned *us* to the walls

You *men* of Angers, and my loving *subjects*

You loving *men* of Angers, Arthur's *subjects*

In brief, *we* are the king of England's *subjects,*
For him . . . *we* hold this town

That can *we* not. . .
To him will *we* prove loyal . . .

We for the worthiest hold the right from both
                                        (my italics)

After the battle, the heralds and kings again address a plural audience, and Hubert uses plural pronouns (*we, our*) twelve consecutive times until he uses *I* when proposing the marriage between Blanche and Lewis: "Vouchsafe a while to stay, / And I shall show you peace and fair-faced league" (II. i. 416–17).

*

Analyses of the Citizen/Hubert problem have been confused through editors' arguing *from* their theories of F's copy *to* this evidence and *from* this evidence *to* conclusions about copy. Inference should instead flow in one direction only: either unequivocal evidence of F's copy establishes a plausible assumption which controls argument here *or* this evidence is logically prior to conclusions about F's copy. The argument probably cannot escape the hermeneutic circle, but we should try to run around that circle in one direction only. Since evidence for F's copy is inconclusive, we are left asking how the problem in Act II might have evolved, and I would like to suggest some inferences from the observations just listed.

First, the compositor probably did not create the difficulty. It is nearly certain that Compositor B read *Hubert* as a speech heading at *John* II. i. 325, and it is probable that he perceived this prefix more emphatically than most other speech headings: economy of space in the line (#1) and his practice else-where in *John* and earlier in F (#2) strongly suggest that his inclination would have been to abbreviate the speech heading. (But, #3, we must remember that Compositor B was now only getting started on a new play and new copy, and we may want to speculate on how *Hubert* came to be or was made emphatic.) Second, anomalous speech headings are concentrated in this unit of *John,* but the Citizen/Hubert problem, like all but two of the other confusions, would not necessarily trouble theatre professionals the way they do a reader (#4). Third, the moment when a character is "named"—either by identifying props or a proper noun—is an important moment for an audience and the dramatist; "Hubert" is not identified until Act III, scene iii, but he is then very deliberately and frequently named (#5, #6). That is, if Hubert speaks from the walls of Angers, the theatre audience could not identify him as "Hubert" until 641 lines after F first assigns him a speech heading.[7] Fourth, if Shakespeare was confused about and/or running short of more-or-less historical names, he may first have wanted a named cit-izen of Angers and then might have decided to make him anonymous, in order to "save" a vaguely historical name for Arthur's jailor and near-murderer. Fifth, F's evidence for the staging of the scene is slightly inconclusive, but it seems most likely that at least one actor might remain *on the walls* during the *excursions* of battle, since *excursions* usually, if not invari-ably, refers to sound effects (#8).[8] If we take F's direction liter-ally, only one actor (*a Citizen*) has been directed to enter, only he remains, and only he addresses the heralds when they appear. We have, however, to take account of the dialogue's consistent testimony that more than one actor has entered *on the walls* (#9).

*

Two principal explanations have been offered for F's evi-dence. J. P. Collier and Aldis Wright suggested that the same actor played the distinct roles of Citizen and of Hubert, and in the middle of the second act someone consequently chose to call Citizen first *Hubert* and then *Hub.* (or something the compositor could plausibly print thus).[9]

It is certainly possible to double Citizen and Hubert; indeed, a minimum casting for the play would assign one actor the roles of James Gurney, Citizen, and Hubert. If the roles were doubled, however, they nonetheless could, and probably would, have remained distinct for the audience. Doubling Citizen and Hubert while keeping them distinct characters assumes, of course, that the actor performs "Citizen" throughout Act II and then appears as "Hubert" in Act III, scene iii. (Otherwise, we must imagine a single actor who exits after his first four speeches and then re-enters, having changed costume or other features of his visual and vocal presence to indicate a new identity!) Moreover, a mixture of speech headings as a consequence of doubling "has no comparable parallel in the canon" as Honigmann says (p. xxxvii; Smallwood, p. 354, concurs); Honigmann continues, "In those plays where doubling is thought to have caused confusion of names only *isolated* instances of confusion are known . . . in *John* Hubert takes over the Citizen's part *systematically* from II. i. 325" (p. xxxvii, n2). This latter comment of course assumes that the parts are the same, or were eventually conceived of as the same (otherwise "takes over" would be illogical).

Dover Wilson and, with more conviction, Ernst Honigmann argued that Shakespeare changed his mind, seeking to make "Citizen" less anonymous and to link the important, named character (Hubert) of the play's second half with an unimportant one in the first half; unfortunately, Shakespeare did not finish (or someone else did not finish for him) rewriting the speech headings of Citizen's first four speeches. The mechanical (or manual) element in this argument is attractive, but reversible. In principle, the "Hubert" of Act II could be in the process of metamorphosing into "Citizen" as plausibly as the reverse.

The further arguments for conflating Citizen and Hubert turn upon assumptions about Shakespeare's techniques of dramatic organization and characterization. It is difficult to find a theatrical or critical justification for merging the two characters.[10] Honigmann offers the best argument (p. xxxvii). He emphasizes three points: the implausibility of the alternative explanation based on doubling (see above); the play's fluctuation between impersonal and individualizing speeches; John's reference to Hubert's "voluntary oath" (III. iii. 23).

Like Matchett (p. xxix) and Smallwood (see especially his pp. 36–37) who accept the argument, Honigmann regards Hubert as a fence-sitter compelled to choose sides; the fearful but politically disinterested "Citizen" (now to be conflated with Hubert) throws in with John and agrees to kill, not keep, his prisoner. Deciding to join John in Act III, scene iii, however, "Hubert still [presumably this *still* refers to the speeches assigned to a named Hubert in Act II] speaks impersonally," and Honigmann guesses that "Shakespeare may have decided to heighten the 'impersonal' impression through identification with the Citizen, so that Hubert's thawing out in IV. i. . . . would give edge to that central scene." Some critics might find Hubert's "thawing out" finely managed within Act IV, scene i itself and his deferential monosyllables in Act III, scene iii a sufficient contrast. Although Smallwood merges Citizen and Hubert, for instance, he explicitly locates the "impersonal" Hubert not in Act II but in the "taciturnity with which he accepted John's terrible commission in Act III, scene 3" (p. 36). Even granting Honigmann's premise of impersonal/personal alternations, one should not fit Hubert into the pattern quite so quickly. While his threats from the walls of Angers may be magniloquence or rant, they do not seem impersonal to the Bastard:

> . . . Here's a large mouth indeed
> That spits forth death and mountains, rocks and seas;
> Talks as familiarly of roaring lions
> As maids of thirteen do of puppy-dogs.
> What cannoneer begot this lusty blood?
> He speaks plain cannon-fire, and smoke, and bounce;
> He gives the bastinado with his tongue.
> Our ears are cudgelled; not a word of his
> But buffets better than a fist of France.
> Zounds, I was never so bethumped with words

Since I first called my brother's father Dad.
(II. i. 458–68)

Nor should we forget that for a theatre audience, Honigmann's version of this change from impersonal to individual requires that we retrospectively integrate the character given a name at III. iii. 19 with the anonymous speaker we last heard 493 lines ago (at II. i. 482).

When he first addresses a character explicitly named "Hubert," John says,

> Come hither, Hubert. O my gentle Hubert,
> We owe thee much. Within this wall of flesh
> There is a soul counts thee her creditor,
> And with advantage means to pay thy love.
> And, my good friend, thy voluntary oath
> Lives in this bosom, dearly cherishèd.
> Give me thy hand. I had a thing to say,
> But I will fit it with some better tune.
> By heaven, Hubert, I am almost ashamed
> To say what good respect I have of thee.
> (III. iii. 19–28)

Honigmann comments, "As the two other voluntary oaths (V. i. 29, V. ii. 10) show, a vassal's oath of allegiance is meant. John's thanks are not altogether too extravagant if *Hubert* swore on behalf of Angiers. The *Citizen* had repeatedly refused to pay allegiance on behalf of Angiers till one king should prove greatest: as John did prove greatest, and Angiers did submit to him (III. iii. 6), continuity of character seems to be urged by the action quite apart from the essential corroboration of the text" (p. xxxvii). At once, we may recall Greg's dry comment: "it is surely not unlike Shakespeare to give solidity to a character by casual allusions to supposed happenings beyond the scope of the action as known to the spectator."[11] (John's "way to win" the nobles' "loves again" [IV. ii. 168] and his "fever" [V. iii. 3] are similarly unexplained.)

Just as the claims about Hubert's impersonality may be the result of unwarranted assumptions, Honigmann's argument here may scant certain evidence. The representative of Angers in Act II (whether "Citizen" or "Hubert") never swears allegiance. "Hubert," it is true, produces an ingenious and cynical proposal—the marriage of Blanche and Lewis—that spares Angers from the united enmity of France and England, but King John fulfills neither *Cit.*'s demand that the winning contestant be "he that proves the King" (II. i. 270) nor *Hubert's* demand that "One must prove greatest" (II. i. 332) in the sense that he demonstrates his superior claim to Angers by right or might. John explicitly exempts Angers from the political settlement and the marriage dowry (II. i. 448–90: "all that we upon this side the sea— / Except this city now by us besieged— / Find liable to our crown and dignity"), and it is King Philip who, much later, calls Angers "lost" in the line Honigmann cites ("III. iii. 6," or III. iv. 6 in most editions) after a battle quite separate from the original argument over Angers.

It is also stretching a point to treat "the two other voluntary oaths" as evidence for regarding "thy voluntary oath" as "a vassal's oath of allegiance." The two other oaths are, respectively, John's allegiance to Rome and the rebellious English nobles' allegiance to the invading Lewis. The only verbal connection is *voluntary* (i.e., unforced, willing). The two later instances may be *oaths* of vassalage and *voluntary,* but that does not mean that "voluntary oath" necessarily means "a vassal's oath of allegiance." The words may mean nothing other than *voluntaries* does at II. i. 67, i.e., that Hubert is a willing, not a compelled, soldier in the English cause (compare *Troilus and Cressida* II. i. 94-95: "Ajax was here the voluntary, and you as under an impress"). Furthermore, *voluntary* is patently ironic in one of Honigmann's examples: it describes John's desperate search for some support against the French. The Bastard's surprise (V. i. 65ff.: "O inglorious league!" etc.) ensures we understand that irony. And *voluntary* certainly could be ironic when it describes the nobles' search, perhaps equally desperate, for some ally to counter John. Thus, for Honigmann and Wilson, whom he follows here, as for all the editors and critics who never boggled at the phrase "thy voluntary oath," the phrase must refer to an unstaged event. Honigmann simply makes a hypothetical interpretation of a hypothetical event.

*

The dialogue of *King John,* Act II virtually stipulates that more than one actor enters on the walls of Angers; I conclude that Citizen and the character the dialogue later names as "Hubert" both enter at II. i. 200.2 and that Citizen speaks the pre-battle speeches and the character eventually identified (in Act III, scene iii) as "Hubert" speaks the post-battle speeches. A defensible, edited direction would thus read:

> *Trumpet sounds*
> *Enter Citizens of Angers, including Hubert, upon the walls*

That is, F's speech headings are accurate and one stage direction is not. This direction might appear to create a technical anomaly: except for the pronouns, the text does not acknowledge plural presences on the walls of Angers and provides neither distinction nor dialogue among these hypothetical citizens.[12] Other Shakespearian and quasi-Shakespearian texts do, however, dramatize episodes very like this one in *King John.* In *3 Henry VI,* Act IV, scene vii, a stage direction reads *"Enter on the Walls, the Maior of Yorke, and his Brethren"* (TLN 2511-12), but only the Mayor appears in speech prefixes, and he employs plural pronouns in his first speech ("We . . . our selues . . . we . . ."), a singular pronoun ("I") in his second, and none at all when he finally concedes to Lord Hastings' demand, "Open the Gates, we are King *Henries* friends," with "I [Ay], say you so? the Gates shall then be opened" (TLN 2526-27). The actor is directed, *"He* descends" (TLN 2528). *The True Tragedy of Richard Duke of York* (anonymous octavo, 1595) bears some close affinity to *3 Henry VI*; in the scene corresponding with Shakespeare's Act IV, scene vii there appears only "Enter the Lord Maire of *Yorke* vpon the wals" (D7),[13] although here too the Mayor uses the first person plural exclusively before speaking in the first person singular and acting as he does in the Folio. A later scene in the octavo, analogous to Shakespeare's Act V, scene i, directs, "Enter *Warwicke on the walles*," and he proceeds to inquire for and then question two messengers and Summerfield. All three interlocutors may be in a different acting space from Warwick (they on the main stage, he "above"), but that leaves little room for the other actors who immediately follow: "Enter *Edward* and his power." The Folio version clears the doubt by directing "*Enter Warwicke, the Maior of Couentry, two Messengers, and others vpon the Walls*" (TLN 2672-73), but only Warwick and the two Messengers have any dialogue. While the octavo and Folio possibly, even probably, reflect different stagings of the respective scenes, the texts variously testify to the following: directions may mention a single actor when more than one has entered; directions may mention more actors than subsequently speak; groups of actors (especially groups designated as a category) may be directed to enter without the text providing them with distinctive actions, different points of view, and so forth; one actor from an otherwise silent group may speak for all until the action requires a specific, personal action or reaction.

If we wish, we may accept Honigmann's critical argument concerning Hubert's move from impersonality to individuality (only four short "impersonal" speeches are given to "Citizen") and locate the first shift when he drops *we* for *I* at II. i. 417, but Honigmann's case is—*in the theatre*—more probable based on dialogue from Act III, scene iii through Act IV, scene i and need not be extended back to Act II, scene i. We do not have to attach the phrase "voluntary oath" to any of the events dramatized in the play.

We may speculate that *"Hubert,"* was a late(r) thought, so emphatically marked in the printer's copy that Compositor B set the full name, but the thought may or may not have been Shakespeare's, may or may not have been prompted by the play's casting-pattern, may or may not have been partially or completely realized in the manuscript the compositors set. Copy for Act II (or "Scaena Secunda") probably comes from an early phase of the play's composition: the apparent uncertainty about the personal name of the French king, the genealogical confusion, and the functional rather than personal designations for Queen Eleanor suggest as much. Finally, since theatre professionals would not have much trouble performing F, there is no reason to suppose that F would have been "corrected" to remove the Citizen/Hubert "confusion" or the other problems I have mentioned even if F's copy originated in the theatre or had been partially marked up for production: the dialogue pretty certainly straightens out the confusion over the French king's name; the audience might not notice the genealogical muddle; Eleanor's speech headings are perfectly lucid since she is the only "queen" on stage. My hypothetical stage direction postulates only that professionals might freely vary, might even expect to vary, the number of characters in a stage direction, without leaving any trace in the script.14 The numerous unspecific directions in *King John,* elsewhere in F, and in manuscript promptbooks make this assumption plausible in genera, although they do not weigh on either side in any specific instance.

Notes

1. Modernized quotations and line references are from my edition of *King John* (Oxford: Clarendon Press, 1989). "F" refers to the first folio edition of Shakespeare (1623). I have adopted the French spelling "Angers" in preference to F's "Angiers" (everywhere except "Angires" at II. i. 536); neither spelling quite represents to a modern eye the likely Elizabethan pronunciation, "Anjers." T[hrough] L[ine] N[umber] references are to the Norton facsimile of F prepared by Charlton Hinman (New York, 1968).

   The editor of this volume and John Jowett, editor of *King John* in *The Complete Works,* gen. eds. Stanley Wells and Gary Taylor (Oxford: Clarendon Press, 1986), commented very helpfully (albeit sometimes in vain) on an earlier version of this essay.
2. J. D. Wilson, ed., *King John* (Cambridge: Cambridge University Press, 1936; slightly revised 1954), xlvff.
3. See, respectively, the following editions of *King John*: E. A. J. Honigmann, ed., Arden Shakespeare, 4th edition (London:

Methuen, 1954); William Matchett, ed., Signet Shakespeare (New York: New American Library, 1966); R. L. Smallwood, ed., New Penguin Shakespeare (Harmondsworth: Penguin, 1974). Hereafter, I cite each of these editions parenthetically and distinguish them by the editor's name.

4. See Charlton Hinman, *The Printing and Proof-reading of the Shakespeare First Folio,* 2 vols. (Oxford: Clarendon Press, 1963), ii. 515, for a summary of the order in which *King John* was composed.

5. See the summary discussion of these two problems in Honigmann's edition, pp. xxxiv-xxxvi and in my edition, Appendix 1. The confusion of *Fra.* and *Hub.* (or their variants) at II. i. 368 poses the harder problem for editorial explanation. Seeking support for his belief that Philip's speeches throughout Act II were headed *King* (or some variant), Honigmann imagines a two-stage process: italic *Hu* misread as *Ki[n.]* or secretary *Hu.* misread as *Ki[n.]* and then normalized to *Fra[ance].* A simpler hypothesis can be offered for a compositor's directly misreading an abbreviation for *Hubert* as *France*: since secretary hand lacked a distinct character for *F,* the form *Hu* (for *Hu[bert]*) in either secretary or italic hands could resemble the secretary *ff*—for upper-case F—followed by the common secretary u-shaped *r* and could thus be misread as *Fr* and set as *Fra* (= *France*).

6. These two characters are similarly merged in the anonymous *The Troublesome Reign of King John* (printed 1591); the relation of this play to Shakespeare's is a matter of interesting debate, but irrelevant to my purposes here.

7. In "Character Identification in the Theatre: Some Principles and Some Examples," *Renaissance Papers 1967* (1968), 55–67, Charles B. Lower describes some ways dialogue identifies a character by function rather than name, even if a name exists in those parts of the text (stage directions, speech prefixes) not spoken in the theatre.

8. For the likely meaning of *excursions,* see e.g., Alfred Harbage, *Theatre for Shakespeare* (Toronto: University of Toronto Press, 1955), 52–53.

9. See W. G. Clark and William Aldis Wright, eds., *The Works of William Shakespeare,* The Cambridge Shakespeare, 9 vols. (New York: Macmillan, 1891), iv. 119 (note xiv) and Honigmann, p. xxxvii.

10. In *The Origins of Shakespeare* (Oxford: Clarendon Press, 1977), 283-85, Emrys Jones also argues against merging the charac-

ters, although he believes Citizen alone speaks from the walls of Angers. Critics have debated whether Shakespeare modelled his Hubert on Hubert de Burgh, mentioned in Holinshed's *Chronicles* and historically a very important personage whose name editors have often given to this character. Jones claims that the play's Hubert is meant to be recognized as the historical Hubert de Burgh, but from "Bigot's contemptuous question at 4. 3. 87," Wilson (xlvii) deduced "that Hubert is of very mean birth," and I doubt the historical identification accepted by Jones and many others.

11. W. W. Greg, *The Shakespeare First Folio* (Oxford: Clarendon Press, 1955), 247, n. 7.

12. Most of these objections were raised privately by John Jowett (see n. 1). Jowett observes, "One might say that the Citizen [in F] exists only in order to be forgotten." Fair enough, but in the Folio and in any editorial reworking of it, the audience will be unable to *remember* "Hubert" as "Hubert" until Act III, scene iii, so forgetting one or more anonymous citizens seems a similar, and similarly negligible, hypothetical price to pay.

13. All quotations are from the facsimile prepared by W. W. Greg (Oxford: Clarendon Press, 1958), with long *s* modernized and signatures cited parenthetically.

14. Most productions place several actors on the walls of Angers, but Arthur Colby Sprague notes a Birmingham production of 1823 which was criticized for using a single citizen, and he defends "stylized treatment of this scene" (*Shakespeare's Histories: Plays for the Stage* [London: Society for Theatre Research, 1964], 24–25). It may be over-literal to demand plural citizens, but the dialogue certainly seems to stipulate them.

Today We Have Parting of Names: A Preliminary Inquiry into Some Editorial Speech-(Be)Headings in *Coriolanus*

Thomas Clayton

This paper represents a preliminary inquiry in which the questions share priority with such answers as the available evidence provides.[1] At the present post-structuralist moment, when the best edition is an "unedited edition," as recent text-theoretical McMissiles and milder salvos either assert or seem to imply,[2] editing a New Variorum Edition of *Coriolanus* might seem almost fashionable, though in my case inadvertently so. But I *have* recently come to think that of three essential kinds of text—the substantive texts unmediated, a pocket-sized reading-edition, and a New Variorum—the last *is* best for purposes that the first two will not serve: it gives a literatim reprint of the copy-text, "according to (or adjusted to) Folio lineation, and with minimal editing" (*Handbook*), together with full data on the transmission of the text and a thorough historical and critical commentary.[3]

Any printed text including F is a more or less accurate redaction—"edition"—of its setting copy. In the case of plays like *Cor.* that survive in only one substantive printed text (F sigs. aa1-cc3v), the nature of that copy is a matter of inference and speculation. In 1985 George W. Williams gave "fair copy" as the consensus of scholars about the copy for *Cor.* (86), and so Albert Gilman had found it in 1954: "a fair copy, in Shakespeare's hand or a scribe's, that *had been used as a prompt-book*" (673). In the *Riverside* edition (1974) G. Blakemore Evans wrote that "there is general agreement that the F1 text was printed from a carefully prepared authorial manuscript, a 'producer's copy' as it has been called, and that this manuscript, though perhaps showing one or two book-keeper's notations, had *never served as a prompt-book*" (1437a, italics mine). Two years later, in the New Arden edition (1976), Philip Brockbank found that "it is consistent with the evidence to suppose that F was set up from autograph copy, at least partly prepared by the playwright for the theatre. It is not possible to be sure that the book-keeper had or did not have a casual, occasional hand in it. Compositors A and B were responsible for adapting their copy to the reading conventions of the Folio, and in particular to the exigencies of its double-column format. Modern editors can at best seek to minimize the damage done in the process to Shakespeare's expressive intentions" (7). That description is both reasonable and open, but if I read William B. Long, McKerrow, Giorgio Melchiori, and even parts of *Coriolanus* right in the matter of speech-headings (hereafter SHs), we may wish to make some further modifications in our view of the printer's hypothetical copy and the extant printed text, and of its doubtful readings, including SHs.

One of Long's examples of recent editorial error that bears on the set text with which the studies in this volume began, McKerrow's "Suggestion Regarding Shakespeare's Manuscripts," is that of the Revels *Women Beware Women*: "J. R. Mulryne believes that the manuscript 'was not thoroughly readied for performance' because Isabella is referred to both as 'Neece' and as 'Isab'; 'we might expect a stage manuscript to avoid this sort of Playwright's confusion.' But the extant evidence shows that players were not concerned with regularizing this sort of playwright's inscription" ("Stage-Directions" 133). Elsewhere, on the basis of his study of surviving manuscript playbooks, he concludes that "there is no evidence . . . that theater personnel removed, simplified, or regularized . . . play-wright's directions in preparing a playwright's manuscript to be a 'promptbook.' Playwrights' manuscripts probably did not go through the 'scribal copy' stage as often as many commenta-tors . . . postulate. It seems to have been much more common for a play to go directly from the playwright to the players without scribal copying and certainly without much annotation or adding or changing of stage-directions by the personnel—as in *Woodstock*" ("A bed" 94). If that is so, the hallowed editorial distinction between author's manuscript and prompt-book may be in many cases and/or to some extent a synoptical illusion and an anachronism retrojected (a contemporary production without a prompt-book is unthinkable). Long "would suggest that Shakespeare's papers were not nearly so foul as that word seems to imply, that they were indeed used as 'prompt' copy, and that they, not a hypothetical 'careful scribal copy,' were the basis of the Folio text" ("Stage-Directions" 124).

There may yet be something in McKerrow's inference that a manuscript in which the SHs "are regular and uniform is more likely to have been printed from some sort of fair copy, perhaps made by a professional scribe" (464), but a *Coriolanus* editor has occasion to regret McKerrow's conceding that "in some, such as the Roman plays, there is little, if any, scope for variation in the names" (463, n. 2). Thus McKerrow's persua-sive case for inconsistent SHs—especially those varying according to changes of role and relationships—as evidence of authorial copy has almost no relevance to *Coriolanus,* where the inconsistencies are of name and spelling only, not of des-cription by function. But other forms of SH-variation are not necessarily less characteristic than those that more strikingly identify a character as "'Father,' 'Servant,' 'Merchant,' or what not, according to the aspect of his personality which is at the moment prominent" (459–60). And if Long is right about the-atrical playbooks, then we might take it provisionally that *Coriolanus* was more than "partly prepared for the theatre" in the original act of playwrighting itself, as would seem to have been the case also with *More* Addition II.D, according to Giorgio Melchiori's recent studies (in "Hand D" [1985] he takes no explicit stand on authorship, but in "The Booke" [1986] D is "most probably Shakespeare," 305).

SHs afford a useful means of assessing the State of the Text of *Coriolanus,* whatever one assumes or *pre*supposes about it, and Brockbank's edition may be taken as expressing the current *consensus magistrorum* as well as his reasoned departures from it. His edition bears scrutiny well, and he has clearly identified the cruxes of the SH kind, which occur at a crossroads where bibliographical, mimesiological, and thematic hermeneutics meet.[4] Brockbank writes in summary that

> Speech-headings present an abnormal number of difficulties, sometimes occasioned by apparent misreadings, sometimes by misinterpretations of alignment, and sometimes by lack of clarity in the playwright's intentions; errors could also arise from the compositor's anticipating the wrong speech-heading or by eye-skip in the margin of the copy. Speech headings are *emended* at I. i. 34, 56 [–165, 13 instances in all]; II. i. 179; III. i. 229, 235, 236, 303; IV. i. 37; IV. ii. 15 [, 25]. They have been *added* at I. vi. 76; III. i. 184, 238; and multiple prefixes (e.g. *All*) have sometimes been clarified (e.g. *all Pleb.*). F's ascriptions at I. i. 27, III. i. 47, and III. i. 202 have been *challenged* [by others] but are retained in the present text. The high incidence of this problem in III. i (affecting both [A's and B's] stints) suggests that the margin of the copy here may have been damaged and the speech-headings therefore illegible [20, italics mine; see "Folio Text of the Editorial Variants" and facsimiles of three F pages following the text of this paper].

Two of the cruxes are major by any measure within the play. The first (#3 below) turns on the question whether speeches in the first scene, which F gives to *2 Cit.* but seem to virtually all editors more characteristic of 1 Cit., should be reassigned or allowed to stand. No modern editor (or RSC director) has followed F in this assignment, but it has come to be strongly advocated by critics, notably Michael Warren and Wilbur Sanders. The second turns on the question whether Virgilia's lines in F IV. ii (#15–16) should stand or be reassigned to Volumnia as they have been in much the same way

by Warburton, Hanmer, and, more recently, Murry and Brockbank. Not to hide my darkness under a bushel, my present
view is that F is correct in the second case, wrong in the first.

2

Editorial Variants

The sixteen-plus cruxes and editorial variants identified in
Brockbank's introduction (20) represent typical editorial problems requiring resolution by applied hypothesis, reasoning, or
coin-toss (Greg). They are editorial—and bibliographical—
problems because they were at first critical. A crux is a reading
that does not satisfy the critically perceived requirements of
sense. Emendation, however supported by hypotheses about
transmission, is action "entailed" by critical interpretation and
the exercise of editorial responsibility and judgment. Moreover,
cruxes are often in large part the basis for the hypotheses by
which they are (hermeneutically, not necessarily vicious-circu-
larly) in turn to be resolved. The editorial variants constitute
four "who's on first?" groups-of-convenience as follows:

    I. *All*—OR SOME(ONE) OR OTHER(S),
SOMEHOW (#1, 2, 4, 7 with 7+)

    II. *CITIZEN* WHICH? (#3: 13 correlative instances in I. i)

    III. *C(O[M<INI>]/[R<IOLAN>])U*S WHO? (#5, 6, 8–10)

    IV. A MISCELLANY (#11-16)

There is too much to be said about the individual cruxes to
be included in an essay of the present kind, but I give the variants in each group with a sampling of general and particular
discussion to indicate the sort of inferences the cases seem to
point to, and (not incidentally) to show how they have been

treated by a sampling of editors from 1951 to 1986.

I. *ALL*—OR SOME(ONE) OR OTHER(S),
SOMEHOW (#1, 2, 4, 7 with 7+)

That the *All* SHs given in F—#1, 2, 7+—are those of the
MS there can be very little doubt. Primary questions about
them are why they are as they are, what they mean, and (for
an editor or director) what to do with them. These three of the
42 instances of *All* (including 2 *Omnes*) in *Cor.* are more complicated but not categorically different from the rest. *All* seems
often to be a blanket—or provisional—SH almost invariably
requiring some disambiguation, by actors, (modern) director,
reader, and (therefore) editor. E. A. J. Honigmann's pioneering
work, "Re-Enter the Stage-Direction," includes attention to *All*
speeches with several examples from *Cor.*: "Shakespeare sometimes used the '*All*' speech prefix loosely, no doubt because he
wrote in haste and thought that he could explain the details
later—just as he might fall back on 'other', or on an actor's
name, when he was too impatient to pause. We learn that an
'*All*' prefix [1] could be reassigned to a single speaker (*Sir
Thomas More*), or [2] could indicate that different consecutive
speakers are required (*M.N.D.*)," and in *Cor.* (3) could indicate
"simultaneous 'confused' speech" (121b).

All occurs twelve times in *More* II.D, once with no further
text (9v) and with one mid-line occurrence (38) deleted by Hand
C in error (see Melchiori, "Hand D" 104a), most instances being
genuine crowd speeches for delivery more or less in unison; for
example, "both both both both" (34). The prominent exceptions
are three speeches toward the end (all on 9r): 96 "marry god
forbid that"; 141 "fayth a saies trewe letts [vs *deleted by C*] do
as we may be doon by" (SH misplaced opposite the last line—
140—of the preceding speech); and 142 "weele be ruld by you
master moor yf youle stand our / friend to cure our don" (D's *all*
replaced by C's *Linco*). Of the change of SH in the last,
Melchiori remarks that it "is fully justified: D, who probably
followed the common practice of adding speech headings only
after completion of the text, seems to have become particularly
careless towards the end of his contribution to the play; he mis-

placed by one line . . . the previous heading, and in this case assigned to the crowd a speech which was surely meant for only one speaker" ("Hand D" 107a). Whether the assignment of *all* was strictly in error and could not have been meant to apply to only one—unspecified—speaker seems doubtful, and C did *not* alter the previous *all* (140 for 141).

In *Cor.* the 42 occurrences of *All* or *Omnes* seem to categorize broadly as follows (by TLN):

A. Simple repetition by "crowd" = same word or phrase repeated twice, occasionally more than twice (ll: 6, 9, 12, 50, 1435, 1891, 1929 [*All Ple.*], 1948, 2015, 2356, 2407).

B. Other collective utterances (7: 359, 823 [*Omnes*], 1070, 3647, 3725 [*All* = lords; 3721 *All Lords*], 3792 and 3804 [both *All Consp.*]).

C. Multiple but not strictly "all" speakers, e.g., "The Gods assist you" (4: 355, 1896, 2915, 2923).

D. Complex, not multiple; = "someone" (10: 36, 547, 549, 1881, 1910, 1913, 2004, 3065 [*Omnes*], 3721 [*All Lords*], 3807 [*Lords, no All*]).

E. Multiple *sentiments*: = more than one speaker, serially or simultaneously (10: 16, 29, 1528, 1564, 1659, 1901, 2391, 2427, 2432, 3793 [*All People*]).

Some of these could be shifted, but there is a spectrum from "Speake, speake" (standing not necessarily for only two but for *n* repetitions) to "Teare him to peeces, do it presently: / He kill'd my Sonne, my daughter, he kill'd my Cosine, / *Marcus,* he kill'd my Father" (*All People*; TLN 3793–95; V. vi. 120–22). *Other* as a MS expedient is different from *all* mainly in being unequivocally singular; both demand disambiguation before performance but not necessarily before rehearsal. Whether there were instances of *other* in the writing stage of *Cor.* cannot be determined; certainly there are no traces. But the example of *More* is instructive: there it is used in decrementally abbreviated form by Hand D and later deleted by C and replaced by named speakers. Along with *Both* (921, 924, 938, 2891), *Both Tri.* (2314, 2924), and *Tri.* (3042), these SHs are not wholly unlike the function-distinctions McKerrow discusses: *other* prescribes a person by relationship to understood "others"; *all* is more open-ended, though it, too, may be singular and not absolutely different from *other*; the referents of *Both* [*Tri.*] are obvious and the delivery is to be near-unanimity, presumably, in some cases ("Well, well, sir, well" 924), and in other cases divided between the two for simultaneous or sequential delivery ("Why? how are we censur'd?" (921; "ho ware" F).

None of the instances of editorial-variant *All* is of easy resolution, but #4, the change from *Cor.* (continuing) to *All*, was made by Brockbank on the assumption that a SH was omitted, as is always possible; but this is the hardest *All* to make stick on critical grounds. #7(+) also could be due to simple omission of one of two intended uses of *All* (still requiring disambiguation; Melchiori argues cogently that two instances of *All* in the same line of *More* 38, the second a later addition by D, mean *some* and *others,* respectively; "Hand D" 101b). Or it could be due to a SH entered, after composition, in the wrong place. Or *All* could have been omitted in TLN 1894 as implicit in the SD, 1893, *"They all bustle about Coriolanus."* But the most vexed and controverted variants are #1–2:

#1 "*All.* Against him first: He's a very dog to the Commonalty" (29; I. i. 27).
#2 "*All.* Nay, but speak not maliciously" (36; I. i. 34).

While they may be left as they are because that is how they surely were in MS, they clearly require resolution—that is, specific sense must still be made of them, and referents identified.

The four preceding *All* speeches are crowd speeches to be delivered more or less "collectively" except for the last: "Speake, speake" (6; I. i. 2); "Resolu'd, resolu'd" (9; 5); "We know't, we know't" (12; 8); and—with a difference—"No more talking on't; Let it be done, away‸" (15, full line, hence no period; 11–12). But as Honigmann notes, in #2 "and in many other places, we have 'All' speeches that are individualized, not ritualistic, and they always sound wrong in the theatre if uttered by more than a single voice" (21a). The question accordingly becomes "which voice?" RSC-Promptbook 1939 (dir. Iden Payne) changed printed "All" to the initials of the actor playing "4 Cit." RSC-PB 1977-79 (dir. Terry Hands) assigned the first part to "6 Cit." and the second to "4 Cit." Jowett (Oxford) assigns #2 to "5 Cit.," having divided #1 between "3 Cit." ("Against him first") and "4 Cit." ("He's . . . commonalty").

However and wherever "we" do it, we *must* interpret, and a reasoned interpretation arguably belongs—in some editions—in the text as well as in the notes. Long's essays are helpful here in reminding us that "play manuscripts originate in an oral, not a written, tradition" ("Stage-Directions" 122) and in arguing that "regularization and completeness simply were not factors in the theatrical marking of an author's papers" (123). In general, *All* must mean "appropriate member(s) of cast, in appropriate manner," "appropriate" to be interpreted by the players concerned according to the composition of the company and the circumstances of performance. Shakespeare would presumably have had his own company in mind and himself been present to interpret, but could doubtless count on being "appropriately" understood even without speaking to and for his script. *All* can certainly speak to companies (and readers) centuries removed, too, but with enough uncertainty that careful editorial aid should seem nearer a service than an imposition or an act of surreptitious authorship.

Obviously, the scene can be played with the speeches emanating from a voice or voices in the crowd, and critical (or theatrical) resolution depends upon differing effects to be achieved by respective assignments. The usual but not universal reassignment of #1 to 1 Cit. and (still more) #2 to 2 Cit. is reasonably well founded in their consonance with the rest of the exchanges between these two in I.i up to the entrance of Menenius. Specifically, it appears that 2 Cit.—who says to the crowd "One word, good citizens" (16; I. i. 13) and is answered at length by 1 Cit.—then addresses "Would *you* proceede especially against *Caius Martius*" (27–28; 25–26) not to the crowd again but to 1 Cit., and in turn would or might be answered not by a voice in the crowd (*All* = "someone" or two) but by 1 Cit. (#1): "Against him first: he's a very dog to the Common-

alty" (29–30); 27-28).[5] Complementing the apparent sentiments of the crowd as well as the assured sentiments of 1 Cit.
("First you know, *Caius Martius* is chiefe enemy to the people,"
TLN 10-11; I. i. 6–7), it *could* go either way. "Nay, but speak
not maliciously," given to 2 Cit. by Malone and most others
since, is much less "ambivalent," because it is temperate and
reasoned, not a crowd sentiment. Finally, however, *All* must
have stood in MS, intended so by Shakespeare, either because
he had not settled on identified speakers (meant to be 1 & 2, as
many editors think) or because he had (voices in the crowd, as
in the Oxford Shakespeare). It seems gratuitous to reassign
one and not the other, if one goes by form and context, and also
gratuitous not to reassign to 1 and 2 Cit. if one goes by these
and critical content. But all "editing" is interpretation, here,
and more than one seems to give a contextually and expres-
sively valid accounting of the text.

II. *CITIZEN* WHICH? (#3: 13 correlative instances in I. i)

Capell's initial reassignment of these speeches from 2 Cit.
(F) to 1 Cit. was later supported by Malone, Dyce, White, and
Hudson (1881). Knight (+ Hudson [1851]) defended F. Malone
had said that 2 Cit. "is rather friendly to Coriolanus," Knight
replying that

> we adhere to the original copy for the precise reason which
> Malone gives for departing from it. The *first* citizen is a
> hater of public *men*—the *second,* of public *measures*; the
> first would kill Coriolanus—the second would repeal the
> laws related to corn and usury. He says not one word
> against Coriolanus [except 'We haue euer your good word'
> (177; 165): 'muttered disgust,' Sanders 141]. We are satis-
> fied that it was not Shakespeare's intention to make the
> *low brawler* [1 Cit.] against an individual argue so well
> with Menenius in the manner of the 'kingly crowned head,'
> etc. This speaker is of a *higher cast* than he who says: 'Let
> us kill him, and we'll have corn at our own price' [1928V
> 29, italics mine].

Wilbur Sanders has a strong recent defense in similar vein:

> 1 Cit. was eloquent (and sincere) enough when it was a matter of telling his supporters what they most wanted to hear, but he is quite unmanned by the new atmosphere of chastened deference [when Menenius arrives]. Who then? The same man who was quirky enough to question the majority view before, who seems to welcome the patrician's arrival as likely to break up the entrenched battle-lines of ignorant confrontation, and who is about to emerge as grasping, better than any, the one unanswerable sanction of oppressed misery. . . . So finally it is 2. Cit.'s stolidly matter-of-fact voice that breaks the silence, at once disowning his primacy in the matter, and accepting with a shrug his necessary implication: "Our business is not unknown to the Senate," etc. (139). . . . Menenius turns this man, potentially his most valuable ally, into the seditious agitator we have watched him refusing to be. And by the time Menenius has enlisted the laughter of his fellows, . . . finally by belching at him for a cheap laugh (the Belly's "smile"), the transformation is complete. Menenius has *made* him "the great toe of this assembly" and feels free, consequently, to treat him as "one o'th'lowest, basest", or (what is the same thing) "poorest of this most wise rebellion" [140].

In an otherwise splendid and often brilliant essay, this elaborate defense is anomalous; but the important thing is that contradictory dialogue, in the very same speech just quoted, has been omitted here. Menenius' speech implies in effect that 1 Cit. is the crowd's leader in the scene from first to last (Sanders's omission in italics):

> For that being one o'th'lowest, basest, poorest
> Of this most wise rebellion, *thou goest foremost:*
> *Thou rascal, that art worst in blood to run,*
> *Lead'st first to win some vantage. . . .*

The italicized lines too could be appropriated to the argument, but they obviously serve it best *in absentia*. I suspect that one

71

not so strongly motivated to make a case for 2 Cit. would associate this description readily with 1 Cit., who *is* the leader at the beginning of the play and the most eligible "great Toe of this Assembly" (163; I. i. 154).

I also think that most see 1 Cit.'s earlier F speeches and "his" (editorial) later speeches as respectively homogeneous and complementary groups; that few would (as in my experience most do not) question the assignment of the later group to 1 Cit. because it seems so much of a piece with the first; and that most have trouble reconciling 2 Cit.'s second (F) group with his first undoubted one. The very lengths and elaborateness of the arguments given in defense of 2 Cit. attest the difficulty of making the case, an instance to prove the inevitable conflict between *lectio difficilior* and Ockham's Razor, and the relative ease of equivocating with either.

But if the later group was supposed to be 1 Cit.'s, why is it not his in F? There are at least two possible reasons. First, as Sisson says (122), "1" and "2" are very easily mistaken for each other in Secretary hand, as indeed they are—but why systematically here but evidently not elsewhere? Second, it is possible that *Cit.* was not identified by number in MS, specification to be added later *or* to be understood but subsequently being *mis*understood in the supplying of "2" by whomever. This possibility is at least consonant with the sort of SH abbreviation in *More* and also with Long's assertions about the nature of playbook copy. It is no more than a possibility, but I think it is not less.

III. *C(O[M<INI>]/[R<IOLAN>])*US WHO? (#5, 6, 8–10)

Of these five instances of *Cor.* vs. *Com.*, #5 and #6 are strictly individual cruxes, whereas #8–10 are related to each other and, bibliographically, to #11–12. In fact, an alternative grouping could have been III: 5-6, IV: 8-13 (bibliographical, 13 an instance separate from the others), and V: 14–16 ("Virgilian"), because 8-12 all occur on F sig. bb2^{v}a, where the multiple SH errors suggest a damaged or illegible margin in the MS, as noted by Brockbank, *or* problems associated with the printing of part of quire bb, or both. The cruxes on bb2^{v}a occur in a span of F lines (TLN 1915–65) that may all have been on the same page of (folio-size) MS, which would presumably have included rather more than the 51 lines of printed F text.[6]

Confusion between *Com.* and *Cor.* as represented in SHs is often, understandably, and perhaps rightly ascribed to misreading abbreviations, presumably on account of ambiguity in terminal *-m/r*. On the only page of *More* plainly legible in facsimile (9r), the terminal *-om* and *-or* are easily distinguishable: *from* 66, *liom* 121, *com* 124; in SH *moor* 144; otherwise *(f)or* 66, 110, 117, 127, 136. Generally speaking, these should not ordinarily have been mistaken for each other (in Hand D, at least), although *Cor.* perhaps *could* be mistaken for *Com.* Editors generally agree that at least three of the five are in error, two with *Com.* for *Cor.* (Wilson thinks three, as I do), one *Cor.* for *Com.*, a much less likely (*More*) mis*reading*.

One would expect—and there is evidence—that SHs would be abbreviated in MS as expediently as possible, in ways quite different from those of the printed texts, where spelling was used to justify as well as identify. In F the prevailing SH forms are *Com.* and *Corio.* The form *Coriol.* occurs ten times only (6 set by compositor B, 4 by A). Four of seven instances of *Cor.* were set by A, all in short lines, three on aa5rb and one on bb1vb; these probably reflect the copy, as A is thought to do otherwise (with *Scici(n).*, etc.). B's three *Cor.* forms—on Bb2ra (sic; B)—are all in crowded lines and probably due to justification. The copy SH(s) for *Cor.* need not have been *Cor*[.] but could just as likely have been *Cor* (*More* has only *yor*), *Co*, or even *C*. And for Cominius *Cõ* (= *Com; More* has only *uppõ*), *Co*, and *C*. *More* manifests variable and often decremental abbreviation in writing SHs in a way that would seem natural to anyone either in the act of original composition *currente calamo* or going back to fill in SHs not supplied while composing dialogue. In *More,* for example (8r), see *other* twice, *oth,* and *o* (4, 7, 10, and 16, respectively); and also—in a series prominently decremental—*Lincolne* (1), *Linco* (5), *Linc* (8, 32, 35, 41), *Lin* (12, 18, 22).

Hinman's analysis of the printing and proof-reading of F adds to complications evident to the naked eye by identifying

problems unique in *Cor.*, problems of printing that overlap
with SH problems as critically perceived. The first two formes
of signature bb—3^v:4 and 3:4^v—were composed in the usual
order and way, but the movement of types shows that what followed was not the rest of bb but the whole of quires kk and ll,
after which the remaining bb formes were printed in the usual
order: bb2^v:5, 2:5^v, 1^v:6, 1:6^v. Hinman found that "this irregularity is without parallel anywhere else in the entire Folio" (ii.
163) and accounted for it by the hypothesis that the present
later-printed bb formes were cancels printed to replace "the
apparently total loss of some 2,400 printed sheets." He thought
that "no eleventh-hour requirement of censorship or difficulty
over copyright seems likely to have produced such results. A
physical cause is more probable; and possibly some kind of
warehouse disaster should be supposed" (ii. 164).

The contents of the deferred bb formes are as follows (with
compositor, TLN, and New Arden refs.):

2^v:5	2^v:	A 1900-92; III.i.190 (Hear)-III.i.261a.
		B 1993-2031; III.i.261aSD-291
	5:	B 2253-2684; IV.ii.41-IV.v.32 (sta-)
2:5^v	2:	B 1768-1899; III.i.75-III.i.190a (Sic.)
	5^v:	B 2685-2816; IV.v.32 (-tion)-159 (cannot)
1^{v}6	1^v:	A 1638-1767; II.iii.233-III.i.74
	6:	A 1247-1376; 4.5.159 (tell)-4.6.45
1:6^v	1:	A 1508-1637; II.iii.116-232
	6^v:	B 2949-3080; IV.vi.46-153

Were the cancels set from the original MS used as setting copy
(presumably) or from earlier-printed copy, damaged on bb2^v? If
the latter, one would perhaps expect evidence of damage on sig.
bb2^{r}b, but there is none, which supports origin in MS and compositor, and a matter possibly of the simple misreading of some
version of *Com.*/*Cor.* in TLN 1954 (III. i. 229b-30)—but not in
the three errors below it (discussed under IV).

Individually, #5, "*Com.* And liue you yet? Oh my sweet

Lady, pardon" (1087; II. i. 179) "palpably belongs to Coriolanus" (Furness, 1928V). Brockbank notes that "only Harrison, among recent editors, retains F's attribution to Cominius. . . . The S.H. [*Com.*] occurs three times in this column of F (with *Corio.* and *Coriol.* also three); it is likely that the transition from *Mar.* to *Cor.* made the slip or misreading *Com.* easier" (161–62).

#6, "*Com.* You are like to doe such businesse" (1734; III. i. 47) is given to Cor. by Wilson and Jowett (Oxford) alone of the editors I surveyed, but time was. "KNIGHT: The modern editors"—contemptuous as usual with Knight—"give the words to Coriolanus as a continuation of his dialogue with Brutus. The words are *not characteristic* of Coriolanus; whilst the interruption of Cominius gives *spirit and variety* to the scene" (italics mine; 1928V 320, n. on III. i. 292–95). Wilson 196: "Little graphical diff. between these abbrev. names. N.B. Brut.'s reply is clearly addressed to Cor.; and Cor. replies in turn." Wilson and Jowett share the company of Theobald, Hanmer, Warburton, Johnson, and others, and I am with them.

#8, "*Com.* That is the way to lay the Citie flat, / To bring the Roofe to the Foundation, / And burie all, which yet distinctly raunges / In heapes, and piles of Ruine" (1915; III. i. 202). This seems not really a problem. The speech cannot be made Cor.'s without gymnastics, and both the *ductus literarum* and Com.'s character make him unquestionably eligible. Given the content, the context, and the possibly defective condition of the MS at this point, it seems not impossible that Menenius was meant to continue after "And so are like to doe" (completing the half-line of *All,* "You so remaine." TLN 1913-14), but probable is another matter. The fact is (and defenses of *Com.* show), any cool head in the vicinity could have the lines in a context where consonant sentiments are expressed by Menenius, *Sen.,* and *2 Sen.,* and, further away, Com.[7]

#9, "*Com.* Stand fast, we haue as many friends as enemies" (1954; III. i. 229). Sisson alone reads with F, commenting that "it is difficult to see why this should be editorially interfered with, as even Alexander does, in obedience to Warburton, who attributed it to Coriolanus. Cominius is more of a soldier than a politician, and is close to Coriolanus. He stands in this scene half-way between Coriolanus and the Senators who counsel discretion. The finer lineaments of character are blurred by this unnecessary emendation. Coriolanus would die fighting one against the world, not considering (as Cominius does here) the balance of forces" (2: 126-27). RSC-PB 1926/33 replaced printed *Com.* with *Cor.*

Cominius' "finer lineaments" here are of Sisson's sketching. My own subjective view is that it is not likely that the patient, reasoning Cominius would, so soon after showing concern for Rome (if #8 is his, as F and most recent editors agree), urge an obliviously defensive and belligerent stand. Compare III. i. 175–78, where Cominius says "Aged sir, hands off" while Martius is saying "Hence, old goat!" and "Hence rotten thing! or I shall shake thy bones / Out of thy garments"; Cominius' "But now 'tis odds beyond arithmetic; / And manhood is call'd foolery when it stands / Against a falling fabric" (243-45); his entry at III. ii. 92–95, "I have been i'th'market place; and sir, 'tis fit / You make strong party, or defend yourself / By calmness or by absence. All's in anger"; and his responding to Menenius' "Only fair speech" with "I think 'twill serve, if he / Can thereto frame his spirit" (96–97).

#10, "*Corio.* Come Sir, along with vs" (1961; III. i. 235). The short of Brockbank's plausible explanation is that the omission of the first of three SHs and the displacement of the proper *Com.* by the *Cor.* belonging to the following speech (#10) elevated *Mene.* to the position that should have been occupied by *Cor.* instead of beginning his proper speech at "Be gone" (210n). Whether this speech *must* go to Cominius might be (mildly) questioned, but it cannot go to Coriolanus. RSC-PB 1952 (dir. Glen Byam Shaw) replaced printed *Cor.* with *Com.*

IV. A MISCELLANY (#11–16)

#11 "*Mene.* I would they were Barbarians, as they are, / Though in Rome litter'd: not Romans, as they are not, / Though calued i'th'Porch o'th'Capitoll" (1962; III. i. 236).

#12 "Be gone, put not your worthy Rage into your Tongue, / One time will owe another" (1965; III. i. 238).

Sisson NR 2: 127: "There can be no real doubt that" the lines of #11, "here opening a speech of Menenius, are spoken by Coriolanus. And so all editors agree. One might suggest that the practice of inserting speakers' names after the dialogue has been written has led here to confusions in the Folio copy. But it seems to me probable that we have here a marginal addition in the copy, prefixed by the compositor in error to the existing speech of Menenius, whose words, *Be gone,* seem to follow directly upon Cominius' *Come Sir*[, along with vs]" (i.e., F2's *Com.,* F's *Corio.,* #10). Such an addition seems to me unlikely on grounds of both meter and sense. Although misaligned with the following line in F, "Be gone" is the fifth foot of the third line of #11; *if* #11 were an addition, "Be gone" would have been a fourth foot (without a fifth) after "Come Sir, along with vs," less unusual as a *three*-foot short line in the text as it is.

The sense of the context proceeds as follows. *Sena.* says, ". . . I prythee noble friend, home to thy House, / Leave vs to cure this Cause"; Menenius adds, "For 'tis a Sore vpon vs / You cannot Tent your selfe: *be gone,* beseech you" 1959-60, italics mine); *Com.* adds, "Come Sir, along with vs" (*Corio.*'s in F). The next lines, of #11, *must* be Cor.'s as the prompting of Menenius' *second* "Be gone" and "put not your worthy Rage into your Tongue," as Cor. does in these very lines.

Too few and misplaced directions after the original writing, a damaged MS, the playwright's writing speeches at speed and putting down a SH but changing his thought instanter, or possibly the bookkeeper's supplying specifications for MS *o(th[er])* as in *More?* (see Melchiori, "Hand D" 106–07). One could imagine a compositor's moving a SH from the MS equivalent of crowded TLN 1965 up to 1962 where there is room, but this hardly makes sense of the space available for compensating or for the "expansive" compositor A, whose misaligning of lines of verse has been shown to be especially characteristic (Prosser; Werstine, "Line Division") and TLN 1964-65 here confirm (1964 has four feet, 1965 six). The MS may have read something like (with F's spelling and punctuation)

Co±   Come Sir, along with vs.

[Co±]   I would they were Barbarians, as they are
         Though in Rome litter'd, not Romans, as they are not,
Men   Though calued i'th'Porch o'th'Capitoll:

Be gone,
Put not your worthy Rage into your Tongue,

with *Men[e]*. (and perhaps also the other SHs) added, after the dialogue was originally written, in the wrong place, like *all* in *More* 140 for 141. If the second *Co±* had been omitted inadvertently, moving *Men* up and ignoring the rule below would probably be the natural thing for a compositor to do.

#13 "*Menen*. The seruice of the foote / Being once gangren'd, is not then respected / For what before it was" (2045; III. i. 303). Despite reading, unusually, with F (*Works* 826a), Sisson has no note in *New Readings*. In an exchange in the *TLS* (1950), H. Eardley-Wilmot pronounced F's ascription to Menenius out of character: "May not either Shakespeare or the printer have made a slip indicating the speaker, Menenius being uppermost in his mind? Warburton and Hanmer both gave the speech to Sicinius; one later editor to Brutus." A. P. Rossiter's reply argued for F's Menenius on the basis especially of "he's a Limbe, that ha's but a Disease / Mortall, to cut it off: to cure it, easie" and its supposed consonance with "The seruice of the foote / Being once gangren'd, is not then respected / For what before it was." "Coriolanus *is* a 'gangren'd' limb, the Fable of the Belly is apposite even here, and the objection about Citizen Great-toe is irrelevant. In any case, a toe is not a foot. . . . As for the personal style of Menenius, . . . dry irony often looks 'flat' in print. But why does Brutus snap back with 'Wee'l heare no more' if Sicinius is the speaker?"

In any case, a foot is not a limb, and Miss Eardley-Wilmot's view is that of most recent editors (and also mine). The better part of a reply may be found in the dialogue in context, Where Menenius is trying to reason with the tribunes, who in shorter speeches take turns rejecting his arguments. After his defense of Cor. in TLN 2033–41 (III. i. 293–301),

Sicinius says "This is clean kamme" (2042; 301a); Brutus para-phrases ("Meerely awry," 2043) and adds the straightforward assessment, "When he did loue his Country, it honour'd him" (2044); Sicinius, drawing on Menenius' earlier figures, now metaphorically diagnoses the loss as a consequence of disease (#13, the lines in question), which is quickly confirmed as such by Brutus' second opinion. There is no more to be said or heard, so Brutus concludes, "Wee'l heare no more" (2048; 305) and passes sentence, prescribing violent remedy: "Pursue him to his house, and plucke him thence, / Least his infection being of catching nature, / Spred further" (2048-51; 305–08). At *this* point Menenius implores "One word more, one word" (2052; 308b), and adds five lines unbidden.

Another case of MS marginal damage or illegibility? Not on the same printed page as the others, but not much further along. Possibly a compositor's change on his noting that *Sicin.* and *Brut.* have just spoken and the speech after this one is *Brut.*'s, so this must be *Menen.*'s. The main reason for reassign-ing is critical, however: Menenius' other speeches in the same context move from cause to the milder course he advocates. This speech, figuratively paraphrasing Brutus' with Menenius' terms, gives justification for action already decided upon and about to be taken.

#14 "*Corio.* O the Gods!" (2477; IV. i. 37). This seems almost to be one of Greg's coin-toss cruxes that on bibliographi-cal grounds favors F's *Corio.* but on critical grounds has been argued both ways. Keightley (1928V 405) gave "this speech to *Vir.*, to whom it is better suited. Her only other speech in this scene is 'O Heauens! O heauens!'" (2448; IV. i. 12a). Chambers: "Coriolanus suddenly realizes how the revenge, which is already beginning to shape itself in his mind, must inevitably bring him into conflict with all that he holds most dear." Of the recent editors sampled, Sisson, Evans, and Bevington read with F, the other five against. "O the Gods!" as Cor.'s could be supported by his somewhat impatient response, "Nay, I pry-thee woman" (2449; 12b) to "O heauens! O heauens!" but the two ejaculations are also complementary as Virgilia's. It is no more than "just conceivable that Coriolanus cries out in apprehension or distress, or even intends a dismissive blasphemy, but either would be inconsistent with the assumed role of 'lonely dragon'" (Brockbank 240)

The heart of Cor.'s speech and action in this scene is "*Cominius,* / Droope not, Adieu: Farewell, my Wife, my Mother, / Ile do well yet" (2457–59; IV. i. 19–21). Misreading seems out of the question here—though it *is* possible in respect of "ye," intended to be "ye" but misunderstood as "the" ("ye"). *Corio.* supplied mechanically because he has had every other speech heretofore? While defending Compositor B in general, Eleanor Prosser concedes that "his settings are littered with unconscious substitutions, probably the result of glancing at his copy, trying to hold too much in his mind, and then setting what his memory dictated. He undoubtedly worked too fast, but he was usually thinking and he was an intelligent man" (113); in her study of *2H4* no evidence bears directly on the error (if it is one) here, but there may be something in his general habits in setting from manuscript copy that makes SHs more vulnerable in that context than in print-to-print transmission. If a SH were missing or illegible in the copy, as is possible, would he not have been likely to supply *Corio.* rather than *Virg.* as the speaker of such an ejaculation? It *is* stronger than "O heauens! O heauens!" It is also somewhat anomalous for Cor., not for Virg., in the scene as a whole.

#15 "*Virg.* You shall stay too: I would I had the power / To say so to my Husband." (2522; IV. ii. 15).

#16 "*Virg.* What then? Hee'ld make an end of thy posterity ∧ [full line] / *Volum.* Bastards, and all" (2536; IV. ii. 25).

BROCKBANK IV. ii. 13–16a, 25c–28:

> *Vol.* If that I could for weeping, you should hear—
> Nay, and you shall hear some. [*To Brutus*] Will you be gone?
> [*To Sicinius*] You shall stay too.
> *Vir.*   I would I had the power
>
> . . . .
> To say so to my husband.
>
> . . . .
> *Vir.*   What then!
> *Vol. He'd make an end of thy posterity,*

Bastards and all.
Good man, the wounds that he does bear for Rome!

Brockbank alone of the recent editors sampled follows
"Warburton and Middleton Murry in assigning these words
['You shall stay too,' IV. ii. 15a] to Volumnia, leaving Virgilia to
speak aside ['I would I had the power to say so to my husband,'
IV. ii. 15b–16a]." His reason is that "the peremptory *shall stay*
is consistent with Volumnia's mood and it precisely anticipates
her exasperation in ll. 22–23 ['I'll tell thee what—yet go! / Nay,
but thou shalt stay too,' IV. ii. 22b–23a]. . . ." "The misinterpretation of the alignment in copy is an easy error" (242), which is
true. He also argues alone with "Hanmer and Murry in assigning this line [i.e., 'He'd make an end of thy posterity,' IV. ii. 26]
to Volumnia, but differ[s] from Murry in retaining *What then!*
(l. 25[c]) as an aside for Virgilia. Since two speech headings
occur in F at this point, it is likely that two stood in the copy;
but the alignment may have been uncertain" (243), which is,
again, plausible. But the reassignment coincides with his having very little to say about Virgilia though implying much, perhaps, in interpreting what Martius calls his (and her) "gracious silence!" (II. i. 174) as due to her being "intimidated by
the clamour of victory" (60), for which I can find no justification in the script. She *may* be laconic to a fault, but in speech
as in architecture sometimes less is more; and taciturnity does
not preclude assertion on occasion.

Volumnia, by contrast, talks so much and often so fluently
(if not always convincingly) that misunderstanding and under-
valuing Virgilia are understandable, especially in the mere
reading. But it would seem editorially as well as critically gratuitous first to decide that Virgilia is reticent, timorous, and
submissive and then to deprive her of dialogue and implied
action that shows her sometimes otherwise, rising to an occasion that justifies anger and demands active response. Given
the size of her speaking role, arguably the smallest "major"
role in Shakespeare, it is a matter of some magnitude whether
she holds or yields her F lines here. Capell found Virgilia
"speaking to Brutus, and stopping him, as Volumnia had done
by his partner. This is thought unfit for the gentle Virgilia by

the Oxford editor [Hanmer]; who, therefore, takes the speech from her, and another at l. 36, giving them to Volumnia; but the gentlest are rouz'd at some times and upon some occasions; nor was it fit that Virgilia should be brought upon the scene to do nothing but cry" (1928V 409).

Generally speaking, Virgilia has seldom had a very good press. Taciturnity is not much valued by persons in the talking and writing professions, especially where aggressive self-assertion holds sway, and her lot in some circles of late is to be contemned as a willing "doormat." Such a perspective has little latitude for a viable, much less sympathetic, even admirable, "gracious silence." Virgilia gets some of her most favorable treatment in J. Middleton Murry's essay, "A Neglected Heroine of Shakespeare" (1922), which evidently expressed his sentiments definitively, because it was reprinted as a substantial part of his *"Coriolanus"* in 1950 (which I cite). The short of his view—which is obviously dated but I give without irony—is that she has an "exquisite, timid spirit" and is "one of Shakespeare's most delicate minor heroines" (233, 240), "the true outline" of which his change of SHs to Volumnia has helped to "disengage." A view that could once have been described without irony as "gallant" (but also without entailed agreement in full) must now seem to some—not merely inaccurate, but—sentimental, patronizing, and "patriarchal."

Wilbur Sanders's more recent reading of Virgilia, in his essay on "An Impossible Person: Caius Martius Coriolanus" (secs. 4–5, "To Please his Mother" and "Great Nature Cries," esp. 172–77 & 180–84), is a searching antidote to much that has been written on the play and its principals since as well as before 1978. His direction is evident in "there seems to be, in the ethos of post-Freudian enlightenment, a terrible gravitation from the self-evident proposition that Coriolanus is given us as very much his mother's son, to the not-at-all-evident proposition that he is given us as *no more than* his mother's son. First Citizen, in other words (the man who wants to kill Martius in order to have corn at his own price), is our hero's most penetrating critic: 'though soft conscienc'd men can be content to say it was for his country, he did it to please his mother . . .'" (173). Similarly, he sees Shakespeare's "sharp eye cast upon the tensions and emulations endemic to this" relationship of son, wife, and mother-in-law as "a radically *comic* eye, and I do find myself doubting that Virgilia's quiet self-possession has ever been seriously breached. Doubting, above all, that the good understanding between wife and husband is vulnerable to the pressures Volumnia brings to bear on it" (175). He says nothing of Virgilia in IV. ii. but much of value on her presence elsewhere in the play, including the butterfly episode (I. iii).

This seems a difficult but not untypical case of reversible arguments bibliographical and critical both. In IV. ii even Volumnia is given pause by tears: "If that I could for weeping, you should heare, / Nay, and you shall hear some. Will you be gone? *Virg.* You shall stay too: I would I had the power / To say so to my husband" (2520–24; 13–16). And by the end of the scene Volumnia's herself again: "Angers my Meate: I suppe vpon my selfe, / And so shall sterue with Feeding: Come, let's go, / Leaue this faint-puling, and lament as I do, / In Anger, *Iuno*-like: Come, come, come" (2565–69; 50–53). *Has* Virgilia asserted herself but lapsed into weeping after the tribunes' departure, or has she confined herself to weeping and the asides allowed her by some of her editors?

3

To summarize the findings of this preliminary inquiry; abbreviation (often decremental), ambiguity, misplaced SHs, and occasional illegibility in an autograph MS possibly used as a "prompt-book," seem as likely an explanation as any other of most of the SH cruxes discussed above. *All* is a multi-purpose heading indicating delivery by appropriate member(s) of cast, in appropriate manner, "appropriate" to be interpreted by the players concerned, and according to the composition of the company and the circumstances of performance. The same would be said of *o(th[er])* in *More,* which does not occur in *Cor.* In the copy for *Cor.,* perhaps some of the *All* SHs, intended as a temporary expedient to be replaced in due course by something more specific, became permanent inadvertently.

Most of the other problems in *Cor.* concern *Cit.* or *Com./Cor.*, and at least some of these may originate in the playwright's abbreviating, and failing to specify what was clear enough to him: which—numerically unspecified—citizen spoke the speeches to Menenius in I. i; and which of two was to be understood from context by *C(o)*. The abbreviations *Co* or *Co^r* could have caused problems, too, and I am gratefully reminded by George W. Williams that in *Romeo and Juliet* "there are many instances in which it is pretty clear that Shakespeare forgot to add the tilde in various contractions" (personal letter, 5 Jan. 1987). And some of the errors could be due to misreading *Com./Cor.*; if on the pattern of *More* Hand D, then more likely *-r* mistaken for *-m* than vice versa. Convincing deductions about the *exact* MS form(s) do not come easy in the case of these SH cruxes.

It is always a source of regret when hypotheses and evidence together fail to yield immediate and satisfyingly universal results, but ambiguity is often inherent in the medium as uncertainty is in many of the exact details of transmission. The major/minor details of Volumnia vs. Virgilia in IV. ii. are a case in point, focal also as an instance of critical disputes not more logical than psychological or ideological, in such a way that they may not be susceptible of any but a coterie consensus. Textual scholars must still, I think, seek *Shakespeare's* "consensus," but such ambiguous cases are more than common enough in textual criticism and practical editing to give some countenance to the position of anti-editors, uneditors, diseditors, and others so minded. Despite unquestionable corruptions, it seems often better to encounter Shakespearean action, character, and dialogue as they are presented in substantive Folio (and quarto) texts than in those tailored to the emergent occasions of posterity according to our varying prejudices in remaking Shakespeare "our contemporary." I do not think it is always so, for every reader, but if editing is to be, it should be open-minded, open-eyed, and circumspect. Better a living doubt than a dead "certainty."

Brockbank's (1976) Sixteen "Editorial Variants"
The Folio Text

No.	Grp.	Arden page, Act Scene-Line	TLN	Sig.	Comp.
1	I	96 1.1.27			
		All. Against him first: he's a very dog to the			
		Commonalty.	29	aal^{r}a	(B)
2	I	97 1.1.34			
		All. Nay, but speak not maliciously.	36	aal^{r}a	(B)
3+n	II	98-107 56-165			
		2 Cit. Our busines is not vnknowne to th'Senat,			
		they	59	aal^{r}b	(B)
4	I	139 1.6.76			
		Oh me alone, make you a sword of me:	697	aa3^{v}b	(B)
5	III	161 2.1.179			
		Com. And liue you yet? Oh my sweet Lady,			
		pardon.	1087	aa5^{r}b	(A)
6	III	197 3.1.47			
		Com. You are like to doe such businesse.	1734	bb1^{v}b	(A)
7	I	207 3.1.184			
		[*2 Sen.* Weapons, weapons, weapons:			
		They all bustle about Coriolanus.]			
		Tribunes, Patricians, Citizens: what ho:	1894	Bb2^{r}b	(B)
		[*All.* Peace, peace, peace, stay, hold, peace.			
		Mene. What is about to be? I am out of Breath,]			
8	III	208 3.1.202			
		Com. That is the way to lay the Citie flat,	1915	bb2^{v}a	(A)
		To bring the Roofe to the Foundation,			
		And burie all, which yet distinctly raunges			
		In heapes, and piles of Ruine.			
9	III	209 3.1.229			
		Com. Stand fast, we haue as many friends as			
		enemies.	1954	bb2^{v}a	(A)
10	III	210 3.1.235			
		Corio. Come Sir, along with vs.	1961	bb2^{v}a	(A)
11	IV	210 3.1.236			
		Mene. I would they were Barbarians, as			
		they are,	1962	bb2^{v}a	(A)
		Though in Rome litter'd: not Romans, as they are not,			
		Though calued i'th'Porch o'th'Capitoll:			
12	IV	210 3.1.238			
		Be gone, put not your worthy Rage			
		into your Tongue,			

		One time will owe another.	1965	bb2^{v}a	(A)
13	IV	214 3.1.303			
		Menen. The seruice of the foote	2045	bb3^{r}a	(B)
		Being once gangren'd, is not then respected			
		For what before it was.			
14	IV	240 4.1.37			
		Corio. O the Gods!	2477	bb4^{v}a	(B)
15	IV	242 4.2.15			
		Virg. You shall stay too: I would I had			
		the power	2522	bb^{v}b	(B)
		To say so to my Husband.			
16	IV	243 4.2. 25*			
		Virg. What then? Hee'ld make an end of			
		thy posterity	2536	bb4^{v}b	(B)

* Not listed in New Arden introduction.

BROCKBANK'S (1976) SIXTEEN "EDITORIAL VARIANTS" COLLATED WITH RECENT SCHOLARLY EDITIONS

51 = Alexander, 1951	74 = Evans, Riverside, 1974
54 = Sisson, 1954	80 = Bevington, Scott, 1980
60 = Wilson, 1960	86 = Jowett, Oxford, 1986
67 = Hibbard, New Penguin, 1967	F = Folio, O = Other

		ARDEN										
No.	TLN	A.S.L.	86	80	ARD 76	74	67	60	54	51	FOLIO	OTHER
1	29	1.1.27	O^1	F	F	O	O	O	O	O	All	1 Cit [Hudson, conj. Malone]
2	36	34	O	O	O	O	O	O	O	O	All	2 Cit [Malone], 5 Cit [Oxford]
3(=13)	59-177	56-165	O	O	O	O	O	O	O	O	2 Cit	1 Cit [Capell]
4	697	1.6.76	F	F	O	F	F	F	F	F	[no SH]	All [Brooke (Soldiers), conj. Style]
5	1087	2.1.179	O	O	O	O	O	O	O	O	Com.	Cor. [Theobald]
6	1734	3.1.47	O	F	F	F	F	O	F	F	Com.	Cor. [Theobald]
7	1894	184	O^2	O	O	O	O	Cries O	O	O	[no SH]	All [Camb.]
7+	1796	186^3	O^4	O	O	O	Men.	O	O^5	O^6	All	[no SH; Camb.]
8	1915	202	O	F	F	F	F	F	F	F	Com.	Cor. [Pope]

86

(Be)Headings in *Coriolanus*

No.	TLN	A.S.L.	86	80	ARD 76	74	67	60	54	51	FOLIO	OTHER
9	1954	229	O	O	O	O	O	O	F	O	Com.	Cor.[Warburton]
10	1961	235	O	O	O	O	O	O	O	O	Corio.	Com. [F2]
11	1962	236	O	O	O	O	O	O	O	O	Mene.	Cor [Steevens, conj. Tyrwhitt]
12	1965	238	O	O	O	O	O	O	O	O	[no SH]	Men. [Steevens, conj. Tyrwhitt]
13	2045	303	O	F	O	O	O	O	F	O	Menen.	Sic.[Hanmer, conj. Warburton]
14	2477	4.1.37	O	F	O	F	O	O	F	O	Corio.	Virg. [Keightley]
15	2522	4.2.15	F	F	O	F	F	F	F	F	Virg.	Vol. [Warburton]
16	2536	25[5]	F	F	O	F	F	F	F	F	Virg.	Vol. [Brockbank; ±Hanmer, Murry]

[1] "[3 Cit] Against him first. [4 Cit] He's ... commonalty."

[2] "[Citizens and Patricians] [*in dispersed cries*]"

[3] Not listed in New Arden introduction.

[4] "[Some Citizens and Patricians]"

[5] "Senators, Patricians."

[6] "Patricians."

The Tragedy of Coriolanus.

Actus Primus. Scœna Prima.

Enter a Company of Mutinous Citizens, with Staues,
Clubs, and other weapons.

1. *Citizen.*

Efore we proceed any further, heare me speake.

All. Speake, speake.

1. *Cit.* You are all resolu'd rather to dy then
to famish?

All. Resolu'd, resolu'd.

1. *Cit.* First you know, *Caius Martius* is chiefe enemy
to the people.

All. We know't, we know't.

1. *Cit.* Let vs kill him, and wee'l haue Corne at our own
price. Is't a Verdict?

All. No more talking on't; Let it be done, away, away

2. *Cit.* One word, good Citizens.

1. *Cit.* We are accounted poore Citizens, the Patri-

1 *Cit.* Soft, who comes heere?

Enter *Menenius Agrippa.*

2 *Cit.* Worthy *Menenius Agrippa,* one that hath al-
wayes lou'd the people.

1 *Cit.* He's one honest enough, wold al the rest wer so.

Men. What work's my Countrimen in hand?
Where go you with Bats and Clubs? The matter
Speake I pray you.

2 *Cit.* Our busines is not vnknowne to th'Senat, they
haue had inkling this fortnight what we intend to do, w̄
now wee'l shew em in deeds: they say poore Suters haue
strong breaths, they shal know we haue strong arms too.

Men. Why Masters, my good Friends, mine honest
Neighbours, will you vndo your selues?

2 *Cit.* We cannot Sir, we are vndone already.

Men. I tell you Friends, most charitable care
Haue the Patricians of you for your wants.
Your suffering in this dearth, you may as well

The way it takes : cracking ten thousand Curbes
Of more strong linke assunder, then can euer
Appeare in your impediment. For the Dearth,
The Gods, not the Patricians make it, and
Your knees to them (not armes) must helpe. Alacke,
You are transported by Calamity
Thether, where more attends you, and you slander
The Helmes o'th State; who care for you like Fathers,
When you curse them, as Enemies.

  2 Cit. Care for vs? True indeed, they nere car'd for vs
yet. Suffer vs to famish, an ... r Store-houses cramm'd
with Graine: Make Edicts for Vsurie, to support Vsu-
rers; repeale daily ... wholesome Act established against
the rich, and prouide more piercing Statutes daily, to
chaine vp and restraine the poore. If the Warres eate vs
not vppe, they will, and there's all the loue they beare
vs.

  Menen. ...ither you must
Confesse your selues wondrous Malicious,
Or be accus'd of Folly. I shall tell you
A pretty Tale, it may be you haue heard it,
But since it serues my purpose, I will venture
To scale't a little more.

  2 Citizen. Well,
He heare it Sir: yet you must not thinke
To fobbe off our disgrace with a tale : .
But and't please you deliuer.

  Men. There was a time, when all the bodies members
Rebell'd against the Belly; thus accus'd it:
That onely like a Gulfe it did remaine

manely : But they thinke we are too deere, the leannesse
that afflicts vs, the obiect of our misery, is as an inuento-
ry to particularize their abundance, our sufferance is a
gaine to them. Let vs reuenge this with our Pikes, ere
we become Rakes. For the Gods know, I speake this in
hunger for Bread, not in thirst for Reuenge.

  2.Cit. Would you proceede especially against *Caius
Martius.*

  All. Against him first : He's a very dog to the Commonalty.

  2.Cit. Consider you what Seruices he ha's done for his
Country ?

  1.Cit. Very well, and could bee content to giue him
good report for't, but that hee payes himselfe with bee-
ing proud.

  All. Nay, but speak not maliciously.

  1.Cit. I say vnto you, what he hath done Famouslie,
he did it to that end : though soft conscienc'd men can be
content to say it was for his Countrey, he did it to please
his Mother, and to be partly proud, which he is, euen to
the altitude of his vertue.

  2.Cit. What he cannot helpe in his Nature, you account a Vice in him : You must in no way say he is co-
uetous.

  1.Cit. If I must not, I neede not be barren of Accusa-
tions he hath faults (with surplus) to tyre in repetition.
Showts within.

What showts are these? The other side a'th City is risen:
why stay we prating heere? To th'Capitoll.

  All. Come, come.

[aa1v (B)]

89

The Tragedie of Coriolanus.

2

I'th midd'ft a th'body, idle and vnactiue,
Still cubbording the Viand, neuer bearing
Like labour with the reft, where th'other Inftruments
Did fee, and heare, deuife, inftruct, walke, feele,
And mutually participate, did minifter
Vnto the appetite; and affection common
Of the whole body, the Belly anfwer'd.

2.*Cit.* Well fir, what anfwer made the Belly.
Men. Sir, I fhall tell you with a kinde of Smile,
Which ne're came from the Lungs, but euen thus:
For looke you I may make the belly Smile,
As well as fpeake, it taintingly replyed
To'th difcontented Members, the mutinous parts
That enuied his receite : euen fo moft fitly,
As you maligne our Senators, for that
They are not fuch as you.

2.*Cit.* Your Bellies anfwer: What
The Kingly crown'd head, the vigilant eye,
The Counfailor Heart, the Arme our Souldier,
Our Steed the Legge, the Tongue our Trumpeter,
With other Muniments and petty helpes
In this our Fabricke, if that they——

Men. What then? Foreme, this Fellow fpeakes.
What then? What then?

2.*Cit.* Should by the Cormorant belly be reftrain'd,
Who is the finke a th'body.

Men. Well, what then?

2.*Cit.* The former Agents, if they did complaine,
What could the Belly anfwer?

Men. I will tell you,
If you'l beftow a fmall (of what you haue little)
Patience awhile; you'ft heare the Bellies anfwer.

2.*Cit.* Y'are long about it.
Men. Note me this good Friend;

Thou Rafcall, that art worft in blood to run,
Lead'ft firft to win fome vantage.
But make you ready your ftiffe bats and clubs,
Rome, and her Rats, are at the point of battell,
The one fide muft haue baile.

Enter Caius Martius.

Hayle, Noble *Martius.*
Mar. Thanks. What's the matter you diffentious rogues
That rubbing the poore Itch of your Opinion,
Make your felues Scabs.

2.*Cit.* We haue euer your good word.
Mar. He that will giue good words to thee, wil flatter
Beneath abhorring. What would you haue, you Curres,
That like nor Peace, nor Warre ? The one affrights you,
The other makes you proud. He that trufts to you,
Where he fhould finde you Lyons, findes you Hares:
Where Foxes, Geefe you are: No furer, no,
Then is the coale of fire vpon the Ice,
Or Hailftone in the Sun. Your Vertue is,
To make him worthy, whofe offence fubdues him,
And curfe that Iuftice did it. Who deferues Greatnes,
Deferues your Hate : and your Affections are
A fickmans Appetite ; who defires moft that
Which would encreafe his euill. He that depends
Vpon your fauours, fwimmes with finnes of Leade,
And hewes downe Oakes, with rufhes. Hang ye; truft ye?
With euery Minute you do change a Minde,
And call him Noble, that was now your Hate:
Him vilde, that was your Garland. What's the matter,
That in thefe feuerall places of the Citie,
You cry againft the Noble Senate, who
(Vnder the Gods) keepe you in awe, which elfe
Would feede on one another? What's their feeking?

170

180

190

101

110

120

130

Mar. Hang 'em: They fay?
They'l fit by th'fire, and prefume to know
What's done i'th Capitoll: Who's like to rife,
Who thriues, & who declines: Side factions, & giue out
Coniecturall Marriages, making parties ftrong,
And feebling fuch as ftand not in their liking,
Below their cobled Shooes. They fay ther's grain enough?
Would the Nobility lay afide their ruth,
And let me vfe my Sword, I'de make a Quarrie
With thoufands of thefe quarter'd flaues, as high
As I could picke my Lance.

Mene. Nay thefe are almoft thoroughly perfwaded:
For though abundantly they lacke difcretion
Yet are they pafsing Cowardly. But I befeech you,
What fayes the other Troope?

Mar. They are diffolu'd: Hang 'em;
They faid they were an hungry, figh'd forth Prouerbes
That Hunger-broke ftone wals: that dogges muft eate
That meate was made for mouths. That the gods fent not
Corne for the Richmen onely: With thefe fhreds
They vented their Complainings, which being anfwer'd
And a petition granted them, a ftrange one,
To breake the heart of generofity,
And make bold power looke pale, they threw their caps
As they would hang them on the hornes a'th Moone,
Shooting their Emulation.

Menn. What is graunted them?

Mar. Flue Tribunes to defend their vulgar wifdome
Of their owne choice. One's *Iunius Brutus*,
Sicinus Velutus, and I know not. Sdeath,

        The.

True is it my incorporate Friends (quoth he)
That I receiue the generall Food at firft
Which you do liue vpon: and fit it is,
Becaufe I am the Store-houfe, and the Shop
Of the whole Body. But, if you do remember,
I fend it through the Riuers of your blood
Euen to the Court, the Heart, to th'feate o'th'Braine,
And through the Cranks and Offices of man,
The ftrongeft Nerues, and fmall inferiour Veines
From me receiue that naturall competence
Whereby they liue. And though that all at once
(You my good Friends, this fayes the Belly) marke me.

   2.Cit. I fir, well, well.

   Men. Though all at once, cannot
See what I do deliuer out to each,
Yet I can make my Awdit vp, that all
From me do backe receiue the Flowre of all,
And leaue me but the Bran. What fay you too't?

   2.Cit. It was an anfwer, how apply you this?

   Men. The Senators of Rome, are this good Belly,
And you the mutinous Members: For examine
Their Counfailes, and their Cares; difgeft things rightly,
Touching the Weale a'th Common, you fhall finde
No publique benefit which you receiue
But it proceeds, or comes from them to you,
And no way from your felues. What do you thinke?
You, the great Toe of this Affembly?

   2.Cit. I the great Toe? Why the great Toe?

   Men. For that being one o'th loweft, bafeft, pooreft
O'this moft wife Rebellion, thou goeft formoft:

[aa1r (B)]

210

220

230

140

150

160

91

16   *The Tragedie of Coriolanus.*

Scici. Heare me, People, peace.

All. Let's here our Tribune: peace, speake, speake,
   speake.

Scici. You are at point to lose your Liberties:
Martius would haue all from you, *Martius*,
Whom late you hang nam'd for Consull,

Mene. Fie, fie, fie, this is the way to kindle, not to
   quench.

Sena. To vnbuild the Citie, and to lay all flat.

Scici. What is the Citie, but the People?

All. True, the People are the Citie.

Brut. By the consent of all, we were establish'd the
   Peoples Magistrates.

All. You so remaine.

Mene. And so are like to doe.

Com, That is the way to lay the Citie flat,
To bring the Roofe to the Foundation,
And burie all, which yet distinctly raunges
In heapes, and piles of Ruine.

Scici. This deserues Death.

Brut. Or let vs stand to our Authoritie,
Or let vs lose it: we doe here pronounce,
Vpon the part o'th' People, in whose power
We were elected theirs, *Martius* is worthy
Of present Death.

Scici. Therefore lay hold of him:
Beare him toth' Rock Tarpeian, and from thence
Into destruction cast him.

Brut. Ædiles seize him.

All Ple. Yeeld *Martius*, yeeld.

Mene. Heare me one word, 'beseech you Tribunes,
heare me but a word.

Ædiles. Peace, peace.

Mene. Be that you seeme, truly your Countries friend,

One time will owe another.

Corio. On faire ground, I could beat fortie of them.

Mene. I could my selfe take vp a Brace o'th' best of
   them, yea, the two Tribunes.

Com. But now 'tis oddes beyond Arithmetick,
And Manhood is call'd Foolerie, when it stands
Against a falling Fabrick. Will you hence,
Before the Tagge returne? whose Rage doth rend
Like interrupted Waters, and o're-beare
What they are vs'd to beare.

Mene. Pray you be gone:
Ile trie whether my old Wit be in requeft
With thofe that haue but little: this muft be patcht
With Cloth of any Colour.

Com. Nay, come away.   *Exeunt Coriolanus and*
                                    Cominius.

Patri. This man ha's marr'd his fortune.

Mene. His nature is too noble for the World:
He would not flatter *Neptune* for his Trident,
Or *Ioue,* for's power to Thunder: his Heart's his Mouth:
What his Breft forges, that his Tongue muft vent,
And being angry, does forget that euer
He heard the Name of Death.   *A Noyfe within.*

Patri. Here's goodly worke.

Mene. I would they were a bed.

Patri. I would they were in Tyber.

Mene. What the vengeance, could he not speake 'em faire?
   Enter Brutus and Sicinius with the rabble againe.

Sicin. Where is this Viper,
That would depopulate the city, & be euery man himselfe

Mene. You worthy Tribunes.

Sicin. He shall be throwne downe the Tarpeian rock
With rigorous hands: he hath resisted Law,
And therefore Law shall scorne him further Triall
Then the feuerity of the publike Power,

2010

2020

2030

1 *Cit.* He shall well know the Noble Tribunes are
The peoples mouths, and we their hands.
All. He shall sure ont.   *Sicin.* Peace.
Mene. Sir, sir.
Corio. Do not cry hauocke, where you shold but hunt
With modest warrant.
Sicin. Sir, how com'st that you haue holpe
To make this rescue?
Mene. Heere me speake? As I do know
The Consuls worthinesse, so can I name his Faults.
Sicin. Consull? what Consull?
Mene. The Consull *Coriolanus.*
Bru. He Consull,
All. No, no, no, no, no.
Mene. If by the Tribunes leaue,
And yours good people,
I may be heard, I would craue a word or two,
The which shall turne you to no further harmes,
Then so much losse of time.
Sic. Speake breefely then,
For we are peremptory to dispatch
This Viporous Traitor: to eie him hence
Were but one danger, and to keepe him heere
Our certaine death: therefore it is decreed,
He dyes to night.
Menen. Now the good Gods forbid,
That our renowned Rome, whose gratitude
Towards her deserued Children, is enroll'd
In Ioues owne Booke, like an vnnaturall Dam
Should now eate vp her owne.

Sicin.

1940

1950

1960

Bru. Sir, those cold wayes,
That seeme like prudent helpes, are very poysonous,
Where the Disease is violent. Lay hands vpon him,
And beare him to the Rock.   *Corio. drawes his Sword.*
Corio. No, Ile die here:
There's some among you haue beheld me fighting,
Come trie vpon your selues, what you haue seene me.
Mene. Downe with that Sword, Tribunes withdraw
a while.
Bru. Lay hands vpon him.
Mene. Helpe *Martius,* helpe: you that be noble, helpe
him yong and old.
All. Downe with him, downe with him.   *Exeunt.*
In this Mutinie, the Tribunes, the Ædiles, and the
People are beat in.
Mene. Goe: get you to our Houses: be gone, away,
All will be naught else.
2. *Sena.* Get you gone.
Com. Stand fast, we haue as many friends as enemies.
Mene. Shall it be put to that?
Sena. The Gods forbid:
I prythee noble friend, home to thy House,
Leaue vs to cure this Cause.
Mene. For 'tis a Sore vpon vs,
You cannot Tent your selfe: be gone, beseech you.
Corio. Come Sir, along with vs,
Mene. I would they were Barbarians, as they are,
Though in Rome litter'd: not Romans, as they are not,
Though calued i'th'Porch o'th'Capitoll:
Be gone, put not your worthy Rage into your Tongue,

[bb2v : 1900-92 (A) ; 1993-2031 (B)]

93

Notes

1. In the interests of economy I use a number of obvious abbreviations, notably: Cit. = Citizen; Cor., *Cor.* = Coriolanus, *Coriolanus*; F = Folio (1623); RSC-PB = Royal Shakespeare Company Prompt-Book (Shakespeare Centre Library, Stratford-upon-Avon); SD = Stage direction; SH = Speech-heading; TLN = Through line-number(s), as used in Charlton Hinman's facsimile of F; 1928V = Furness's Variorum edition of *Cor.* (1928). I follow (±) *The MLA Style Manual* (1985), abbreviating references to as little as necessary for recognition. For lines in the play I generally quote from F, using the parenthetical reference-format, "(697; [I.vi.]76)," meaning TLN 697, I. vi. 76 in the New Arden edition (act-scene-omitted when redundant).

   Appended materials include, above, (1) the F text of the sixteen editorial variants discussed or noted here, (2) a collation of these in several academic editions from 1951 to 1986, and (3) reduced photo-facsimiles of F sigs. aa1r+v, which contain #1–3; and bb2v, which contains #8–12 (nearly a third) of the sixteen editorial variants (the facsimiles give a detailed bibliographical and critical context for the discussion); and, below, (4) a list of Works Cited and Consulted.

   Coriolanus is not a play long on sympathetic readers. A fairly typical reaction is implied in the title of a recent *Drama* interview, "Crunching Butterflies for Breakfast," which perpetuates a hoary misrepresentation of Coriolanus, Jr.'s, butterfly chase in I. iii and often belongs to the summary-court-martial school of criticism convicting Martius as an "oppressor-class-bozo." G. K. Hunter's judgment is less categorical and rests on different ideological foundations and generic criteria, but its valence and purport are not very different in his finding the play (after Shaw) "a comedy of self-ignorance" in which "with immense labour and the deployment of transcendent talent Coriolanus engineers his own irrelevance" and is finally incapable of "a genuine anagnorisis" ("Traditions of Tragedy" 135–36). This Cor. is reminiscent of F. R. Leavis's Othello.

   I confess myself by contrast a member of an audience I think fit and know few, who agree with T. S. Eliot that "*Coriolanus* . . . is, with *Anthony and Cleopatra,* Shakespeare's most assured artistic success" ("Hamlet and His Problems," 1919). My commitment to a New Variorum *Coriolanus* began with special enthusiasm for the play and even its protagonist, in better ways as well as worse "an impossible person," in the phrase of one of not many critics to write of this play and its principals with sympathy, Wilbur Sanders.

2. See McGann, McLeod, and Warren. McGann's materialist position includes a correlative view of canonical works and authors as "modern national scriptures," giving textual critics the somewhat limited option of being priests or commissars.

3. If "essential" editions were synonymous and coextensive with "indispensable" editions, then at the present writing I should gladly add for *Coriolanus* Philip Brockbank's New Arden edition (1976) and that in the Oxford Shakespeare (1986) for which John Jowett has "prime responsibility" (v).

4. S. P. Zitner rightly notes that "Not all cruxes in Shakespeare arise from language or idea"; there are also "cruxes of physical action in which the choice of stage business can alter significantly how we see character and plot" (139), as can variant SHs still more emphatically.

5. I take it that the use in the first line of the play, "1. *Citizen.* / Before we *proceed* [move forward] any further, heare me speake" (4-5; I.i.1), is different in sense from that in TLN 27–28 (take action against), which relates less well to the crowd than to 1 Cit., who has said, "Let vs kill him, and wee'l haue Corne at our own price. Is't a Verdict?" (13–14; 9–10).

6. *More* averages 49 *written* lines per page with crowding in the last line or two of 8^v (four verse lines in two written lines) and 9^r (1 1/2 lines).

7. "*Mene.* Fie, fie, fie, *this is the way* to kindle, not to quench.
"*Sena.* To vnbuild the Citie, and *to lay all flat*" (1906–08, italics mine). In Cor.'s mouth the speech would exult in the prospect of total destruction, plausible enough in the abstract, and apparently consonant with some sentiments expressed elsewhere in the play, but in the immediate context quite at odds with his own dialogue and actions otherwise, as numerous editors have noted.

Works Cited and Consulted

Bowers, Fredson. "The Copy for Shakespeare's *Julius Caesar.*" *South Atlantic Bulletin* 43 (1978), 23–36. Cf. Jowett.

————. "Foul Papers, Compositor B, and the Speech-Prefixes of *All's Well That Ends Well.*" *Studies in Bibliography* 32 (1979), 60–81.

Brockbank, Philip, ed. *Coriolanus.* New Arden edition. London and New York: Methuen, 1976.

Clayton, Thomas. *The "Shakespearean" Addition in "The Booke of Sir Thomas Moore": Some Aids to Scholarly and Critical Shakespearean Studies.* Center for Shakespeare Studies Monograph No. 1. Dubuque: Wm. C. Brown, 1969.

Davis, Tom. "Textual Criticism: Philosophy and Practice." Review article. *The Library,* Sixth Series, 6 (1984), 386–97.

Eardley-Wilmot, H. *Times Literary Supplement,* 13 October 1950: 645. On Menenius/Sicinius SH at *Cor.* 3.1.304-306; see Rossiter for an answer.

Farmer, John S., ed. *The Book of Sir Thomas Moore: Harleian MSS. 7368.* Tudor Facsimile Texts. 1910. Rpt., New York: AMS Press, 1970.

Furness, Horace Howard, Jr., ed. *The Tragedie of "Coriolanus."* New Variorum Edition. Philadelphia: Lippincott, 1928.

Gilman, Albert. "Textual and Critical Problems in Shakespeare's *"Coriolanus."* Ph.D. diss. University of Michigan, 1954. *DA* 14 (1954): 673–74.

Greg, W. W. *Dramatic Documents from the Elizabethan Playhouses: Stage Plots: Actors' Parts: Prompt Books.* 2 vols. Oxford: Clarendon Press, 1931.

Gross, Mary J. H. "Some Puzzling Speech Prefixes in *Richard III.*" *Papers of the Bibliographical Society of America,* 71 (1977), 73–75.

Hinman, Charlton. *The Printing and Proof-Reading of the First Folio of Shakespeare.* 2 vols. Oxford: Clarendon Press, 1963.

Honigmann, E. A. J. "Re-Enter the Stage Direction: Shakespeare and Some Contemporaries." *Shakespeare Survey 29* (1976), 117–25 (*All* SH, 120–22).

————. *The Stability of Shakespeare's Text.* London: Arnold, 1965.

Howard-Hill, T. H. Letter responding to Gross. *Papers of the Bibliographical Society of America,* 71 (1977), 311–12.

————. *A Reassessment of Compositors B and E in the First Folio Tragedies.* Columbia, S.C.: privately printed, 1977.

————."Varieties of Copy: Possibilities and Probabilities." Unpublished paper delivered at meeting of New Variorum editors, MLA, Chicago, December 1985. (Heard and also read, thanks to Richard Knowles's kindly sending me a copy.)

Hunter, G. K. "Shakespeare and the Traditions of Tragedy." *The Cambridge Companion to Shakespeare Studies.* Ed. Stanley Wells. Cambridge: Cambridge University Press, 1986. 123–41.

Jackson, MacD. P. "Compositors B, C, and D and the First Folio Text of *Love's Labour's Lost.*" *Papers of the Bibliographical Society of America,* 72 (1978), 61–65.

———. "Compositor C and the First Folio Text of *Much Ado about Nothing.*" *Papers of the Bibliographical Society of America,* 68 (1974), 414–18.

Jowett, John, ed. *Coriolanus.* The Oxford Shakespeare, 1986. 1201–39.

———. "Ligature Shortage and Speech-Prefix Variation in *Julius Caesar.*" *The Library,* Sixth Series. 6 (1984): 244–53. Cf. Bowers.

Long, William B. "'A bed / for woodstock'; A Warning for the Unwary." *Medieval & Renaissance Drama,* II (1985), 91–118.

———. "Stage-Directions: A Misinterpreted Factor in Determining Textual Provenance." *TEXT: Transactions of the Society for Textual Scholarship,* 2 (1985), 121–37.

McGann, Jerome J. *A Critique of Modern Textual Criticism.* Chicago: University of Chicago Press, 1983.

———. ed. *Textual Criticism and Literary Interpretation.* Chicago: University of Chicago Press, 1985.

———. "The Monks and the Giants: Textual and Bibliographical Studies and the Interpretation of Literary Works." McGann, ed., *Textual Criticism.* 180–99.

McKerrow, R. B. "A Suggestion Regarding Shakespeare's Manuscripts." *The Review of English Studies,* 11 (1935), 459–65.

McLeod, Randall. "No more, the text is foolish." Taylor and Warren, eds., *The Division of the Kingdoms.* 153–93.

———. "Spellbound: Typography and the Concept of Old-Spelling Editions." *Renaissance and Reformation,* New Series, 3 (1979), 50–65.

———. "Un*Editing* Shakespeare." *Sub-Stance,* 33/34 (1982), 26–55.

Meagher, John C. "Conrade Conned: Or, the Career of Hugh Oatcake." *Shakespeare Quarterly,* 24 (1973), 90–92.

Melchiori, Giorgio. "*The Booke of Sir Thomas Moore*: A Chronology of Revision." *Shakespeare Quarterly,* 37 (1986), 291–308.

———."Hand D in 'Sir Thomas More': An Essay in Misinterpretation." *Shakespeare Survey,* 38 (1985), 101–14.

Murry, John Middleton. "A Neglected Heroine of Shakespeare [Virgilia]." *Countries of the Mind: Essays in Literary Criticism.* London: Collins, 1922. 31–50. Reprinted as a substantial part of

"*Coriolanus*" in *John Clare and Other Studies.* London: Peter Nevill, 1950. 231–42 of 222–45 (the latter quoted here).

Oxford Shakespeare, The. *William Shakespeare: The Complete Works.* Gen. Eds. Stanley Wells and Gary Taylor. Oxford: Clarendon Press, 1986.

Prosser, Eleanor. *Shakespeare's Anonymous Editors: Scribe and Compositor in "2 Henry IV."* Stanford: Stanford University Press, 1981.

Proudfoot, Richard. Rev. of New Arden *Coriolanus,* ed. Philip Brockbank. *Shakespeare Survey,* 30 (1977), 203-205.

Reid, S. W. "B and 'J': Two Compositors in Two Plays of the Shakespeare First Folio." *The Library,* 6th ser. 7 (1985), 126–36.

Riverside Shakespeare, The. Ed. G. Blakemore Evans. Boston: Houghton, 1974.

Sanders, Wilbur. "An Impossible Person: Caius Martius Coriolanus." In *Shakespeare's Magnanimity: Four Tragic Heroes, Their Friends and Families.* By Wilbur Sanders and Howard Jacobson. New York: Oxford University Press, 1978. 136–87.

Rossiter, A. P. *Times Literary Supplement,* 20 October 1950: 661. On Menenius/Sicinius SH at *Cor.* 3.1.304-6; answer to Eardley-Wilmot.

Shakespeare Survey 29 and *30,* ed. Kenneth Muir; *38* ed. Stanley Wells. Cambridge: Cambridge University Press, 1976, 1977, and 1985.

Shakespeare Variorum Handbook. By Richard Hosley, Richard Knowles, and Ruth McGugan. New York: MLA, 1971. Intermittent supplements to date.

Sisson, C. J. *New Readings in Shakespeare.* Vol. 2 of 2 vols. Cambridge: Cambridge University Press, 1956.

———., ed. *William Shakespeare: The Complete Works.* New York: Harper, 1954.

Taylor, Gary. "Henslowe's, *and* Shakespeare's, Book of Sir Thomas More." Unpublished Paper ("Working Draft," 17 pp., ts, 3-11-83).

———., and Michael Warren, eds. *The Division of the Kingdoms: Shakespeare's Two Versions of "King Lear."* Oxford: Clarendon Press, 1983.

TEXT 2. Eds. D. C. Greetham and W. Speed Hill. New York: AMS Press, 1985.

Warren, Michael. "Textual Problems, Editorial Assertions in Editions of Shakespeare." In McGann, ed., *Textual Criticism.* 23–37.

Werstine, Paul. "The Editorial Usefulness of Printing House and Compositor Studies." *Play-Texts in Old Spelling: Papers from the Glendon Conference* [1978]. Ed. G. B. Shand with Raymond C. Shady. New York: AMS, 1984. 35–64. Reprint (35–42), with Afterword (42–64), of "Compositor B of the Shakespeare First Folio." *Analytical & Enumerative Bibliography,* 2 (1978), 241–63.

———. "Folio Editors, Folio Compositors, and the Folio Text of *King Lear.*" Taylor and Warren, eds., *The Division of the Kingdoms.* 247–312.

———. "Line Division in Shakespeare's Dramatic Verse: An Editorial Problem." *Analytical & Enumerative Bibliography,* 8 (1984), 73–125.

"All things is hansome now": Murderers Nominated by Numbers in Variant Texts of 2 *Henry VI* and *Richard III*

Steven Urkowitz

In the earliest printed texts of *Henry VI, Part 2* and *Richard III*, parallel sets of variants in the characterizations and actions of two pairs of murderers—nominated by their function or by numbers—reveal finely detailed, lively, and surprisingly consistent alterations in the scripted portrayals of psychological brutality, cynicism, remorse, and repentence. Created by manipulation of speech prefixes, formal stage directions, and dialogue, these patterned textual variants suggest (1) that significant artistic attention was paid to these minor, anonymous characters at some stage in the process of composition, (2) that the same agency—author, acting company, reviser, or illicit pirate—generated at least these parts of the alternative versions of *Henry VI, Part 2* and *Richard III*, (3) that modern editorial practice which often builds an eclectic text from the alternative early versions inadvertently distorts self-consistent readings of the early versions, and (4) that modern editorial practice both arises from and perpetuates a general insensitivity of theatrical nuance governing the relationships between dramatic characters discoverable in these early variant scripts.

This essay departs in several ways from the traditional opinions concerning the derivation and relationships of the texts of *Henry VI, Part 2* and *Richard III* and the usual consequences of these opinions. Based upon theories of "memorial reconstruction" which gained a form of bibliographic legitimacy after W. W. Greg applied them first to the 1602 Quarto of *The Merry Wives of Windsor* and again in *Two Elizabethan Stage Abridgements,* Peter Alexander and D. L. Patrick argued that the earliest printed texts of these history plays resulted from a similar process: Alexander proposed that *Henry VI, Parts 2 and 3* were pirated by one or possibly several actors, and Patrick contended that *Richard III* was memorially reconstructed by an entire acting company dictating its recollection to a scribe in order to replace a lost or unavailable promptbook. Elsewhere I have shown that the evidence offered by Patrick and Alexander fails to support their memorial reconstruction hypotheses.[1] The main flaws in their arguments are their misunderstandings of basic practices of Elizabethan acting companies, their confusion of literary taste with bibliographic evidence, and their inadequate, reductive, and denigrating models of composing processes which may have led to theatrical scripts played by Shakespeare's actors.

In the following essay I do not argue that one version of a passage under discussion is necessarily superior to another: such evaluation becomes necessary only in the context of editing when only a single version is to be established as "authoritative." An editor usually must decide which of two or more versions he or she is to print in the body of an edition and which versions will be relegated to notes, to textual collations, to appendices, or to other loci of typographic oblivion. Instead of concentrating solely upon one "best" text or "original" or "final authorially intended" version, I believe that we can learn more from these alternative texts by examining them as independent theatrical documents, just as we may look at independent stage productions or video or film versions of any particular play. Questions of "better" and "worse" have traditionally interfered with or completely prevented comparative analysis of underlying purposes in the early, radically variant quartos of Shakespeare's plays, and in textual studies such aesthetic evaluations often have led to a rhetoric of angry disdain for rather than understanding of the efforts of players and playwrights, adapters and publishers. We have had many constructively comparative studies examining Shakespeare's plays in contrast to their narrative and dramatic sources, as well as equally valuable comparative studies relating Shakespeare's plays to later plays derived from them.

Very few readers, actors, or teachers of Shakespearean drama have ever looked closely at the earliest printed versions of Shakespeare's plays. Editors and textual critics who have had occasion to work with these texts report that they do indeed have surprising (though often only grudgingly acknowledged) value, particularly to anyone interested in theatrical performance. For example, G. Blakemore Evans suggests the First Quarto printing of *Henry VI, Part 2,* is "especially valuable as giving us some insight into at least one Elizabethan production of the play.[2] But recent criticism explores the possible ramifications of this insight only to generate a single "authorial" text (as in the new Oxford edition of the complete works) or to demonstrate the superiority of the Folio version over the earlier printed texts.[3] The following essay looks at one set of differences found in a few of these early texts: the two versions of murderers' scenes in *2 Henry VI* and *Richard III.*

First published in 1594 as *The First Part of the Contention betwixt the two famous Houses of York and Lancaster . . . , 2 Henry VI* was printed in a radically different and longer form in the 1623 Folio; the first printed text of *Richard III* is dated 1597 and differs only slightly but often significantly from the 1623 Folio version.

The murderers of Duke Humphrey in *2 Henry VI* and of Clarence in *Richard III* have no names, only numbers or titles indicating their functions, but they demonstrate the practical dimensions and techniques of craftsmanship applied by a playwright and an acting troupe in the task of character-building. We find carefully manipulated motivations for actions, articulated and possibly changing attitudes toward their tasks, and identifiable mannerisms of speech, such as emotional reticence or exuberance and verbal deference or insolence to characters of higher rank.

In the course of this essay I will treat the earliest published versions before the later published versions. My own opinion is that the earlier printed texts were indeed composed before those printed later; and in my opinion the same agents,

Shakespeare and his fellow players, were responsible for the early versions and the later versions. But observations about these differences may be separated from theoretical speculation about their sources. Indeed, in the heated atmosphere of contemporary textual debate, such abstraction of observation from theory is necessary for any change of opinion to occur.[4] In short, the observations may prove interesting whether or not the theory which drives them is acceptable.

* * *

Here is the simplest instance. The murderers of Duke Humphrey in the first printed version of *2 Henry VI* are designated simply "two men" in the stage direction at their entrance, and in speech prefixes they are called *"One."* and *"2."* The scene in which they appear contains in the 1594 Quarto a long stage direction and five speeches and in the 1623 Folio a shorter stage direction—calling for radically different action—and eight speeches.

> Then the Curtaines being drawne, Duke Humphrey is discovered in his bed, and two men lying on his brest and smothering him in his bed. And then enter the Duke of Suffolke to them.
> *Suffolk*. How now sirs, what have you dispatcht him?
> *One*. I my Lord, hees dead I warrant you.
> *Suffolke*. Then see the cloathes laid smooth about him still,
> That when the King comes, he may perceive
> No other, but that he dide of his owne accord.
> *2*. All things is hansome now my Lord.
> *Suffolke*. Then draw the Curtaines againe and get you gone,
> And you shall have your firme reward anon.
> *Exet* murtherers.
> (III. ii. 1–14; Quarto, E2)[5]

Murderer One gives a triple affirmation that their job was fully accomplished, "I my lord," "hees dead," and "I warrant you," where a simple "Aye," or "Yes," would have sufficed. The script does not dictate the First Murderer's attitude toward the task, but through repetition it insists on intensity. At Suffolk's command, "Then see the cloathes laid smooth," I imagine that the other executioner, 2, goes to plump up dead Humphrey's pillows and smooth the bed clothes. Or, perhaps, he has already neatened them without being asked, before Suffolk's command. In either case, this executioner gives a jolly reply. "All things is hansome now my Lord," rings with brisk engagement in the work, a proud craftsman satisfied with his job. The Duke of Suffolk promises his employees, worthy of their hire, a "firme reward," quite as if there were a contract or an established set of rates. Upon his command, they draw the bed-curtains and depart. The violent opening tableau of this scene thus ends in a grisly but orderly domesticity.

Between the 1594 printing and the 1623 Folio version, labor diffidence and unprofessional confusion seem to have infected the Murderers Guild. Our friends, 1 and 2, commit their crime offstage rather than in sight of the audience; they burst onstage in a vivid display of mixed motives and disjointed actions, and when questioned by their employer only Murderer 1 responds.

> *Enter two or three running over the Stage, from the*
> *Murther of Duke Humfrey.*
>   *1.* Runne to my Lord of Suffolke: let him know
> We have dispatcht the Duke, as he commanded.
>   *2.* Oh, that it were to doe: what have we done?
> Didst ever heare a man so penitent?   *Enter Suffolke.*
>   *1.* Here comes my Lord.
>   *Suff.* Now Sirs, have you dispatcht this thing?
>   *1.* I, my good Lord, hee's dead.
>   *Suff.* Why that's well said. Goe, get you to my House,
> I will reward you for this venturous deed:
> The King and all the Peeres are here at hand.
> Have you layd faire the Bed? Is all things well,
> According as I gave directions?
>   *1.* 'Tis, my good Lord.
>   *Suff.* Away, be gone.   *Exeunt.*
>   (III. ii. 1–14; Folio, TLN 1690–1705)

In contrast to the orderly progress of the crime in the Quarto, the Folio begins with running figures and rapid commands, "Runne . . . let him know . . . " Significantly, these first commands are not obeyed; instead the Second Murderer voices his regrets for the action, and then immediately Suffolk enters and makes the initial commands unnecessary. Like the dialogue between the murderers, Suffolk's opening question to them again is indirect rather than straightforward: "have you dispatcht this thing?" instead of "have you dispatcht him?" Suffolk's order for the murder, not the murderers' deed itself, takes precedence in this text. In the opening moment, rather than witnessing the murder itself, we see men running from an event initially unspecified to the audience. Then we hear that the Duke has been killed on Suffolk's command. Where the Quarto calls for two enthusiastic scoundrels doing in the good Duke Humphrey in plain sight, a feature so attractive that it is mentioned on the Quarto's title page, in the Folio we miss the homicidal display, initially see confused movement, hear Murderer One speak more like a laconic functionary— without his assertive "I warrant you" of the Quarto tagged onto "he's dead"—and we observe Number Two as a querulous repentant—"What have we . . . ?", and "Didst ever heare . . . ?"

While the minor characters, 1 and 2, seem far less colorful than in the Quarto version, Suffolk in contrast vigorously dominates the stage in the Folio. Suffolk raps out questions and instructions, and no fearsome corpse upstage draws our attention away from the First Murderer's prompt and deferential responses. Further, Suffolk sends the murderers to his own home, perhaps as a place both for refuge and for payment. They seem more under his control, more within his power, than do the more vividly characterized and independent murderers of the Quarto.

Suffolk's manner of dismissing the murderers was part of a long, friendly sentence in the Quarto: "Then draw the Curtaines againe and get you gone, / And you shall have your firme reward anon"; his equivalent in the Folio is an officious and repetitious order following on suspicious interrogation: "Have you layd faire the Bed? Is all things well, / According as I gave directions? . . . Away, be gone." Suffolk's questions may also generate an interrupted exit, momentarily calling back

106

the murderers (after the command, "Go get you gone . . . "), and so may indicate an improvisatory quality in the Duke's actions. (Similar variants in *Richard III,* at III. v. 75–108, also impel and then delay an equivalent exit from a murderous moment, the delivery of Hastings' head.) Further, instead of a "firm reward" as in the Quarto, Suffolk speaks of a reward for "this venturous deed": in F for Suffolk the murder is a chancy adventure rather than a "firm" job of work meriting a "firm reward."

We notice that Suffolk in Q is a vicious noble among knaves similarly confirmed in vice, all three relishing their own evil. They have no secrets from one another; we receive no surprises. In F however Suffolk stands as both the primary motivating force for wickedness and the most wicked of the men before us, displayed between one repentant sinner and one colorless operative.[6] From the outset we have unexpected disclosures and actions: first an unknown offstage event signalled by the running men, then disclosure that the murder occurred, then the Second Murderer's humane sympathy for the victim, then Suffolk's dispatch and recall of the murderers.

We are dealing with radically different conceptions of the scene, each with its own integrity, rhythms of action, and theatrical values. Most modern editions follow the Folio version. However, in the tradition of textual eclecticism, Andrew Cairncross in his Arden edition attempts to make the best of possible worlds from his variant sources. Onto the Folio's laconic First Murderer's final speech, he grafts a stub of the Quarto's exuberant Second Murderer's "All things is hansome now." Rather than the Folio's "'Tis, my good Lord," the Arden text reads: "'Tis handsome, my good lord" III. ii. 13. Reproducing neither of the two alternative texts from Shakespeare's time, the Arden editor invents an interesting but inconsistent third. In his collation and his explanatory note, he fails to indicate that the fragments he joins together come from speeches assigned to distinct roles in distinct conceptions of the passage.

We have here two alternative "authorial" strategies for handling the murder. We just do not know certainly how to name their author or authors, we do not know whether one or the other or both versions resulted from individual or group efforts, and we cannot be sure which of the two versions came first. But we do have the alternative versions, and if we only know to look we could discover much about the abstract process we call "dramatic characterization" simply by examining both texts at once. G. Blakemore Evans asserts that "Q1 has no basic authority" (p. 665), but scholars and theater historians should be shown that although the Quarto is not much help in determining details of the lost manuscript (or irrecoverable performances) that lies somewhere behind the Folio text, Q1 does have impressive, indeed unique, "authority" for exactly the version which it first prints: the equally lost manuscript (or performances) used to generate Q1.[7]

* * *

Richard III, in its 1597 Quarto and 1623 Folio versions,[8] offers a far more intricate set of variants in the characterizations of two other "enumerated murderers," the men who kill the Duke of Clarence. The First Murderer in both versions takes the more active role as executioner. He alone stabs Clarence, and he alone hauls the dying man out for drowning in malmsey. The Second Murderer initially is reticent in both texts, then he appears fiercely committed to the task, and finally, within moments of the crime, he repents. But in the Folio version alone the Second Murderer is more forceful in his initial reticence. In the Folio he oscillates more violently between holding back or going on. Only in the Folio does he take a small rather than an equal part in the grim debate with Clarence over the merits of Clarence's execution. And only in the Folio at the last instant of Clarence's life in the Folio does he futilely warn him of the fatal attack from his fellow.

The following argument about the murderers in *Richard III* presupposes that scripted characters in plays, especially in plays by Shakespeare, behave as understandably and consistently human. Their actions and motives may waver, but these should be recognizable as "normal" human waverings. This acceptance of an Aristotelian "imitation of human action" for minor as well as major characters is one of the basic principles of modern criticism and dramatic production. Contemporary productions by first-class repertory companies demonstrate how an accomplished actor may discover the same intense life in a well-drawn messenger as in a prince.

Antony Hammond argues to the contrary that Shakespeare generated apparently inconsistent murderers in this scene—"These minor figures have no 'characters' in any consistent sense . . . ; they act according to the immediate dramatic needs of the moment" (Arden ed., p. 177). The Furness Variorum, in contrast, quotes Cowden-Clarke: "The two Murderers are drawn with a terribly bold and masterly hand. They are not only designed with a marked difference from any others of Shakespeare's murderers . . . , but these have such perfect individuality as to be unlike and quite distinct from each other" (Variorum ed., pp. 85–86). Recognizing consistency of characterization in a script depends very much upon one's own literary taste, theatrical imagination, and basic principles of analyzing human behavior.

After the Keeper of the Tower leaves the murderers alone with sleeping Clarence, both texts give roughly identical dialogue for the opening exchange between 1 and 2. Murderer Two voices his first qualms:

> 2 What shall I [we *in F*] stab him as he sleepes?
> 1 No then he will say twas done cowardly
> When he wakes.
> 2 When he wakes,
> Why foole he shall never wake till the judgement day.
> 1 Why then he will say, we stabd him sleeping.
> 2 The urging of that word Judgement, hath bred
> A kind of remorse in me.
> 1 What art thou afraid.
> 2 Not to kill him having a warrant for it, but to be damnd
> For killing him, from which no warrant can defend us [me *in F*].
> 1 Backe to the Duke of Glocester, tell him so.
>   (I. iv. 100–116; Quarto, D1v)

The Quarto reading presents the last quoted speech in the form of a command; *1* tells *2* he should bring his theological cavil back to their employer.

109

The Folio has two speeches not found in Q, and in contrast the last speech becomes a threat by the First Murderer to inform against his fellow. Significant variants in spoken dialogue appear in italics:

> *1* What? art thou affraid?
> *2* Not to kill him, having a Warrant,
> But to be damn'd for killing him, from the which
> No Warrant can defend *me.*
> *1 I thought thou had'st bin resolute.*
> *2 So I am, to let him live.*
> *1 Ile* backe to the Duke of Glouster, and tell him so.
> (I. iv. 109–116; Folio, TLN 947–52)

With this threat, and reminded of the fee he will earn, Murderer Two puts aside his reservations and even attacks the idea of Conscience in a style matching Falstaff's anatomy of Honor in *1 Henry IV*: "Ile not meddle with it, it makes a man a Coward: A man cannot steale, but it accuseth him: A man cannot Sweare, but it Checkes him: A man cannot lye with his Neighbours Wife, but it detects him," etc. (I. iv. 134–37; Folio, TLN 968–71).

As the two murderers get ready to fall to their work, the next segment of dialogue is roughly the same until the moment they see Clarence awaken. Murderer Two delays the killing in the Quarto, taking a step back from his momentary enthusiasm for it:

> *2* . . . Come shall we to this geere.
> *1* Take him over the costard with the hilts of thy sword,
> And then we wil chop him in the malmsey But in the next roome.
> *2* Oh excellent device, make a sop of him.
> *1* Harke he stirs, shall I strike.
> *2* No, first lets reason with him.
> (I. iv. 153–160; Quarto, D2)

In contrast to his delay in the Quarto version, Murderer Two in the Folio urges immediate action to fulfill their charge. But here Murderer One calls for delay: he will play even though Richard warned against talking with "well-spoken" Clarence (in I.iii).

> *2* O excellent device; and make a sop of him.
> *1* Soft, he wakes.
> *2* Strike.
> *1* No. wee'l reason with him.
>> (Folio, TLN 989–92)

Both men take roughly equal parts in the succeeding dialogue in the Quarto, but in the Folio—where the delay was introduced by Murderer One—Murderer Two has many fewer speeches and fewer lines. Murderer One speaks eleven speeches comprising seventeen typeset lines when Murderer Two has ten speeches on fourteen lines in the Quarto; they share four speeches (marked *Am.*, for *Ambo* or "both"). In the Folio, Murderer One has fourteen speeches on twenty-three lines compared to Two's ten speeches on thirteen lines; they share only one speech. More important than the shifting number of speeches, however, Murderer Two in the Folio speaks all the statements sympathetic to Clarence, and only he displays any of the hesitancy shared by both in the Quarto. The differences may be seen in the dialogue immediately following Clarence's awakening. The Quarto reads:

> *2* No, first lets reason with him.
> *Cla.* Where art thou keeper, give me a cup of wine.
> *1* You shall have wine enough my Lo: anon.
> *Cla.* In Gods name what art thou.
> *2* A man as you are.
> *Cla.* But not as I am, royall.
> *2* Nor you as we are, loyall.
> *Cla.* Thy voice is thunder, but thy lookes are humble.
> *2* My voice is now the Kings, my lookes mine owne.
> *Cla.* How darkly, and how deadly doest thou speake:
> Tell me who are you, wherefore come you hither?
> *Am.* To, to, to.
> *Cla.* To murther me. *Am.* I.
>> (I. iv. 160–74; Quarto, D2)

The Folio reverses the speech prefixes for One and Two in this segment and gives the stammering, "To, to, to—" as a speech to the Second Murderer alone.

> *1* No, wee'l reason with him.
> *Cla.* Where art thou Keeper? Give me a cup of wine.
> *2* You shall have Wine enough my Lord anon.
> *Cla.* In Gods name, what art thou?
> *1* A man, as you are.
> *Cla.* But not as I am Royall.
> *1* Nor you as we are, Loyall.
> *Cla.* Thy voice is Thunder, but thy looks are humble.
> *1* My voice is now the Kings, my lookes mine owne.
> *Cla.* How darkly, and how deadly dost thou speake?
> Your eyes do menace me: why looke you pale? Who sent
> you hither? Wherefore do you come?
> *2* To, to, to——
> *Cla.* To murther me?
> *Both.* I, I.

> (Folio, TLN 992–1006)

In the third speech of the passage above, "You shall have wine enough my Lord anon," the Folio speech-prefix here allows only the Second Murderer to address Clarence respectfully as "my Lord," in contrast to the Quarto which has both murderers use the form.

Speech prefixes regulating the dialogue continue invariant in both texts until we come to a series of ironic responses shared by both murderers or spoken by the Second Murder alone in the Quarto. With the exception of Murderer Two's speech immediately after Clarence awakens ("You shall have wine enough my Lord anon"), each of these sardonic rejoinders appears only in the First Murderer's part in the Folio. Here is the Quarto version:

> *2* You are deceiv'd, your brother Glocester hates you.
> *Cla.* Oh no, he loves me, and he holds me deare,
> Go you to him from me.
> *Am.* I, so we will.
> *Cla.* Tell him, when that our princely father Yorke,
> Blest his three sonnes with his victorious arme:

And chargd us from his soule, to love each other,
He little thought of this devided friendship.
Bid Glocester thinke of this, and he will weepe.
    Am. I, milstones as he lessond us to weepe.
    Cla. O doe not slaunder him for he is kind.
    1 Right as snow in harvest, thou deceiv'st thy selfe,
Tis he hath sent us hither now to slaughter thee.
    Cla. It cannot be, for when I parted with him,
He hugd me in his armes; and swore with sobs,
That he would labour my delivery.
    2 Why so he doth, now he delivers thee,
From this worlds thraldome, to the joies of heaven,
      1 Makes peace with God, for you must die my Lo:
                (I. iv. 232–49; Quarto, D3)

Both ironic speeches designated "*Am.*" in the Quarto are marked for "*1*" in the Folio. The nasty jest in the next-to-last speech about delivering Clarence "to the joies of heaven" is marked for "*1*" in the Folio, and the final speech prefix in this segment is for "*2*" rather than "*1*." A contrasting effect appears in the speech prefixes for the two speeches which advise Clarence to prepare himself for death: ". . . my Lord, therefore prepare to dye" TLN 1012, and "Make peace with God, for you must die my Lord" TLN 1082. The Quarto divides these between the two murderers; the Folio however gives both expressions of concern for Clarence's soul to Murderer Two. Again, in this text only the Second Murderer addresses Clarence respectfully as "my Lord."

In the last major segment, the Second Murderer turns in both texts to express his resurgent hesitation: "What shall we do?" Then Clarence addresses him individually, making a direct appeal to one murderer in an attempt to split them apart. The alternative texts again heighten the differences between the two men: we see the Second Murderer mute and helpless in the Quarto, and in contrast we see his vain effort to warn Clarence of impending attack in the Folio.

    2 What shall we doe?
    Cla. Relent, and save your soules.
    1 Relent, tis cowardly and womanish.
    Cla. Not to relent, is beastly, savage, divelish,

My friend, I spie some pitty in thy lookes:
Oh if thy eye be not a flatterer,
Come thou on my side, and intreat for me,
A begging Prince, what begger pitties not?
     1 I thus, and thus: if this wil not serve,   *He stabs him.*
Ile chop thee in the malmesey But, in the next roome.
                       (I. iv. 256–70; Quarto, D2-D3ᵛ)

The Folio text includes five lines not in the Quarto version of Clarence's first speech quoted above. These stress Clarence's appeal to both murderers at first: they create a greater contrast in F than in Q when he turns to address Murderer Two as "My Friend" in his last speech. Murderer Two replies to Clarence only in this version. The two passages unique to F appear below in italics.[9]

    2 What shall we do?
    Clar. Relent, and save your soules:
Which of you, if you were a Princes Sonne,
Being pent from Liberty, as I am now,
If two such murtherers as your selves came to you,
Would not intreat for life, as you would begge
Were you in my distresse.
    1 Relent? no: 'Tis cowardly and womanish.
    Cla. Not to relent, is beastly, savage, divellish:
My Friend, I spy some pitty in thy lookes:
O, if thine eye be not a Flatterer,
Come thou on my side, and intreate for mee,
A begging Prince, what begger pitties not.
    2 Looke behinde you, my Lord.
    1 Take that, and that, if all this will not do, *Stabs him.*
Ile drowne you in the Malmesey-But within.   *Exit*
                     (Folio, TLN 1089–1104)

The Second Murderer's useless outcry includes a final, poignantly respectful address to Clarence, "Looke behinde you, *my Lord*" rounding off the usage of this form, consistently spoken only by this character in the Folio.

The remainder of the scene appears roughly the same in both versions, the major differences occurring in patterns of alliteration and interrogation in both roles.

> *2* A bloudy deede and desperately performd,
> How faine like Pilate would I wash my hand,
> Of this most grievous guilty murder done.
>   *1* Why doest thou not helpe me,
> By heavens the Duke shall know how slacke thou art.
>   *2* I would he knew that I had saved his brother.
> Take thou the fee, and tell him what I say,
> For I repent me that the Duke is slaine.   *Exit.*
>   *1* So do not I, go coward as thou art:
> Now must I hide his body in some hole,
> Untill the Duke take order for his buriall:
> And when I have my meede I must away,
> For this will out, and here I must not stay.   *Exeunt.*
>   (I. iv. 271–83; Quarto, D3v)

The Folio reads "desperately dispatcht" for "desperately performed" in the first line quoted, and instead of "Why doest thou not helpe me," Murderer One in the Folio asks, "How now? What mean'st thou that thou help'st me not?"

The Second Murderer's belated repentance and the First Murderer's mercenary, opportunistic professionalism set out in both texts the same emblematic alternatives that we see repeated by Richard's other agents as they are seduced and corrupted. By using speeches and speech patterns common to both men, the Quarto creates a pattern close to that found in the Quarto version of *2 Henry VI*; by distinguishing between the two men more consistently, the Folio resembles the polar opposition between the two murderers found in the Folio version of *2 Henry VI*.

***

These two sets of anonymous murderers in variant texts of *2 Henry VI* and *Richard III* change their characteristics by what seems the simplest of textual manipulations—speech prefix variants—as well as by the most complex: additions, rearrangements, excisions of lines, and changes in stage-action.

Abjuring debate about the authenticity or the derivation of the earliest printed texts of Shakespeare's multiple-text plays,

I believe it is sufficient to note that these alternative texts exist and that—in addition to and perhaps even more than our contemporary, modern, edited versions of the same plays—they properly claim our attention. And if the reader wishes to believe that pirates or players "memorially reconstructed" the 1594 text of *2 Henry VI* or the 1597 *Richard III,* then such a reader may be pleased to have discovered the demonstrably sensitive workings of those agents: witnesses of or participants in the plays' performances in the 1590s, therefore, remembered or reconstructed the versions printed in 1594 and 1597 when they perhaps saw performed the texts represented in the 1623 printing. We may learn much about these playgoers or about playgoers in general by examining their systematic patterns of "memorial error." Such a task should appeal to adherents of "memorial reconstruction." Alternatively, we may hold tentatively to a hypothesis of authorial revision as the source of these alternative texts. In that case, examination of the multiple-texts may give us insight into the author's revising process, perhaps when he was at his desk, perhaps during initial polishings of foul papers before handing fair copy to the acting company, perhaps after he tested his earlier versions in performance, or perhaps after having seen in print the versions found in the quartos. Or we may consider that the printed scripts of plays usually represent a confluence of pressures and contributions generated by an extended literary, theatrical, and publishing community: authors, shareholders, journeyman actors, apprentice boys, playhouse scribes and bookkeepers, different versions of chronicle histories, rival playwrights, theatrical censors, publishers, compositors setting from the initial manuscript copy, proofreaders, compositors setting from printed and possibly annotated copy in later quartos, and compositors setting Folio copy. Given such a melange of influences, authorship necessarily loses some of its vatic mystery. But we may look at the variant products of different momentary resolutions of these forces to see how we impose our own values and imagined reconstructions upon them.

We cannot tell with any certainty beyond guessing who is responsible for the first versions; we cannot tell who is respon-

116

sible for the second versions either. This is not a big problem. And the issues of authorship and authority become critical only because editors, propelled by the economic demands of their publishers, claim to produce a single item to be marketed as the genuine, authoritative, Shakespearean version, a cultural icon likely to be purchased in large numbers by high schools and by college students. As publishers quickly learned during his lifetime, Shakespeare's name on the title page sells books, and "Newly imprinted and enlarged to almost as much againe as it was, according to the true and perfect Coppie" encourages faith in the buyer that the goods are genuine. But if we are interested in these scripts not as icons but as dramatic documents, if we consult them for the theatrical possibilities they suggest for enactment in our own theatres, then the appeal of any singular "authority" should not replace the potentialities of divided authorities. Just as we learn more about *Hamlet* after having seen Laurence Olivier, Richard Burton, and Derek Jacobi in the leading role, we learn more about Humphrey's and Clarence's murderers when we see them in the two early texts than when we read them in a single, "authoritative" Arden or Riverside edition. What we lose, however, is any reassuring notion of "Shakespeare's" version. It seems clear that the historical figure known to his contemporaries by that name was not very much concerned with leaving such singular records of his dramatic compositions.

No matter what one concludes about the authority of these documents, literary scholars, theatrical historians, students or idolators of Shakespeare, or performers of his plays may profitably turn to examine the earliest printed versions themselves.

Notes

1. Steven Urkowitz, "Reconsidering the Relationship of Quarto and Folio Texts in *Richard III*," *English Literary Renaissance*, 16 (1986), 442-66, and "'If I mistake in Those Foundations Which I Build Upon': Peter Alexander's Textual Analysis of *Henry VI Parts 2 and 3*," *English Literary Renaissance*, 18 (1988), 230-56.

2. G. Blakemore Evans, ed. *The Riverside Shakespeare* (Cambridge, Mass: Houghton Mifflin, 1974), p. 665. One of the few recent applications of Evans' suggestion is Scott McMillin, "The Queen's Men in 1594: A Study of 'Good' and 'Bad' Quartos," *English Literary Renaissance,* 15 (1985), 55-69. The continuing debate over the *King Lear* Quarto and Folio texts revolves about the interpretation of evidence which some critics believe points to early production but which others feel could only have arisen from errors in transcription or typesetting.

3. Claire Saunders, "'Dead in his Bed': Shakespeare's Staging of the Death of the Duke of Gloucester in *2 Henry VI,*" *Review of English Studies,* N. S. 35 (1984), 19-34; Saunders argues that an acting company on tour created the Quarto as a spectacular but reductive adaptation of Shakespeare's single version.

4. See, for example, Random Cloud, "The Marriage of Good and Bad Quartos," *Shakespeare Quarterly* 33 (1982), 421-31; Jonathan Goldberg, "Textual Properties," *Shakespeare Quarterly* 37 (1986), 213-17; Paul Werstine, "Narratives about Printed Texts: 'Foul Papers' and 'Bad' Quartos," *Shakespeare Quarterly* 41 (1990), 65-86; Marion Trousdale, "A Second Look at Critical Bibliography and the Acting of Plays," *Shakespeare Quarterly* 41 (1990), 87-96.

5. In all quotations from the early texts, u and v, i and j, long s and typographic ligatures have been normalized according to modern conventions; turned-over or turned-under lines are regularized; and italicized proper nouns in the dialogue of the original are here given in roman type. Act-scene-line numbers are taken from *The Riverside Shakespeare,* Through Line Numbers from *The Norton Facsimile: The First Folio of Shakespeare,* ed. Charlton Hinman (New York: W. W. Norton, 1968).

6. A somewhat similar variant may be found in *King Lear,* V. iii, where the Folio text lacks the reply of Edmund's captain: "I cannot draw a cart, nor eate dride oats, / If it bee mans work ile do't" Quarto, K4v. In consequence, Edmund himself stands out as a villain against a neutral background rather than allied with an articulate opportunist in a world of desperate scoundrels.

7. A similar, thematically related, and highly theatrical variant appears later in this play when Jack Cade meets his death in the garden of Eyden or Iden, "Esquire of Kent." Unlike the supine Duke of Gloucester, Cade challenges the man who arrests him: "I have eate no meate this five dayes, yet and I do not

leave thee and thy five men as dead as a doore nayle, I pray God I may never eate grasse more." Eyden replies, "Nay, it never shall be saide whilst the world doth stand, that Alexander Eyden an Esquire of Kent, tooke oddes to combat with a famisht man, looke on me, my limmes are equall unto thine, and every way as big, then hand to hand, ile combat thee" (Q, G4; IV. x. 38-52.). Just as one jolly and one intense murderer in Q gave way to one repentant and one laconic murderer in F, the two combatants here whose "limmes are equall" give way to one slight and one massive actor in F: " . . . to combate a poore famisht man. / Oppose thy stedfast gazing eyes to mine, / See if thou canst out-face me with thy lookes: / Set limbe to limbe, and thou art farre the lesser: / Thy hand is but a finger to my fist, / Thy legge a sticke compared with this Truncheon, / My foote shall fight with all the strength thou hast, / And if mine arme be heaved in the Ayre, / Thy grave is digg'd already in the earth" (TLN 2948-56). Dramatic characterization is tailored to fit the actors available as well as the particular dramatic sensibilities of the writer/reviser/memorial reconstructer.

8. The bibliographic rather than theatrical variants found in five quarto editions reprinted from Q1 before the Folio offer a daunting barrier to facile discussions of the texts of *Richard III*. Alternative readings from the later quartos have little impact upon the passages discussed here. For a recent summary of the *Richard III* texts, see Antony Hammond, ed. *King Richard III*, The Arden Edition (London: Methuen, 1981), 21-50. Only one variant speech-prefix, at TLN 998, is involved in the complicated discourse of error and influence of different quartos on the Folio, but that one prefix has little bearing on my argument.

9. Hammond repositions these lines in his text so they follow ". . . beastly, savage, divellish," two lines below. Following a suggestion by Harold Jenkins, he claims the Folio arrangement is an error, "sundering the coherent argument on the merits of relenting" (Arden ed., p. 337). I do not see why a character at the edge of death must necessarily argue with logical coherence: Clarence voices a series of desperate tries while scrambling for his life.

Speech Prefixes, Compositors, and Copy: Illustrated from Speech Prefixes in Plays of the Shakespeare *Apocrypha*

Richard Proudfoot

Searching for a point of theory to which to relate various and miscellaneous instances of interest in speech prefixes from the group of plays which I am engaged in editing, I found that one issue which cropped up all the time was how far and in what respect speech prefixes in printed plays could be identified as reflecting copy and in what circumstances anomalies could reasonably be attributed to compositors. The examples from plays in the Shakespeare *Apocrypha* which follow have in common some relation to these questions: in addition, they permit occasional speculation about the character or detail of the lost copy manuscripts. The examples comprise: variations in designation of characters by speech prefixes; variations in spelling or form of speech prefixes for a given character; anomalous or missing speech prefixes; and textual puzzles traceable to irregular placing of speech prefixes in the copy manuscript. Strictly speaking, my topic is itself anomalous as few if any of my examples are even imaginably Shakespearian. But though the *Apocrypha,* as defined by Tucker Brooke's fourteen-play collection (Oxford, 1908: 1929), may lack some of the more entertaining and striking kinds of evidence to be found in the Shakespeare quartos printed from 'foul papers', its plays neverthless yield a wide range of cases of interest.

Radical variation in the form of the speech prefix for a given character must generally derive from copy. Thus in *The Two Noble Kinsmen* (1634: printed by Thomas Cotes for John Waterson) the character who is *Iailor* in other scenes (abbreviated speech prefix *Iai.* or *Iay.*) appears in II. ii as *Keeper* (*Keep.*). Less noticeably, the spelling of the name of Theseus' friend Peirithous varies between *Pirithous* (*Pirith.* or *Pir.*) and *Perithous* (*Perith.* or *Per.*). In an avowedly collaborative play such variation at once suggests different authorship of the scenes in question, once it is established that the variation relates to scenic rather than to bibliographical units of text. This may be the true explanation of the *Pir./Per.* alternation. *Pir.* forms are used consistently in four scenes generally assigned to Shakespeare: I. i, iii; V. iii, iv (a single *Per.* early in V. iii seems to mark the compositor's change back from the consistent form of the previous three acts to a section of copy with *i* forms).

After a similar single *Pirith.* at the opening if II. iv (the first Fletcher scene in which the character appears), *Per.* forms only are used throughout the three middle acts, up to and including the short Fletcher passage which opens V. i. *Per.* forms are associated with the correct classical scansion of the name as a tetrasyllable, accented on the second and fourth syllables, while *Pir.* forms occur in scenes where the full name is scanned as a trisyllable, accented on the first and third syllables (the scansion used by Chaucer in his *Knight's Tale,* from which the play is largely derived). An odd anomaly is that the classical scansion of the name is associated in Fletcher's scenes with Chaucer's preferred *e* spelling, while Shakespeare's scenes show the *i* spelling found in North's translation of Plutarch's *Lives,* which more accurately reflects the Greek *ei* diphthong.

The case of *Iailor / Keeper* is less clear-cut. II. i, where he first appears, as *Iailor,* and II. ii, where he is *Keeper,* may indeed be the work of Shakespeare and Fletcher respectively, but in his later scenes (mostly by Fletcher) he is always *Iailor* or *Iaylor.* One explanation might be that Fletcher has learned to conform to Shakespeare's usage, but there is another possibility. Of all his scenes, only II. ii contains no reference to his daughter. It may be that the later predominance of *Iaylor* owes something to the fact that she—a far more prominent character than her father—is early established as *Iaylors Daughter.*

Striking variation of speech prefixes for the same character occurs likewise in *The Merry Devil of Edmonton* (1608: printed by Henry Ballard for Arthur Johnson). Here it seems clear that the variations stem from the copy manuscript. As W. W. Greg pointed out in a review of the edition of the play by W. A. Abrams (*The Library,* Fourth Series, 25 (1944–45), 129), this must have been an abbreviated acting version with many features suggestive of imperfectly revised "foul papers." The variations are of different kinds, but some relate to scenic units, where they may derive from local circumstances. To start with a simple instance: Banks the miller and Sir John the priest are generally *Banks., Bank.,* or *Ban.* and *Sir Ioh.* or *Sir Io.* In IV. iii (E3–4), after an initial speech prefix *Ban.,* Banks becomes *Mill., Milla.,* or *Mille.,* while Sir John is *Priest., Prie.,* or *Pri.* throughout. One further *Pri.* speech prefix is found, in the final scene, V. ii (F4). One explanation for the speech prefixes in IV. iii may be that the scene dramatizes an episode which is wholly independent of the play's main narrative source, being a jest, from the highly popular *A Hundred Merry Tales,* whose characters have no names. But a further possible explanation exists. Only in IV. iii and V. ii are the two characters' occupations of any significance. Banks, in his white miller's clothes, is taken for a ghost, while Sir John appears, first in the churchyard of his parish church, then to officiate at the final wedding. Whatever the origin of the divergent speech prefixes, they seem to reflect the author at work, influenced either by a change of source material or by the action of particular scenes.

Other variations in *The Merry Devil* result from the presence of three pairs of fathers and sons. They are: Sir Arthur Clare and his son Harry; *Sir* or *Old* Mounchensey and his son Raymond; and Sir Ralph Jerningham (*Sir Ar.* once on D2: no doubt a misreading of *Ra*) and his son Frank. Speech prefixes reflect great indecisiveness. In the early scenes, where the generations do not mix on stage, *Clar.* and *Cla.*, *Mount.* and *Moun.*, and *Ier.* are used indiscriminately for father or son. More distinctive forms gradually establish themselves. The Clares become *Sir Ar.* and *Ha. Cla.* or *Har.*; the Mounchenseys, *Sir Moun.*, *Old Moun.* or *Old Mo.*, and *Ray.*; and the Jerninghams, *Sir Ier.*, *Sir Raph.*, *Sir Rap.*, or *Sir Ra.* and *Yong Ier.*, *Frank.*, *Fran.*, *Fra.*, and *Fr.* Though inconsistencies do still occur and the Mounchenseys fade out of the action in the middle acts, the two other father/son pairs eventually settle down as *Sir Ar.* and *Cla.* and as *Sir Rap.* and *Ier.* The *Merry Devil* used to be thought of as a memorial text, a 'bad quarto'. The speech prefixes are among features which would seem to point rather to 'foul papers' as the copy manuscript (though there are also substantial grounds for supposing that the text has undergone abridgement on a major scale).

To offer the foregoing examples under the heading of "Speech Prefixes" is to concede that speech prefixes are, among other things, one of the three or four places where characters' names will usually be found in a text (the others being, of course, stage directions, dialogue, and, on occasion, lists of Persons). Where speech prefixes may be deemed distinctive is that they are habitually abbreviated—so habitually, indeed, as to draw attention to texts which make frequent use of the full forms of names in their speech prefixes, such as *Fair Em* ([1592]: printed probably by John Danter for Thomas Newman and John Winnington) or *The First Part of Sir John Oldcastle* (1600: printed by Valentine Simmes for Thomas Pavier). What is often hard to tell is how far compositorial variations of abbreviation may correspond to copy. It is hard to imagine, for instance, that all the variant speech prefixes for the title character in *The Tragedy of Locrine* (1595: printed by Thomas Creede) are faithful reflections of copy. He figures as *Locrine.*, *Locrin.*, *Locr.*, and *Loc.* A similar economy yields for Corineius, *Corin.*, *Cori.*, and *Cor.*; for Humber, *Humb.* and *Hum.*; likewise, we find *Strumbo.*, *Strum.*, and *Stru.*; *Brutus*, *Brut.*, and *Bru.* Such variations show no consistent relation to either scenic or bibliographical units.

Where manuscript copy used either full forms or unambiguous abbreviations, compositors would not be unduly prone to error, though they might well vary their own practice of abbreviation in reponse to the immediate pressures of time, spacing, or type depletion. Misprinting of speech prefixes may often reflect ambiguity or illegibility in copy, and in a place where contextual clues are not always present, especially when composition is by formes. Such misprints or errors may offer clues to several aspects of the printing process as well as affording occasional insights into the nature of the copy manuscript.

The early scenes of *The Reign of King Edward III* (1596: printed by Thomas Scarlet) contain two minor characters with names that yield similar speech prefixes, Lorraine and Lodwike. Lorraine appears in the first two scenes (I. i, ii), Lodwike in the next two (II. i, ii). The speech prefix for Lorraine is *Lor:* (A3^v, 4; B3) or *Lor.* (A4^v). Lodwike's first speech is on B3^v. It comes as a surprise, as no entry direction for the character has preceded it. The speech prefix is *Lor:*. On B4^v, his three speeches are headed *Lo:*. By now, he has been named in the dialogue, and on B4^v his re-entry has the stage direction *Enter Lodwike*. In quire C his speech prefixes are as follows: *Lor:* (C1, 2^v); *Lor.* (C1); and *Lo:* (C1^v, 2). He next enters on D3 and has one speech, headed *Lo:*, while *Lo.* is the form used for his final two speeches on D3^v. In quires B and C the explanation for these errors seems quite simple. The inner forme of B and the outer of C were set by the compositor who had previously set inner A, with its *Lor:* speech prefixes. Meeting the copy form *Lo:* for the first time on B3^v and lacking the guidance of any explanatory stage direction, he took it for the same character, set it as *Lor:* and proceeded to do likewise in outer C. Meanwhile, the other compositor, who met *Lo:* for the first time only after setting the entry direction for Lodwike on B4^v, rightly preserved the copy form both there and in inner C. By quire D, both were using the form *Lo,* though they punctuated it differently. Here, the variation in forms of a speech prefix offers a scrap of evidence both for compositor identification and for setting by formes, at least in B and C, while also strongly implying copy forms of *Lor:* or *Lor.* for Lorraine and *Lo:* or *Lo.* for Lodwike.

Other anomalous speech prefixes in *Edward III* are less illuminating. On D2ᵛ the final line of a speech by Audley to Derby is given the speech prefix *King:*, while on I1 the speech prefix *Vil.* (for Villiers, who is not on stage) is found before a speech clearly belonging to Charles, Duke of Normandy, the Dauphin (speech prefix *Ch:* or *Ch.*). Either could just conceivably be a misreading—of 'Ed' or 'Ch'—induced by ignorance of context as a result of setting by formes, but other explanations seem equally possible. *Vil.* for *Ch.* may result from an associative lapse by either compositor or scribe: Villiers has just been named in the dialogue, which concerns his obtaining a passport for the Earl of Salisbury. The intrusive *King* speech prefix, though, is harder to explain, as it occurs against the final line of a speech. However, it comes near the head of an outer forme verso page, so that the compositor setting it, not having set consecutively from the start of the scene, had no way of knowing that the king was not yet on stage and may have been the readier to misinterpret whatever he saw in the left margin of his copy as a speech prefix for him.

Before leaving *Edward III,* I might add that it lacks a total of thirteen necessary speech prefixes. Eight are simply accounted for as they affect speeches immediately following entry directions for their speakers: they occur on B1ᵛ, F1,1ᵛ, G1,4 and I2, where there are no fewer than three. It seems likely that they figured also in the copy manuscript. Cast-off copy, and possibly a change of compositor, must be involved in III. i. Despite the catchword "*K. Io.* Now" on E3, the first line on E3ᵛ lacks the speech prefix for King John of France. Perhaps the speech prefix in the copy manuscript was written so high as to be separated from the line by the marking of cast-off. Earlier, on C4-4ᵛ, the speech prefix is missing both from the catchword and the dialogue, suggesting its likely absence from the copy manuscript. The other omissions are on B3, D4ᵛ, and F4ᵛ, which my provisional analysis would assign to the same compositor, raising the likelihood that his carelessness is their cause.

Anomalous speech prefixes in *The London Prodigal* (1605: printed by Thomas Creede for Nathaniel Butter) offer a somewhat different point of interest, though, once more, the ignorance of context imposed on a compositor setting from cast-off copy may be seen as a factor contributing to error. The play contains two pairs of characters with names that are easily confused, especially in the truncated form of speech prefixes. They are: Sir Lancelot Spurcock and his daughter Luce; and Sir Arthur Greenshield and Artichoke, Spurcock's servant. The respective speech prefixes for these characters are: *Lance.*, *Lanc.*, *Lan.* / *Luce.*, *Luc.* (including the error of *Luce.* for *Lance.* on D2ᵛ); and *Arthur.*, *Arth.*, *Art.*, *Ar.* / *Arti.*, *Arty.*, *Art.*, *Ar.* (in addition to the total ambiguity of the two shortest forms, the error *Arty.* for *Arth.* is found on E4ᵛ). In each case of error a normal ambiguity of Elizabethan secretary hand is involved: *n* and *u* are indistinguishable without the guide of context and the forms *h* and *y,* each with a prominent loop below the line, are also easily confused. An incidental inference suggested by the *h* / *y* error is that the speech prefixes in the copy manuscript had at least some mixture of secretary forms and may have been in a secretary hand throughout.

Variations in the form of speech prefixes may sometimes provide sharp and clear evidence for compositor identification. *A Yorkshire Tragedy* (1608: printed by Richard Bradock for Thomas Pavier) provides an instance of unusual clarity. A single compositor set quires A-C. The presence of a second compositor in quire D, where he set the three pages of the outer forme (D1, 2ᵛ, 3), is revealed at a glance because, unlike his colleague, he used no indentation before speech prefixes and the opening lines of speeches.

A less clear situation obtains in *The Puritan* (1607: printed by George Eld). The protagonist, George Pieboard, has six forms of abbreviated speech prefix: *Pye.*, *Py.*, *Pie.*, *Pyb.*, *Pib.*, and (once) *Peb.* The forms *Py[e].*, *Pie.*, and *Pyb.* (*Pib.*) cluster in such a way as to suggest that each is the preferred form of a different compositor. Another variant speech prefix is *Moll.* / *Mol.*, the former showing some association with *Pyb.*, the latter with *Pie.* A third, for Captain Idle, varies between *Capt.* and *Cap.*: here the former goes with both *Pyb.* and *Pye.*, while *Cap.* is almost invariable on *Pie.* pages. Though these three speech

127

prefixes alone leave many pages without evidence and though their own patterns are not always clear-cut and unambiguous, they do seem to offer adequate evidence for presuming that three compositors shared the setting of *The Puritan.*

Among the simplest and most frequent ways in which speech prefixes can induce textual corruption is by appearing in the copy manuscript out of alignment with the speeches to which they belong. This seems to offer the clue to a puzzling passage of dialogue in *The Two Noble Kinsmen.* Unfortunately I saw the significance of the quarto's layout both here and in the other passage I shall discuss only after publication of my edition of the play in the Regents Renaissance Drama Series in 1970, so that it does not contain the emendations I would now adopt (although I am glad to see that the second of them has been adopted by the editors of the new Oxford *Complete Works* (Oxford, 1986)). As layout is crucial, I reproduce both passages in facsimile from the 1634 quarto.

Figure 1.

Pal, She met him in an Arbour :
What did fhe there Cuz?play o'th virginals ?
Arc. Something fhe did Sir.
Pal. Made her groane a moneth for't;or 2, or 3.or 10.

Figure 1 shows a section of III. iii as it appears on G2. It is hard to read the marked lines (III. iii. 33–36: TLN 1504–47), as consistent with what is going on in the scene, namely the teasing of Arcite by Palamon about an alleged love affair with the steward's daughter. The difficulty is that Arcite's role of prompting and provoking Palamon's speeches becomes blurred at lines 1505–6. Editors, however, have let the passage stand, never questioning the assignment to Palamon of the questions

in line 1505 and to Arcite of the first phrase of the answer. In
fairness, it must be conceded that the dialogue can be played
as it stands, but reassignment of these two lines serves to clarify the tone and the tendency of the dialogue. What I believe to
have happened—very easily in such a passage of rapid exchange of part-lines—is that the speech prefixes at 1506 and
1507 were printed a line too low, perhaps through sheer carelessness, perhaps because of misalignment in the copy manuscript. I propose that the passage should read as follows:

> *Pal.* She met him in an Arbour.
> *Arc.* What did she there Cuz? play o'th virginals?
> *Pal.* Something she did Sir, made her groane a moneth for't;
> Or 2. or 3. or 10.

Figure 2

2.*Fr.* Not well? ———*Wooer,* No Sir not well.
Woo. Tis too true, fhe is mad.

The second passage I wish to consider is the repetition of a
speech prefix for consecutive speeches on 12 (Figure 2: IV. i.
45–6: TLN 2169–70). Again, the editorial tradition has been
conservative. The orthodox cure, involving the minimum intervention, has been to suppress the speech prefix *Woo.* But further thought may lead to a questioning of the function of the
dash in line 2169. Nothing like it is found elsewhere in the
quarto. It becomes comprehensible if we visualize the copy
manuscript. A short speech was apparently omitted in error by
the transcriber—perhaps confused by the repetitive turn of the
dialogue—and was then added in the right margin, with a line
to indicate where in the text it belonged. The compositor, mis-

taking the intention of the line, simply set what he saw, representing it as a long dash. This led him to place the wooer's first speech a line too low, after, rather than before, the words of the Second Friend. The correct sequence, comprising two full verse lines, is:

> *Iay*. Well Sir.
> *1. Fr*. Not right?
> *Wooer*. No Sir not well.
> *2. Fr*. Not well?
> *Woo*. Tis too true, she is mad.
> *Fr*. It cannot be.

In fairness to the compositor, he seems not to have thought that he was setting the same speech prefix in consecutive lines. The fact that he used the full form *Wooer* in 2169 and followed it with a comma indicates that he read the phrase after the dash as part of the Second Friend's speech.

These disparate examples may serve as a reminder of the range of bibliographical interest to be found in speech prefixes. Apart from their general exemplary interest, though, they are drawn from play quartos several of which come from shops that also printed Shakespeare quartos. John Danter, Thomas Creede, Valentine Simmes, Richard Bradock, and George Eld are printers whose apocryphal quartos have their own right to a place in the canon of works of bibliographical relevance to the study of Shakespeare's text.

What's the Bastard's Name?

Random Cloud.

for Tom Berger

Her name was McGill,
She called herself Lil,
But everyone knew her as Lee. Ta.
She was Lo, plain Lo, in the morning, standing four feet ten
in one sock. She was Lola in slacks. She was Dolly at school. She
was Dolores on the dotted line. But in my arms she was a l w
a
y

Alexander Pope in the Preface to his 1723 edition of "The Works of MR *William Shakespeare*" seems to have intended praise:

> *every single character in Shakespear is as much an Individual, as those in Life itself; it is as impossible to find any two alike; . . . had all the Speeches been printed without the very names of the Persons, I believe one might have apply'd them with certainty to every speaker.*[1]

The editor's confidence that one could supply a whole corpus' worth of missing speech tags (!) must reflect his conception of the distinct in-dividuality (hence the distinct unity) of each of this playwright's dramatic characters. He *is* onto something, of course, for life-like characterizations (in the major roles, if not in "every single character") is one of Shakspere's most conspicuous achievements.

But Pope is also quite off track. However unified the interpretation of a Shakespearean role can be made to seem in performance or in modern editions, the very names of the Persons in the earliest Shakespear texts very frequently vary. (That you don't know *what* the hell I am talking about shows how poped your Shakespeare is.) In order to contradict the editor it is not even necessary that we deny his critical premise, of Shakesper's appeal to Life itself; one merely has to read the evidence of the earliest quartos and folios. So, if you like: *when it comes to the very names of the Persons, every single character in* Shakespear *is as Dividual as those in Life itself.*

Pope's fantasy about speech tags is scarcely innocent. In openly praising Shakespeare's artistic coherence, he secretly congratulates his own reductive editing; for Pope played fast and loose with the evidence of Shakspear's text, suppressing the *artistic* variation of names that contradicts the *editorial* notion of unity.

With how much certainty would Pope's imagined restorer cope with this passage from the 1599 quarto of *Romeo and Iuliet* (shown on top of the next page), if its speech tags were actually removed?[2] Essentially the same four lines are assigned not only to a young man passionately in love for the first time, but also to an old and mortified friar. That Shakespeare assigned

Ro. Would I were fleepe and peace fo fweet to reft
The grey eyde morne fmiles on the frowning night,
Checkring the Eafterne Clouds with ftreaks of light,
And darkneffe fleckted like a drunkard reeles,
From forth daies pathway,made by *Tytans* wheeles.
Hence will I to my ghoftly Friers clofe cell,
His helpe to craue,and my deare hap to tell.

           Exit.
  Enter Frier alone with a basket. (night,
 Fri. The grey-eyed morne fmiles on the frowning
Checking the Eafterne clowdes with ftreaks of light:
And fleckeld darkneffe like a drunkard reeles,
From forth daies path,and *Titans* burning wheeles:
Now erethe fun aduance his burning eie,

this speech to such very different roles suggests that its duplica-
ted words have little to express of the Personal experiences of either of them. Isn't it better to say that precisely *because* they are
repeated, these four lines have an *im*Personal expression; that
the speech primarily tells time (a function discharged elsewhere
in this play by an *im*personal Chorus); or that it creates an
ambiance verbally, whereas the modern stage may do it with
lighting; or that it serves to close or open a scene in a *play*: that
it is thus *dramatically* or *scenically* functional, and not unmedi-
atedly *mimetic* or redolent of the *Personal* character of Life itself?

Or consider the passage in the 1623 folio *All's Well* shown
on the top of the next page.[3] Although there are two speech tags
here, there is only one speech and only one speaker, to whom,
as we read along, Shakspeare gives a new name in the very
midst of his speech. Now, once an actress intones the words of
Shakespeare's dialogue, they become her own, as it were, in
the service of the role she performs. The residual variant
speech tags, however, remain behind in Shakespere's "voice";
for surely they are all his vocatives. To whom else can we
ascribe his naming? Certainly to no one *in* the fiction.

Cou. You haue difcharg'd this honeftlie, keepe it to your felfe, manie likelihoods inform'd mee of this before, which hung fo tottring in the ballance, that I could neither beleeue nor mifdoubt : praie you leaue mee, ftall this in your bofome, and I thanke you for your honeft care : I will fpeake with you further anon.   *Exit Steward.*

Enter Hellen.

Old.Cou. Euen fo it vvas vvith me when I was yong:
If euer vve are natures, thefe are ours,this thorne
Doth to our Rofe of youth righlie belong
Our bloud to vs, this to our blood is borne,
It is the fhow, and feale of natures truth,
Where loues ftrong paffion is impreft in youth,
By our remembrances of daies forgon,
Such were our faults, or then we thought them none,
Her eie is ficke on't, I obferue her now.

Surely they are all Shakspere's vocatives.

What caused Shakespear to rename the role during the speech, I don't know either. But playing with names, as Samuel Johnson so sympathetically observed, was Shakespeare's "fertile Cleopatra." In fact, during the course of the play the author used five different speech tags for this one role:

Mother, Countess, Old Countess, Lady and *Old Lady.*

One of the simplest explanations for the repeated and augmented speech-tag is that it marks a seam in the layering of composition. The second part of the speech could easily have been scripted first, or, if it came second, it may have been written at some remove from the first part. The ideal unity we *read into* such a text runs up against a fragmentation or a multiplicity that we actually *read.* It is a problem of interpretation whether such supposed traces of construction are to be swept under the rug in production, as if they were mere noise, or whether they are to be attended to as messages—as discontinuities in tone, or in action, or in what interests me most here, in dividual characterization.

Understandably, an actress of this role is liable to be focused (in a way Pope would understand intuitively) on her own *character*; she may most readily come to conceive an individual identity (especially before rehearsals) from the inside out, as it were—from reading all the dialogue assigned to her, as if she is centered in what she says. So, let's imagine for contrast how a director might view the overall flow of *action* during this speech, and from that outward perspective counsel the actress. The director may feel that the Steward's exit and Hellen's entrance mark a pause or turning of the action which will orient the audience to new themes and new relationships, in the course of which the audience's perception of this role will be reassessed. (As she is about to initiate talk about the new themes of youth and age, it should be easy for actress and director to talk each other's language, though they come from different directions.)

Suppose, for the ease of argument, that the director wants the audience to see the young woman's entrance slightly before the Countess does. From our point of view, Helen's entrance onto a silent stage occupied only by the Countess would, without a word's yet being spoken, offer us an emblem of *Youth vs Age*; we would perceive the Countess now not solely from her own perspective (built up from the dialogue she has spoken, or from that she is about to speak), but rather relatively, ironically, and from the outside. In this silent moment she would be re-perceived by the audience as an *Old* countess—not because she *is* old (though she is), but because with Hellen beside her she suddenly *looks* old.

Now, this moment of silence is nevertheless textual (though you won't find it in modern editions). Its text is that of the new speech tag, which states, *in the author's voice,* that the speaker of the dialogue to follow is *Old*. When the silence ends, the first line of her resumed speech discovers, as I said, that age is a theme there too: "it vvas . . . when I was yong". But age and youth are, crucially, not the only themes. The rest of the Old Countess's first line, "Euen so . . . vvith me", can be read as affirming that the two women are alike in their capacity for love, and this theme is not directly about age. The redundancy of the new tag and the dialogue it ushers in is thus *selective* redundancy; and selective redundancy between such internal textual categories as tag and dialogue externalizes itself as *interpretation*. (And whose interpretation, do you suppose?)

Later in the play Shakespeare switches to *Old Lady* as the tag for this role, again during conversation with Hellen. (She is "*Old*", by the way, *only* when Hellen is present.) If, in the speech we have been analyzing, Shakespeare had switched to the *Old Lady* tag after Hellen's entrance (instead of *Old Countess*), might we not have felt that the thematic redundancy of tag and dialogue was now less about age than about *Being Female*? Do you see why I say that selective redundancy is interpretive? Or imagine this: elsewhere Shakespeare tags Hellen as "*La*." Suppose Shakspeare called them both "Ladies" in the speech we have been considering. In addition to the *Female* theme, might we not detect that of *Gentility*?

Here are the lines that immediately follow the passage already photoquoted.

> *Hell.* What is your pleafure Madam ?
> *Ol.Cou.* You know *Hellen* I am a mother to you.
> *Hell.* Mine honorable Miftris.
> *Ol.Cou.* Nay a mother, why not a mother? when I
>   fed a mother
> Me thought you faw a ferpent, what's in mother;
> That you ftart at it ? I fay I am your mother,

At the start of the play Shakespeare's speech-tag name for the Countess was *Mother*. Suppose Shakespeare had reverted to this tag at the entrance of Hellen. Would not such a redundancy direct our attention to the *Maternal-Filial* dynamic of the encounter, which is strongly borne out in these later lines, rather than to the theme of *Age vs Youth*?

Of course, an actress can convey her age and be simultaneously womanly and motherly and ladylike. My fancied substitions from among Shakespeer's other variant speech tags are intended to show merely that each of his options for naming this character could be redundant of *some*thing in the dialogue, but not of everything; Shakespeare's specific choices of tag do interpret dialogue through selective emphasis. It is helpful to remember that no one speaks in Shakespeare's plays without being summoned by a name for each speech. Each time he summoned a character, Shakespeare was free to rename her, and he was just the author to exploit that freedom. He is thus, thank God, unpredictable. Pope's nomenclature for Shakespeare's characters is highly predictable; Shakespeare's is not. So I'll put it to you. When you read Shakespeare do you want to read Shakespeare? or do you want to read Pope?

March 5, 1834

COLER: *Shakespeare's intellectual action is wholly unlike that of Ben Jonson or Beaumont and Fletcher. The latter see the totality of a sentence or passage, and then project it entire. Shakespeare goes on creating, and evolving B out of A, and C out of B, and so on, just as a serpent moves, which makes a fulcrum of its own body, and seems for ever twisting and untwisting its own strength.*

My remarks suggest that the identity of dramatic character need not be an internal affair; it can be externally relational and interactive—an interaction no less between one role and another on stage, than between a role and its scriptor. Such an approach also suggests the inherently social nature of drama and theatre, and argues for a competing primacy to the one that Pope celebrated—of action and confrontation, as in the struggle between hero and antagonist. Not only is it not philosophically necessary to ascribe a primary or a transcendent unity to the notion of individual, isolated Character that so obsesses modern history, but also the text and Shakespeare's nomenclutter resists such appropriation.

No one can say how Ed Pope would have assigned the tags for this speech in *All's Well* if, as he fantasized, they were stripped away from the original evidence. However, his actual edition cuts out the Countess's *"Old"*—and voilà, by *reductio editionis*, a Shakespearean Individual.

Count. You have difcharg'd this honeftly, keep it to your felf; many likelihoods inform'd me of this before, which hung fo tottering in the ballance, that I could neither believe nor mifdoubt : pray you leave me, ftall this in your bofom, and I thank you for your honeft care ; I will fpeak with you further anon.
6   [*Exit Steward.*

SCENE

All's well that Ends well.   381

S C E N E VII.

Enter Helena.

Count. Ev'n fo it was with me when I was young ;
    If we are nature's, thefe are ours : this thorn
Doth to our rofe of youth rightly belong,
    Our blood to us, this to our blood is born ;
It is the fhow and feal of nature's truth,
Where love's ftrong paffion is impreft in youth ;
By our remembrances of days foregone,
Such were our faults, or then we thought them none.
Her eye is fick on't, I obferve her now.

Curiously, Pope repeats the tag *"Count.*", but this is not because he is conserving this rare example of Shakespeare's multiple naming. Rather Pope himself had a neo-classy notion of scene divisions. For him an entrance or exit during a speech could initiate a new editorial scene, and the first speech of such a new scene required an editorial speech tag—even if there is no interruption of the flow of speech. Thus, Pope would have had a tag here even if Shakespear hadn't! Although Pope idealized the unity of character, we can surmise that this now-unpopular editorial practice tended to atomize Shakespearian action, a sin comparable to the editorial division of the action into acts, which is still much in vogue, though there is no basis for it in many of Shakesper's early publications. In any case, we certainly may edit the quotation with which this paper opened:

> Pop: *Had all the speeches been printed with Shakespear's very names of the Persons, I believe an Editor may apply his own names with certainty to every speaker.*

*

Pope was only the second "editor" of Shakespeare, as we have come to use that term. The first was Rowe, whose edition appeared in 1709, almost two decades before that of Pope, who closely followed Rowe's lead in renaming characters. Prior to them, and the age of Shakespeare Editing which they initiated, stretched a century and more, back to the quarto editions of Shakespeare's individual works, which began appearing before his death, and to the collected editions in folio, which came out after. During that century, these quartos and folios were frequently reprinted, one printing often serving uncritically as copy for the next, the compositors modernizing graphic features and punctuation, for example, as they went. Compositors would attempt to correct what seemed to be obvious mistakes, but, human nature being what it is, would also create new errors. And so this pre-Editorial era of transmission evidences a gradual corruption and naive sophistication of Shakespeare's texts. Perhaps the simplest way to characterize this period is to say that Shakespeare's text was drifting.

Such a process can be tolerated at first by wary and ingenious readers, but it must inevitably have a break-point, when the textual errors become so grossly compounded that average readers can no longer understand the text, or when the text deviates so considerably from whatever early versions may have survived, that collation of them produces a list of variants longer than the original work. But such cumulative drift of the reprinted texts in the 17th century can scarcely account in itself for the birth of Editing. True, the fourth folio at the end of this period has its sorry moments textually, but Renaissance readers did not expect the kind of accuracy in printed books that we do. 17th-century readers must have been astute at detecting error and double-guessing authorial intent behind the frequent, palpable errors. In any event, Shakespeare at this time was merely a good read. Luckily, he had died before he had become the Bard, whose every word was sacred. (He had to wait for Editing to be so canonized.) I suggest, therefore, that the impetus for Editing lay outside the internal problems posed by the drifting texts, just as I suggest that the impetus for continued Editing in the 20th century lies outside the internal problems of the text. The urge to edit stemmed from the profound transformation of English culture in the 18th century, which was typified by its fascination with Taste, Propriety, and Criticism as preceptors to art. The age had its positive sides, no doubt, but its stuffiness can be measured by the passionate reaction to it (to look ahead) in Romanticism, just as much as in the freedom and wildness (to look back) of the Elizabethan texts that it sought to discipline, tidy and regulate.

A corollary of the editorial reform of speech tags is the creation of editorial dramatis-personae lists. No Shakespeare text published before his death has such a list, and only a handful exist in the folio tradition after his death. Why editors should inflict dramatis-personae lists on plays, and not novellae-personae lists on novels or sonnetae-personae lists on sonnet sequences, is not clear to me. For the most part, editors act, they do not explain. It is not that such lists are not helpful to a reader who is open to such intro-textual Aids; but that they take the conservative form they do in edition after edition, when there are a thousand different ways to help a reader, is strange. The crucial thing to observe is that the dramatis-personae list has insinuated itself between the title page and the opening of Act 1, Scene 1. These editorial lists have now become as sacrosanct as the very body of Shakespeare's play-tex

*

t.It was decades ago that the battle was joined to check the critical tendency to count Lady MacBeth's children—or to project "the Girlhood of Shakespeare's Heroines", to use Mary Cowden Clarke's telling phrase. But can such a battle ever be won as long as dramatis-personae lists continue to infiltrate Shakespare's text? These lists imply that characters are solid entities,

THE COUNTESS

that pre-exist their functions in the play, rather than illusions

now *Mother* now *Old Countess* now *Lady* . . .

built up out of the simultitudinous dynamic of *all* the ingredients of dramatic art, of which character is only a part.

Edition after edition suggest that editors do not read Shakespeare's text afresh to compile such lists. No, they read and crib them from other editors, in a tradition that stems from Pope's appropriation of Rowe (see the next opening).

Both their editions were published by the astute Tonson, who claimed his copyright, I understand, not in *Shakespeare's* but in his *editors'* words. (Do you $mell a fault?) But ever since Tonson's rights ran out, it seems always to be the same originally-arbitrary, now-traditional list—the same Peckering Order, men above women, gentle above common—and only so much info, and of such and such a slant. Lear is *King,* but not a Father, or a Fool. Albany is *Husband to Goneril*; but she is *Lear's Daughter,* not Albany's Wife—or Edmund's Lover, or her Sisters' Rival, or a Suicide. Duke Frederick is *the Usurper of Duke Senior's dominions*; the latter *lives in banishment.* MacBeth, however, is merely *a General in the King's army.* It doesn't say where *he* lives; nor does it say he is a King-Killer. Bertram is *Count of Rossillion,* not an Egotistical Snob; yet

Parolles is his *Parasitical Follower*. Julius Caesar is, comfortingly, plain Julius Caesar. But Marc Antony is one of the *Triumvirs*—a position he achieved after Caesar's death, even though at this early point in the unfolding of the action of the plaI mean in the unfolding of the dramatis-personae list—Caesar is evidently not dead yet. At least not very dead.

Dramatis Perfonæ.

KING *of* France.
Duke of Florence.
Bertram, *Count of* Roffilion,
Lafeu, *an old Lord.*
Parolles, *a Parafitical Follower of* Bertram, *a Coward, but Vain, and a great* Pretender *to Valour.*
Several Young French *Lords, that ferve with* Bertram *in the* Florentine *War.*
Steward, } *Servants to the Countefs of* Roffilion.
Clown,

Countefs of Roffilion, *Mother to* Bertram.
Helena, *Daughter to* Gerrad de Narbon, *a famous* Phyfician, *fome time fince dead.*
An old Widow of Florence.
Diana, *Daughter to the Widow.*
Violenta, } *Neighbours and Friends to the Widow.*
Mariana,

Lords attending on the King. *Officers, Soldiers,* &c.

The SCENE *lyes partly in* France, *and partly in* Tufcany.

(Rowe, 1709)

Obviously the dramatis-personae lists' perspectives on Shakespeare's characters are as crock-eyed as those in a cubist painting. Of such stuff is Editorial Unity made. . . .

Dramatis Perſonæ.

KING of France:
Duke of Florence.
Bertram, *Count of* Rouſillon.
Lafeu, *an old Lord.*
Parolles, *a paraſitical follower of* Bertram, *a coward, but vain, and a great pretender to valour.*
Several young French *Lords, that ſerve with* Bertram *in the* Florentine *war.*
Steward,⎫
Clown,　⎭ *Servants to the Counteſs of* Rouſillon.

Counteſs of Rouſillon, *mother to* Bertram.
Helena, *daughter to* Gerard de Narbon, *a famous phyſician, ſome time ſince dead.*
An old widow of Florence.
Diana, *daughter to the widow.*
Violenta, ⎫
Mariana, ⎭ *Neighbours and friends to the widow.*

Lords attending on the King, Officers, Soldiers, &c.

SCENE, *lyes partly in* France, *and partly in* Tuſcany.

The plot taken from Boccace, *Decam.* 3. *Nov.* 9.

(Pope, 1723)

145

S C E N E III.

Enter Helena *and two Gentlemen.*

1 Gen. Save you, good madam.

Hel. Madam, my lord is gone, for ever gone.

2 Gen. Do not fay fo.

Count. Think upon patience: 'pray you, gentlemen,
I've felt fo many quirks of joy and grief,
That the firft face of neither on the ftart

Can

All's well that Ends well.   413

Can woman me unto't. Where is my fon?

2 Gen. Madam, he's gone to ferve the Duke of *Florence.*
We met him thitherward, from thence we came;
And after fome difpatch in hand at court,
Thither we bend again.

Hel. Look on this letter, madam, here's my pafsport.

*When thou canft get the ring upon my finger, which never
fhall come off, and fhew me a child begotten of thy body that I
am father to, then call me husband: but in fuch a* Then *I write
a* Never.

This is a dreadful fentence.

Count. Brought you this letter, gentlemen?

1 Gen. Ay, madam, and, for the contents fake, are forry
for our pains.

Count. I pr'ythee, lady, have a better cheer.
If thou engroffeft all the griefs as thine,
Thou robb'ft me of a moiety: he was my fon,
But I do wafh his name out of my blood,
And thou art all my child. Towards *Florence* is he?

2 Gen. Ay, madam.

Count. And to be a foldier?

2 Gen. Such is his noble purpofe; and believe't

Enter ▓▓▓ *and two Gentlemen.*

▓▓▓ Saue you good Madam.

▓▓▓ Madam, my Lord is gone, for euer gone.

▓▓▓ Do not fay fo.

▓▓▓ Thinke vpon patience, pray you Gentlemen,
I haue felt fo many quirkes of ioy and greefe,
That the firft face of neither on the ftart
Can woman me vntoo't. Where is my fonne I pray you?

▓▓▓ Madam he's gone to ferue the Duke of Flo-
rence,
We met him thitherward, for thence we came:
And after fome difpatch in hand at Court,
Thither we bend againe.

▓▓▓ Looke on his Letter Madam, here's my Pafport.

When thou canft get the Ring vpon my finger, which neuer
fhall come off, and fhew mee a childe begotten of thy bodie,
that I am father too, then call me husband: but in fuch a (then)
I write a Neuer.
This is a dreadfull fentence.

▓▓▓ Brought you this Letter Gentlemen?

▓▓▓ I Madam, and for the Contents fake are forrie
for our paines.

▓▓▓ I prethee Ladie haue a better cheere,
If thou engroffeft, all the greefes are thine,
Thou robft me of a moity: He was my fonne,
But I do wafh his name out of my blood,
And thou art all my childe. Towards Florence is he?

▓▓▓ I Madam.

▓▓▓ And to be a fouldier.

▓▓▓ Such is his noble purpofe; and beleeu't

And <u>noooow</u> it's **your** turn at the exciting new Family Game, **WHAT'S THE BASTARD'S NAME?**®. Yes, it's time for <u>everyone</u> across America and, now thanks to satellite, all our friends in Europe and Asia to PL*And Canada*—to PLAY with these challenging concepts—And to <u>HAVE FUN</u>!!! We'll begin on page 146 with the celebrated POPE version, in which all the names are apply'd for you *with certainty*. This, Contestants, is the ANSWER. <u>Your job</u> is to identify the QUESTION! Not so easy as you might think! <u>Weeeellll</u>, we've given you a headstart, for on the facing page, 147, is the rough-hewn Shapeshift version with **OBLITERATURE**® of the very names of the Persons. Remember: you have only *five* names to chose from for the *one* role (which I can't name—because that would be cheating, wouldn't it?)—and HEEERE they are: *Mother, Countess, Old Countess, Lady* and *Old Lady.* But hold your applause until you hear what's next. Our dear *Madame fLexicon* is not the **only** test of your Editorial Wits. In today's **WHAT'S THE BAS-TARD'S NAME?**® there are other characters with tags you'd NEVER have *guessed*: there are EXTRA*POINTS for figuring out how many of Shakespeare's dozen are <u>Substantively</u> Conserved in Traditional Editing! Not so easy as you might think! Soooo, ready, Contestants? In the next sixty seconds make a *Reasoned Hypothesis* on the basis of what you have learned todaSorry, Time's Up. **Stopwritingnow,** the exam is **over**. Make sure your **names** appear in the upper right-hand corner of each examination booklet, that the **same form of your name** is used on each booklet to avoid CONFUSION *and otherwise they won't be marked,* and that booklets are inserted one inside another in numerical order. Then surrender surrender your scripts to the center aisle and remain seated **and silent** until I have collected and counted them all.

**NOW GRADE YOURSELF,
YOU STUPID BASTARDS**

*

Enter Hellen and two Gentlemen.

French E. Saue you good Madam.

Hel. Madam, my Lord is gone, for euer gone.

French G. Do not say so.

La. Thinke vpon patience, pray you Gentlemen,
I haue felt so many quirkes of ioy and greefe,
That the first face of neither on the start
Can woman me vntoo't. Where is my sonne I pray you?

Fren.G. Madam he's gone to serue the Duke of Flo-
rence,
We met him thitherward, for thence we came :
And after some dispatch in hand at Court,
Thither we bend againe.

Hel. Looke on his Letter Madam, here's my Pasport.

*When thou canst get the Ring vpon my finger, which neuer
shall come off, and shew mee a childe begotten of thy bodie,
that I am father too, then call me husband: but in such a (then)
I write a Neuer.*
This is a dreadfull sentence.

La. Brought you this Letter Gentlemen?

1.G. I Madam, and for the Contents sake are sorrie
for our paines.

Old La. I prethee Ladie haue a better cheere,
If thou engrossest, all the greefes are thine,
Thou robst me of a moity: He was my sonne,
But I do wash his name out of my blood,
And thou art all my childe. Towards Florence is he?

Fren.G. I Madam.

La. And to be a souldier.

Fren.G. Such is his noble purpose; and beleeu't

These iditorial D.P. lists are *soooo* straight. No thought of the artistic ambition a ploywright could have had toward them. Let me sketch some possibilities with reference to five modern scripts.

A painful question for Didi in *Waiting for Godot* is whether the child who comes at the end of both acts claiming to be dispatched by Godot is the *same* boy. The bearer of the message in the second act says that he has not been here before, but Didi initially thinks he has. His attempts to verify that supposition and his reluctant acceptance that this is a different boy bear crucially on his grasp of reality and consequently on ours. For our reality not only includes him as an abject, but also is filtered through his subjectivity.

Now, the dramatis personae records only *one* "Boy"; casting based on this list therefore provides the audience with a certainty that coincides with Didi's initial, but not with his subsequent, opinion. A gap opens—but is it between us and Didi? or between both of us and Godot? Is one actor (the practical-minded member of an audience might ask) doubling Boy roles as a cost-cutting measure?—or is there really only one Boy represented? *We* can plainly see there is only one and the same actor in both acts, but *Didi* ultimately can't be sure today's Boy is yesterday's as well, because he doesn't trust his eyes to tell him the truth. The Boy may have "doubled" himself by lying, of course. Alternatively, if there *is* only one Boy, is he as confused about his identity as Didi is, and simply can't remember where he was yesterday? Or is it Beckett (the pervert) who abandons mimesis, and, simply mixing his signals, cooks up something absurd? The rival authorities of the dramatis-personae list, dialogue, speech tags and stage directions do not constitute a problem to be resolved before producing the play: the play *is* this problem.[4]

*

Wilde's dramatis-personae list for *The Impotance of Being Earnest* begins with an entry for "JOHN WORTHING, J.P." When this character enters in the first scene, he is announced as "Mr. Ernest Worthing", and is addressed by Algernon Moncrieff, as "Ernest". The name "Jack", however, appears in both stage directions and speech tags. Eventually this *literary* discrepancy becomes a topic of discussion in the dialogue, and so becomes available to the *audience*: true, his *calling card* may read "Ernest," but the testimony of his *cigarette case* is plain "Jack". (Have you ever known a cigarette case to lie?) Exposed, the character divulges his secret—he is Ernest in *town,* Jack in the *country*. But life is not as simple as a play. Eventually Jack learns not only the truth about his parentage, but also what a terrible thing it is to discover that all his life he has been speaking nothing but the truth: he actually *is* both Ernest and John (though a Moncrieff not a Worthing). During all this turmoil, his speech prefix continues unruffled "Jack"—though "Jack" at the tape can scarcely *mean* what "Jack" off the blocks did. If Wilde had not written his own dramatis-personae list, might not a zealous editor be tempted to Pope one up?

JOHN WORTHING, J.P., disguised in town as Ernest

—or more perspicaciously

JOHN ERNEST MONCRIEFF, who mistakenly thinks of himself as John ("Jack") Worthing in the country, and Ernest Worthing in the city; unbeknownst brother to Algernon Moncrieff (as we shall see!)

Wilde's own list and its mixture of agreement with and contradiction of the dialogue and such non-spoken parts of the play as the title, the names in directions and speech tags, a calling card, and even an engraved cigarette case (perhaps *especially* an engraved cigarette case) is Wilde's strategic *dis*information. The dramatis-personae list does not aspire to an editorial transcendence. It is projected from a point or points shy of the protagonist's moment of truth.[5]

*

In Lorca's *Bodas de Sangre* (*Blood Wedding*) we are offered a dramatis-personae list which includes this entry:

LA MUERTE *(como mendiga)*

—DEATH *(as a Beggar Woman)*. (This is the only one in the more than a dozen entries in the *personajes* with a parenthetical addition (which in turn offers the only use of lower case there). As we read through the script, "MUERTE" is not named in the stage directions or speech tags. Eventually, in Act 3, Scene 1, however, *una anciana* (an old woman) is bid enter, and her speech tag is MENDIGA, who in a subsequent direction is equated with death, though that interpretation is never used to name the role.[6]

(Desaparece entre los troncos, y vuelve la escena a su luz oscura. Sale una anciana totalmente cubierta por tenues paños verdeoscuros. Lleva los pies descalzos. Apenas si se le verá el rostro entre los pliegues. Este personaje no figura en el reparto.)

MENDIGA.
Esa luna se va y ellos se acercan.
De aquí no pasan. El rumor del río

He disappears among the trunks, and the stage goes back to its dark lighting. An Old Woman comes out completely covered by thin green cloth. She is barefooted. Her face can barely be seen among the folds. This character does not appear in the cast.

BEGGAR WOMAN.
That moon's going away, just when they's near.
They won't get past here. The river's whisper

Curiously consonant with this oddity is Lorca's specification, *"Este personaje no figura en el reparto."* ("This character does not appear in the cast [list].") Whether this puzzling phrase means that Lorca did not want this character to be identified in the playbill (Anonymous Death will take audiences by surprise.), or whether, more simply, he is registering his recognition of an inconsistency of his own nomenclature (he disdains merely to correct it.), I don't know. Either possibility is mist for my grill. The former argues what the previous two examples have: a dramatist can use the (peripheral) *reparto* deliberately to confuse an audience; the latter argues that a dramatist, having recognized a variant in his naming, can not only tolerate it, but also inscribe his recognition of it into the (central) script—where an editor's hobgoblin instinct would be to revise to achieve consistency, and so to harmonize the literary and dramatic aspects of text. But Lorca created distinctly different experiences for reader and viewer, and both of them are paradoxical. The imposition of editorial consistency may not seem hard to arrive at, for the reader at least. One could bulldoze MUERTE through the speech tags, and drop the reference to her absence from the *reparto*. A touch of the cosmetic. But the result would be a literary blandscape. *Exit Mysterium. Exit Lorca.*[7]

The whole question can be referred nicely to the theatre. Lorca was very close to productions in Madrid in 1933 at the Teatro Beatriz and in Buenos Aires in 1934 at the Teatro Avenida. Characters are identified in the program for the former production once only, in the order of their appearance on stage, whereas for the latter, they are identified repeatedly in the order of appearance in each new scene. The Madrid program names the role "La Muerte (como Mendiga)"—allegorically first, and then representationally, as in the published *Personajes*; but in Buenos Aires, where it was much easier for a member of the audience to search out the identity of this figure in the program when she appeared on stage, she was named merely "La Mendiga", without allegorizing. Of course, members of an audience do not have to read the program in order to interpret a character, and, if reading it, need not swallow any allegory proffered there, or, finding none, resist allegorizing the character to their own taste; moreover, actors may have learned their parts in ignorance of the *reparto* (and much else of the script!) and so be slanting their interpretations variously. It would thus be ridiculous to legislate an interpretation from the program; I am merely illustrating the textual resources and their potential dynamic for a specific crux, for readers inside the theatre and outside. Certainly if we insisted that the Madrid audience would *have* to prioritize—Muerte *first,* Mendiga *second,* it would be hard to square such literary necessity with the eyewitness account by Carlos Morla Lynch of the opening of the play at Teatro Beatriz on March 8, who seems to reverse the order.[8]

> . . ."aparece, entre los troncos negros del bosque, 'la mendiga', que se detiene en medio de la escena con el manto inmensamente abierto como las grandes alas de un pájaro oscuro. La muerte . . ."

> . . ."appears, between the black trunks of the wood, 'the beggar woman', and stops in the middle of the stage with her immense cloak open like the giant wings of a dark bird. Death . . ."

*

Alain Resnais' *Hiroshima mon amour* opens with the mute, languorous embrace of male and female. It is fitting, then, in Marguerite Duras' script (to separate it from Resnais' film), that when eventually the lovers start their incantation (of his denial and her affirmation), they should be distinguished by merely generic tags.[9]

> LUI.—Tu n'as *rien* vu à Hiroshima. Rien. . . .
> ELLE.—J'ai *tout* vu. *Tout.*

From the dialogue and directions we eventually do learn particulars: that SHE is a Frenchwoman (from Nevers on the Loire) and HE a Japanese (from Hiroshima on the Ota). But these fictional revelations, diametrical expressions of the real historical globe, as the documentary images of wartime devastation compel us to remember, do not, as we might expect them to, convert the pronoun tags, which are in the sexual embrace of "ELLE" and "LUI" on the last page as on the first.

What's the Bastard's Name? Random Cloud.

Duras' Synopsis is explicit about naming. The name of "this anonymous woman" "will never be given in the film". The tag "ELLE" thus seems to be precipitated not only from our sexual first glimpse of the heroine, but also from this deliberate authorial namelessness. As with the heroine's name, so with those of the other characters.

But anonymity does not say it all. There *are* names, and they are crucial. They are not, however, for direct disclosure. Naming is mysteriously at issue, for example, in the following bizarre exchange in Part IV (pp. 72–3), in which to her latest lover the heroine reveals her wartime madness, the consequence of the killing of her first lover, a German soldier in the army occupying Nevers. (Curiously, both ELLE and LUI collude in fusing the German and Japanese men (though not their separate nationalities), who, both "being dead", are shrunk in her memory to an *unspecified*, German name.)

ELLE.— . . . Je t'appelle doucement.
LUI.—Mais je suis mort.
ELLE.—Je t'appelle quand même. Même mort. . . .
LUI.—Tu cries quoi?
Elle.—Ton nom allemand. Seulement ton nom. Je n'ai plus
qu'une seule memoire, celle de ton nom.

Surprising, therefore, is the reader's discovery in a direction midway through Part IV (when the camera discovers the heroine's bleeding hands) that Duras abruptly states her name (p. 71).

Caves de Nevers. Mains saignantes de Riva.

Half a dozen subsequent directions over as many pages repeat this strikingly unFrench name, and once, in Part V (pp 94–95, in an early Gallimard edition), "RIVA" even serves as a speech tag for a monologue substantially repeating a speech in Part I, which had been tagged "ELLE" (pp 26–27).

Succession des rues de Hiroshima et de Nevers.
Monologue intérieur de Riva.

155

RIVA.—Je te rencontre.
Je me souviens de toi.
Cette ville était faite à la taille de l'amour.
Tu étais fait à la taille de mon corps même.
Qui es-tu?
Tu me tues. . . .

"RIVA" and "Riva" continue, moreover, several dozen times in the appendices. In the latter half of the book it seems that, despite her denials, Duras did know this character's name, and divulged her secret (to the *reader,* if not to the *viewer*).

Is there allegory here? Well, in the film there *are* tenderly filmed shots of *Riva* on the *banks* of the Loire. Is that it? Is she a "genius of the shore"? Riva's German lover, who has no speaking part (and hence no speech tag), is also named in the appendices—"Fresson" (p. 116). Does the international allegory thicken? An Italian name for a Frenchwoman, but a French name for a German—and a German name for a Japanese? Is Fresson her *frisson*? And why should his name sound like German for "gobble"? Is he *gefressen*, "devoured" by his death on the *banks* of the Loire? Whatever it means, Fresson is named, as is Riva, only in the silent parts of Duras' text, never in the dialogue; again the *reader* may have an insight (however murky) not afforded the *viewer*.

In neither of two English translations I have consulted are found the prefatory cinematic credits in the two Gallimard editions I have to hand—where one learns that Emmanuelle Riva and Bernard Fresson acted in the film. Duras did indeed have a name for ELLE; and it was a reel-life not a literary name. It is, therefore, only the Poor English Readers who are obliged to have Special Insight into the Names Secreted from the Viewers. The viewers of the credits in the theatre (as well as the French readers) have access to the names "Riva" and "Fresson" from the very start, and as soon as they encounter them will know (in the case of viewers) and can easily learn by flipping a few pages (in the case of French readers) to dismiss them as irrelevant to any allegorical interpretation.

Now, Duras' Preface and a footnote in Part I (p. 17) record that her scripting was not entirely separate from production. It evolved through her almost daily conversations with Resnais and with Gérard Jarlot, the literary advisor, who commented on her recent work before she proceeded. Her schematic initial text was modified and enlarged during cutting of the film, and parts of it (for example the mushroom cloud from which the lovers' embrace at the start of the film was to have emerged) were either cut or not used by Resnais; such may be printed in the Gallimard editions, but are bracketed as "abandonned". (They are bracketed *or deleted* in my English editions.) Finally, Duras tells us that Resnais commissioned the appended "Notes on Nevers" *pre-posterously*: as if annotations not on a *future* film, but on a *finished* one. The script is thus partly fashioned by that which it fashioned; it is a composite text—of *before, during* and *after* production. The same can be said from the point of view of production: that it is *before, during* and *after* the script. Not only are the script and film temporally disjunct, but also they are not commensurate with each other. And neither the director nor writer thinks to pretend otherwise.

Surely, therefore, the "*Riva*" directions in Part IV and the one "Riva"-tagged speech in Part V must indicate a late stratum of the script. In fact, the Preface implies that these highly charged portions of the story dealing with Nevers, and in which the heroine is referred to by the actress's name, were all written after the original scenario (July 1958), but before shooting in France (December, 1958), which followed filming in Japan. Taken together, this information suggests, unanonymously, that this actress influenced Duras' still-evolving conception of her heroine: that, as the text seems *literally* to indicate, Riva did not merely act ELLE: she *became* her. (Thus, the editorial spirit that normalized the speech tag from Riva to ELLE in the later Gallimard edition—even should it prove authorial—strikes me as particularly unimaginative and unhistorical. Of course, that it does not normalize the *Riva* name in the *directions* also registers the editing as inconsistent.)

Nevertheless, and despite Duras' avowal of anonymity, her heroine *is* climactically named where it counts—*in the dia-*

logue—and named in a way that corresponds to the allegorical naming of her partner. Yes, he is named too. In the face, paradoxically, of a "universal oblivion" stipulated in the direction, their anonymity ends. Stunned, but seemingly visionary, Lui and Elle call each other by names already well known to us (and which are all but etched on our retinas in the closing minutes of the film by the lyrical crescendo of cuts back and forth between their native Japanese and French cities).

> . . . *Elle a réussi à le noyer dans l'oubli universel. Elle en est emerveillée.*

Elle.—Hi-ro-shi-ma.
Elle.—Hi-ro-shi-ma. C'est ton nom.

> *Ils se regardent sans se voir. Pour toujours.*

Lui.—C'est mon nom. Oui.
[On en est là seulement encore. Et on en restera là pour toujours.] Ton nom à toi est Nevers. Ne-vers-en-Fran-ce.

FIN

In these final speeches, where the romantic and political statements of the work coalesce, we may come to understand retrospectively that his name had been declared "all along", as it were—in the very first word of the title, *Hiroshima mon amour,* now revealed as vocative. As her lover he was never really anonymous to us—if only we had had the wits to see it. The work now stands revealed as a long ceremony of naming. (And as knowledge is everywhere assailed by forgetting, it promises an equally long ceremony of blind departure from this intense vision.)

She too was never anonymous, though, until she remembers and relives her suffering, she is merely too sane, too partial to recognize as her own, inescapable, tragic name, the name of the little place of her wartime awakening, ecstacy, humiliation and derangement. At the very start of Part IV (where, we are told in a direction, the "miracle" takes place of the "resurgence of Nevers" (p. 70) her lover asks whether "Nevers" means anything (other than the designation a French town). The question seems contrived by Duras to make us see through the negative reply.

LUI.—Ça ne veut rien dire, en français, Nevers autrement?
ELLE.—Rien. Non.

Her unknowing answer, that "Nevers" has no exceptional significance, anticipates but also postpones their ultimate recognition—and ours—that her war loss has been written so deeply into the heroine, that she cannot even begin to remember to forget it, without taking on the sign—and in this most word-conscious script that will mean the *name*—of her community of suffering. Preparing to take on that name, as a direction in Part V allegorizes, is ironically a "«mariage»" (p. 97). (This term is always used metaphorically in the text, as the guillemets which regularly accompany it show; but its two other related uses are straight—at the end of Part III (p. 63), where it styles the rapture of the young French and German lovers, and in the appended lyrical commentary on it (p. 115).) Here in Part V, in the ironic sense of the marriage, it is only as the forlorn bride of a banal "Histoire de quatre sous", as she now regards it, that this "petite fille de Nevers", this "Morte d'amour à Nevers" (p. 97) can grow to witness her—Hiroshima (p. 94),

Cette ville [qui] était faite à la taille de l'amour

—which, with a change of gender, metamorphosizes before us in the next line as her lover:

Tu étais fait à la taille de mon corps même.

Witnessing Hiroshima. The last words of the script clarify its opening *récitative*: there LUI denied, despite his lover's dutiful attendance at the hospital, and her *four* visits to the Peace Memorial Museum, her having seen the photographs, learned the History . . . that she had seen anything at all of Hiroshima. Her climactic realization of the *Japanese* name of her lover is Duras' symbol that the heroine may have ceased to be a tourist, even perhaps a voyeur, and may have witnessed at last—if not the inconceivable All of it, then as much as *anyone* from Nevers is ever able to witness without vaporizing—the incomprehensible inexpressible searing atomic meaning of Hiroshima. She becomes able to bear witness to it by taking the measure of her own suffering. Then, on the diminutive scale of the heart of HIM and HER, "Nevers" and "Hiroshima" may vastly balance translate and articulate each other pain fully in love.

*

Anthony Shaffer's *sleuth* offers this dramatis-personae list:[10]

> SLEUTH was first presented at the St. Martin's Theatre, London, on February 12th, 1970, after a pre-London tour of Oxford, Leeds, Brighton and Eastbourne, with the following cast:

ANDREW WYKE	Anthony Quayle
MILO TINDLE	Keith Baxter
INSPECTOR DOPPLER	Stanley Rushton
DET. SGT. TARRANT	Robin Mayfield
P. C. HIGGS	Liam McNulty

> The play was directed by Clifford Williams.

Andrew (Anthony Quayle) murders Milo (Keith Baxter) in the first part of the play, hence the Inspector Doppler (Stanley Rushton), who comes to solve the murder. So, three roles—though in a pinch two actors (with make-up and props) would be enough to play them all. Yes?

In the following quotation (from a turning point in the action) two actors are on stage, the murderer and the policeman—but you will see that, curiously, there are *three* speech tags.

What's the Bastard's Name? Random Cloud.

ANDREW. Who the hell are you?

DOPPLER. Detective Inspector Doppler, sir, spelt as in
C. Doppler 1803-1853 whose principle it was that when
the source of any wave movement is approached, the
frequency appears greater than it would to an observer
moving away. It is also not unconnected with Doppler
meaning double in German - hence Doppleganger or
double image. And of course, for those whose minds
run to these things, it is virtually an anagram of the
word Plodder. Inspector Plodder becomes Inspector
Doppler, if you see what I mean, sir!

ANDREW. (a shriek) Milo!

MILO. (normal voice) The same.

(MILO peels off his disguise which apart from elaborate
face and hair make-up - wig, false nose, glasses,
cheek padding and moustache, also includes a great
deal of body padding, and elevator shoes, which have
had the effect of making him taller than ANDREW,
where in reality he is a fraction shorter)

ANDREW. You shit!

It is the *playwright* who is the shit, because he has fooled
us. There *is* no murderer, and no victim—*yet*, at least (for he'll
fool us again). Nor is there an Inspector Doppler, and hence no
Stanley Rushton, you Stupid Bastard. Moreover, the lie,
"Doppler", is truer than we thought—as a description of the
"Double" rather than as a proper name. Now, can you imagine
evaporating the very names of all the actors and then editorially reconstituting them

JUST ADD WATER AND STIR

and still coming up with Stanley Rushton?

*

Each of these dramatis-personae lists has a unique and
complex sem antic relationship with the rest of the text.
Suppose we know that four centuries ago authors such as
Beckett, Wilde, Lorca and Shaffer participated in the ancient

convention of dramatis-personae lists, but that these parts of their *oeuvres* had not survived into modern times. Do you think that an editorial reconstruction would stand one chance in a thousand of hitting on the authors' texts or the authors' intents? Suppose we knew that Shakespear had never written a dramatis-personae list. Do you think that an editor would stand *any* chance of applying the names with certainty to the list that Shakespeare would have written?—or that he would understand what Shakespeare would have meant? Do you respect the argument that since *we* live in an ironic age, our playwrights feel free to be play full, creative, mysterious with the literary parts of their playtexts and to pit them against the theatrical—but that Shakespeare lived in the plodding Classic Age and would not, therefore, have taken liberties? That Shakespeare was straight?

For argreement's sake, let's take one of the few of his plays to have a "Names of all the Actors". The unique authority for *Measure for Measure* is the First Folio. Typically, the folio lists appear *after* their plays, where they can hardly set us up. The *Measure for Measure* list begins with

Vincentio : the Duke.

Suppose this list had never made it into the First Folio. No editor could possibly regenerate it, for the name "Vincentio" occurs nowhere else in the work—whether in dialogue, stage direction, speech tag or title. Nowhere.

If our sense of the names of dramatic characters were based on what we heard in the theatre, would we know the King in *Hamlet* as "Claudius"—for that name appears only in a single stage direction? Its existence is purely literary, therefore, not spoken. Theatrically speaking, it doesn't exist. But some editors multiply this single occurrence into a dominant fact—in the dramatis-personae list, in every stage direction and speech prefix in which the character figures. Thus "Claudius" rather than "King" or "Uncle" has become the name of choice when literates discuss this character.

What's the Bastard's Name? Random Cloud.

A similar situation exists in *Waiting for Godot*. The literary names for the protagonists are Vladimir and Estragon, and so they are generally referred to in academic criticism. But in the theatre one knows them primarily as Didi and Gogo, though they also answer to names like Abel and Mr. Albert. Which names we call them by profoundly registers our oral or anal mean *written* biasses.

*

Now, unlike Shakespeare, Beniamin Ionson regularly used "Persons of the Play" lists, and he placed them before his opening scenes, where they can cast long shadows over subsequent reading.

The Persons of the Play

MOROSE, *a gentleman that loves no noise.*
SIR DAUPHINE EUGENIE, *his nephew.*
CLERIMONT, *a gentleman, his friend.*
TRUEWIT, *another friend.*
EPICOENE, *supposed the Silent Woman.*
SIR JOHN DAW, *a Knight.*
SIR AMOROUS LA FOOLE, *a Knight.*
THOMAS OTTER, *a land- and sea-captain.*
CUTBEARD, *a barber*
MUTE, *one of* MOROSE'S *servants.*
PARSON.

LADY HAUGHTY
LADY CENTAUR } *Ladies Collegiates.*
MISTRESS MAVIS
MISTRESS OTTER, *the Captain's wife*
MISTRESS TRUSTY, *the* LADY HAUGHTY'S *woman* } *Pretenders.*[1]

PAGES, SERVANTS, &c.

THE SCENE: *London*

This photoquote clearly showing the title character (fifth in the list) is from the Norton Critical Editiobert M. Adams is one of the editors of the distinguished *Norton Anthology of English Literature.*[11] A professor emeritus of English at the University of California at Los Angeles, he received his PhD. from Columbia University and has taught at ColumbiaWis consinRutgersandCornell. He has held two Guggenheim Fellowships and a Hudson Review Fellowship in Literary Cri-

163

(528)

The Persons of the Play.

MOROSE. *A Gent. that loues no noise,*

DAVP. EVGENIE. *A Knight his nephew.*

CLERIMONT. *A Gent. his friend.*

TRVE-WIT. *Another friend.*

EPICOENE. *A yong Gent. suppos'd the silent Woman.*

IOH. DAW. *A Knight, her seruant.*

AMOROVS LA FOOLE. *A Knight also.*

THOM: OTTER. *A land, and sea-Captaine.*

CVTBERD. *A Barber.*

MVTE. *One of* MOROSE *his seruants.*

MAD. HAVGHTY.

MAD. CENTAVRE. } *Ladies Collegiates.*

M^{r}. MAVIS.

M^{rs}. TRVSTY. | *The La.* HAVGHTIES *woman.*

M^{rs}. OTTER. | *The Captaines wife.* { *Pretenders.*

PARSON.

PAGES.

SERVANTS.

DRAMATIS PERSONÆ.

MOROSE, a Gentleman that loves no noise.
Sir DAUPHINE EUGENIE, a Knight, his nephew.
NED CLERIMONT, a Gentleman, his friend.
TRUEWIT, another friend.
Sir JOHN DAW, a Knight.
Sir AMOROUS LA-FOOLE, a Knight also.
THOMAS OTTER, a land and sea Captain.
CUTBEARD, a Barber.
MUTE, one of Morose's servants.
Parson.
Page to Clerimont.
EPICŒNE, supposed the SILENT WOMAN.
Lady HAUGHTY, ⎫
Lady CENTAURE, ⎬ Ladies Collegiates.
Mistress DOL MAVIS, ⎭
Mistress OTTER, the Captain's Wife, ⎫ Pre-
Mistress TRUSTY, Lady Haughty's woman, ⎭ tenders.

Pages, Servants, &c.

The SCENE—*London.*

ticism. He is one of the editors of the distinguished *Norton Anthology of English Literature.* His volume presents a new and fresh selection of Jonson's dramatic works, including the three greatest and most accessible comedies, among which is *Epicoene,* OK?

As Adams reveals, his critical edition is *not* based on the 1616 folio of Ionson and his printers (the Approach Direct), no, but on the text established, yes the *Established Text* by William Gifford in 1816 (a *full* two centuries later, you seebut *collated* against the *standard* 20th-century edition of Herford and Simpsthough as the collation is *silent* SSSHHHHHHHH

165

we are not to look for collationalno notes. But Herford and Simpson they *did* look at the 1616 folio (when they weren't taking their readings from Dr Aurelia Henry's 1906 edition as L. A Beaurline[12] shows it was faster, you see, than doing all the collations yourself, generating the text freshly yourself. Thanks Henry. Thanks Les. For greater ease of access, all has been freshly modernized and fully annotated to make a proper conservative text for American students. No, madame, I do not think that there is any basis whatsoever to your allegation (which hardly befits a Woman) that editing is driven by base market forces.

So look back to the previous opening at the "Perfons" list in Ionson's 1616 folio (the *Un*established text) and in Gifford's first—well actually we don't have his 1816 edition here in Trona, but as his text is carried on in the Mermaid edition,[13] I'll just substitute it. No harm done. Look especially at the title name, "EPICOENE", and its place in the two sequences. No harm done.

But first, in *viewing* the play we are stunned in the last moment to discover, with the removal of her peruque, that Epicoene is really a man under her skirt! (I hope I didn't spoil the plot for you.) But in our *reading* of the play Ionson has contrived to blow this disguise from the outset. Ionson, as it were, projected his (Excuse my English)—he projected his "Persons" list from the *anagnorisis* (where ironic distance collapses). Not only did he range the name "Epicoene" among the MenComeFirst (Guilt by Association), but more definitively, Ionson also specified that the character <u>is</u> "A *yong Gent.*". (I guess I can't spoil your surprise if there wasn't one to begin with.) So what's my point? What Epicoene is "*suppos'd*" to be, therefore, <u>must</u> be (as we read to the end of the line) "*the . . . Woman*"—but <u>may</u> also be "*silent*". It's all a question of emphasis.

But Gifford, ô rare Ben Gifford, did something *very* clever (You'll love it) when, as if acting on etymology, he relocated his EPICOENE *between* the male roles above and the female roles below in his—well, now it's called DRAMATIS PERSONAE (no harm done)—where its very *placement* is epicene. Neat, eh? It's PLACEMENT is epicene. The males are on top and the women are Get it? Coordinately, he *deleted* the stipulation of male gender ("*A yong Gent.*"), so that the dramatis-personae list is now projected from the *disguise* rather than from the *recognorisis*. (I hope I'm not spoiling your lack of surprise.) The phrase which remains at the end of Gifford's truncated line, "supposed the SILENT WOMAN", now may seem to take its stress more on "silent" than, as it did in the 1616 folio, on "woman"—as if it now served to symbolize one's surprise on learning that Epicoene was *loud*, rather than that she is *he*. Because in Gifford you don't *know* her gender. See? Same words. Different meaning.

But now back to the new and fresh Norton Critical Edition, a proper text for American students (p. 163). It doesn't matter that Gifford's approach was devilishly witty. No. Modern editing must respect textual authority and evidence, and so have recourse to the 1616 folio. *Back* comes Ionson his original title for the list. *Back* comes his original sequence of names, even if they seem rather unIonsonian, even if they seem respectively neither as classically learned nor as funny as the old Gifford's. Good. However, where "EPICOENE was situated in Gifford's sequence (look back, please to page 165) there now appears a

Did you see it, class? Look again.

How to *read* this blank? Well, it is not just an *emptiness*. After all, anyone—**anyone** could just say it's empty. You don't need a PhD for *that*. No, there must be more than that. Isn't it, class—isn't it the empty*ing* of a specific editorial content?— Gifford's? Very good! It's *Gifford's* content. It is a—what shall we call it? It's a "fissure" in the surface of the Norton text that marks editorial struggle: where one editor sought (without complete success) to disestablish the work of his predeceasor. Ironically, where Gifford's placement of EPICOENE brilliantly out-Jonsoned Ionson, and charged his "Persons" text with equivocal gender, Adams' disestablishment of Gifford thrusts assunder its male and female parts, unequivocates its genders, denies the epicene. (And who would ever want such behaviour inscribed into his Work RECORD?)

One might suppose that Adams' editorial repositioning was undertaken in the name of the 1616 text. In the name of *Ionson*. But, here is where it gets real subtle: it is *Gifford* who lives on in this very line, not Ionson; for Adams has restored that editor's *shortened* version of Ionson his line:

EPICOENE, *supposed the Silent Woman.*

In other words, Adams' version of the title role is missing the author's UNEQUIVOCAL MALE INDICATOR—"*A yong Gent.*" (It may be deemed, however, by really close readers, that Adams' repositioning of this line back with the boys (its authorial position) sublimanaly marks Epicoene (despite her name) as male—as merely *supposed* a woman.)

And more: Adams' next line

SIR JOHN DAW, *a Knight.*

is also essentially Gifford's, not Ionson's. Gifford had deleted the folio's "*her seruant*"—as he was logically obliged to, when he relocated the previous line, which contained the referent of the "*her*" he deleted.

Now, let me ask you, What could Ionson have meant by "*her*" in the phrase "*her seruant*"? Whatever sense it makes must be in terms of the preceding line, right? Since Ionson himself defined Epicoene there as "*A yong Gent.*", "*her*" cannot refer grammatically to "*Gent.*" (a "*him*"), to the *name* "Epicoene" (an "*it*"), or, obviously, and by definition, to the *concept* of the epicene (a "*him*"/"*her*"). It can refer only to the *suppos'd* . . . "*Woman*", which words cannot point to a female *fact* in the world of the play, but merely to a deceitful *projection* of a female identity. Serving this "*her*", therefore, Daw serves a man. *Her* is *him*. In other words, the epicene connotations of Ionson's feminine pronoun, "*her*", in his Persons list is, when you think it through, of an order of paradoxical wit not uncomparable to that of Gifford's relocations in his DRAMATIS PER-

SONÆ list—who had to cut Jonson's witty equivocation of gender from the text in order to make his own epicene joke—which Adams undid, seemingly without understanding the wit of either his authorial or editorial predecessors. This is further textimony that distinguished Norton Critical editing *freshly* approaches the question of text not by a radical derivation from authority, but merely (Good Luck!) by trying to fix what seems broken in the received text. Do you smell aught of the Assbackwords? The whole OPERATION is as arbitrary as Bush in Panama, making a proper text for fresh American students JUST BECAUSE

DRAMATIS PERSONÆ.

orose, *a gentleman that loves no noise.*
r Dauphine Eugenie, *a knight, his nephew.*
ed Clerimont, *a gentleman, his friend.*
ruewit, *another friend.*
ir John Daw, *a knight.*
ir Amorous La-Foole, *a knight also.*
Thomas Otter, *a land and sea captain.*
Cutbeard, *a barber.*
Mute, *one of Morose's servants.*
Parson.
Page *to Clerimont.*

Epicœne, *supposed the* SILENT WOMAN.
Lady Haughty, .
Lady Centaure, } *ladies collegiates.*
Mistress Dol. Mavis.
Mistress Otter, *the Captain's wife.* } *pretenders.*
Mistress Trusty, *lady Haughty's* } *pretenders.*
woman.

Pages, Servants, &c.

The SCENE London.

[handwritten annotations:]

George —— Finally got to NYC (after submitting copy to Jack at AMS) and Randy-vous'd with 1816 Gifford (no copy in Trona) — as opp'd to MERMAID I posed to built my argument on. GUESS WHAT?

The BLANK LINE certifies ← with GIFF! He was as flat-footed as Adams It was ∴ some MERMAID – MERMAN editor that ♂ and ♀!

So... don't set type for any of the London section. I'll have to cut most of it. There goes all my jokes!

Sorry, Randy, time's up. Too late. GW

*

On the other hand, what if it's not editors, but actors and directors who eliminate not only Ionson's *"A yong Gent."*, but also his *"suppos'd"* from the definition of the role of Epicoene

CAST IN ORDER OF APPEARANCE

Ned Clerimont, *a gentleman*	**Jared Harris**
A Boy	**Liza Hayden**
Truewit	**Richard McCabe**
Sir Dauphine Eugenie, *a knight, nephew to Morose*	**Peter Hamilton Dyer**
Sir Amorous La Foole, *a knight*	**Michael Mears**
Morose, *a gentleman who hates noise*	**David Bradley**
Mute, *Morose's servant*	**Graham Turner**
Cutbeard, *a barber*	**William Chubb**
Sir John Daw, *a knight, servant to Epicoene*	**John Ramm**
Epicoene, *the silent woman*	**Hannah John**
Master Otter, *a land and sea captain*	**David Shaw-Parker**
Mistress Otter, *his wife*	**Jennie Heslewood**
A Parson	**Paul Lacoux**
Madame Haughty) *Ladies*	**Amanda Bellamy**
Madame Centaur) *Collegiates*	**Rebecca Saire**
Mistress (Dol) Mavis)	**Sarah Crowden**
Mistress Trusty, *Madame Haughty's woman*	**Polly Kemp**

—who was played by Hannah John, according to the "programme/text" published by Methuen in 1989 for the production which opened in June at the Swan Theatre. Only if you go looking for this actress in the "Biographies" will you figure out what a dumb bastard you are.

What's the Bastard's Name? Random Cloud.

JOHN HANNAH *Epicoene*
Theatre: Gus in *Waiting for Shuggie's Ma* (Royal Court), Johnnie in *The Gorbals Story* (Glasgow Citizens) John in *The Philanthropist* (Mobil Tour), Caspian in *Voyage of the Dawn Treader*, Bandy Corner in *The Gambling Man*, Robert in *Rents* (Newcastle Playhouse), Phil in *Rents* (Palace Theatre Westcliffe), Pie McKay/Susie Creamcheese in *The Innocent* (Traverse Theatre), Jerry in *The Zoo Story* (Tron Theatre), Malcolm in *Macbeth* (Royal Exchange), Joe in *The Daughter-in-Law* (Bristol Old Vic).
RSC: This season: Epicoene in *The Silent Woman or Epicoene*.
Television: Pretty Boy in *Reasonable Force,* Johnny in *Bookie, Brief Encounter,* Robert in *Brond,* Keith in *These Colours Don't Run.*
Film: Tommy in *Losers Blues.*

*

OLD ▆▆▆▆▆▆. So, what *is* the Bastard's name? "Edmund", right? No problem.

▆▆▆▆▆▆ Answer me this first: What is the hero's name in *Richard 2?*

▆▆▆▆▆ "Bolingb*no,* "Henry 4"—I'd call him by the name he achieved. Or "Richard", you could consider "*King* Richard", rather, to be the hero.

▆▆▆▆▆ You seem to have different names for a role at different moments in the play.

▆▆▆▆▆ To reflect their changing status. It's only neutural. It wouldn'tI mean *natural*. It wouldn't do to call Richard "King" after he was deposed, would it? Or Lear after he relinquished his crow

▆▆▆▆▆ Or John after he abdicates? And even if Shakespeare does?

▆▆▆▆▆ The less Shakespeare he. Anyway, you're changing the topic. But, we don't have to stick with the author when we're *editing* their works. That's elitism. We have to consider the needs of our readers. And of common sense. Some of these Elizabethans were asleep at the wheel, and readers need to have the authors' intents protected from misunderstandings. And what identity would editing have if it were merely a derivative *copy* of an author's words. And one thing at a time. You've changed the topic. What *is* the Bastard's name? What are you driving at?

▆▆▆▆▆ It depends on whom you attend to:

171

Corn. True or false, it hath made thee Earl of Gloucester. 3.5.17
Gon. My most dear Gloucester! 4.2.25
Osw. And give the letters . . . To Edmund Earl of Gloucester; 4.6.248
Alb. Thou art armed, Gloucester, let the trumpet sound. 5.3.90
Edg. What's he that speaks for Edmund Earl of Gloucester? 5.3.125

If you follow the *evil* characters, the Bastard's name becomes "Earl of Gloucester." *But* if you follow the *good* characters, his name becomes "Earl of Gloucester." So you're answered.

████████ But that's stupid. He's a plain Bastard. He *usurps* the title of Earl of Gloucester.

████████ What about your King Bolingbroke?

████████ That's different, and you *know* it is. Bolingbroke *succeeded*—and where he didn't, Hal forgave him. Henry IV wasn't a *bad* king. Anyway, I've read *Lear*, and Shakespeare calls this character sometimes "Edmund" and sometimes "Bastard"; so an editor should prick one of those to avoid confusing readers and actors, because that's the important ████ and run with it, I think, and not start calling him Gloucester *halfway through the play* (how confusing that would be), just because that's his new title throughout the dialogue, especially when his legitimate father is still living. Besides, this is a moral play, and Bastards have no right to inherit. Your standing up for bastards would make a civil war in the reader's head.

████████ m. Precisely.

████████ p. Is that all there is?? When you came on all hot and heavy with this "What *IS* The Bastard's Name?" business, I thought you had some insight. You're just an anarchrist.

Old ████ c. OK, I'll give you one more chance. What's the Bastard's name—in *King John* this time?

████████ I haven't read *King Joh*you know I mean in a long time. So, you tell me.

████████ The character in question and his brother are entered and speak under the names *"Robert Faulconbridge"* and *"Philip"*.

172

> *Enter Robert Faulconbridge, and Philip.*
> *Philip.* Your faithfull fubiect, I a gentleman,
> Borne in *Northamptonſhire*, and eldeſt ſonne
> As I ſuppoſe, to *Robert Faulconbridge*,
> A Souldier by the Honor-giuing-hand
> Of *Cordelion*, Knighted in the field.
> *K. Iohn.* What art thou?
> *Robert.* The ſon and heire to that ſame *Faulconbridge*.
> *K. Iohn.* Is that the elder, and art thou the heyre?
> You came not of one mother then it ſeemes.
> *Philip.* Moſt certain of one mother, mighty King,
> That is well knowne, and as I thinke one father:

Philip, being older, is the heir, but Robert challenges his parentage, suggesting he, Robert, may be the first *true*-born, and therefore the heir. Finally, Queen Elinor, who notices a royal-family resemblance in Philip, asks him if he'd rather continue as the Faulconbridge heir, or be reputed the bastard son of Richard the Lionhearted. Before he can speak, none other than Shakespeare himself answers for him: the character's response is tagged proleptically *"Bast."*, no longer *"Phil."*— though bastardy is so far "demonstrated" only in this character's doubts, in his (and Robert's) growing wish, and in the gleam in Queen Elinor's eyes—none of it hard evidence.

> *Phil.* Of no more force to difpoſſeſſe me ſir,
> Then was his will to get me, as I think.
> *Eli.* Whether hadſt thou rather be a *Faulconbridge*,
> And like thy brother to enioy thy land:
> Or the reputed ſonne of *Cordelion*,
> Lord of thy preſence, and no land beſide.
> *Baſt.* Madam, and if my brother had my ſhape
> And I had his, ſit *Roberts* his like him,

King John asks him what his name is. The "Bastard" replies *"Philip"*, whereupon John knights him "Sir *Richard* . . . *Plantagenet*", and the Queen Mother addresses him as "Richard".

173

> *K.John.* What is thy name?
> *Baſt.* Philip my liege, ſo is my name begun,
> Philip, good old Sir *Roberts* wiues eldeſt ſonne.
> *K.Iohn.* From henceforth beare his name
> Whoſe forme thou beareſt
> Kneele thou downe *Philip*, but riſe more great,
> Ariſe Sir *Richard*, and *Plantagenet.*
> *Baſt.* Brother by th'mothers ſide, giue me your hand,
> My father gaue me honor, yours gaue land :
> Now bleſſed be the houre by night or day
> When I was got, Sir *Robert* was away.
> *Ele.* The very ſpirit of *Plantaginet* :
> I am thy grandame *Richard*, call me ſo.
> *Baſt.* Madam by chance, but not by truth, what tho;

Notwithstanding, Sir Richard's speech-tag and stage-direction name remains "*Bastard*", for the rest of the play, even when the King and Philip both speak the name "*Richard.*" (The King's "*Faulconbridge*" in the first line following designates Robert, by the way, who is now the Faulconbridge heir. As he does not speak again, we have no chance to see if his tag changes too.)

> *K.Iohn.* Goe, *Faulconbridge*, now haſt thou thy deſire,
> A landleſſe Knight, makes thee a landed Squire:
> Come Madam, and come *Richard*, we muſt ſpeed,
> For *France*, for *France*, for it is more then need.
> *Baſt.* Brother adieu, good fortune come to thee,
> For thou waſt got i'th way of honeſty.
> *Exeunt all but baſtard.*

> *Baſt.* A foot of Honor better then I was,
> But many a many foot of Land the worſe.
> Well, now can I make any *Ioane* a Lady,
> Good den Sir *Richard*, Godamercy fellow,
> And if his name be *George*, Ile call him *Peter*;
> For new made honor doth forget mens names:

And the tag remains "*Bast*" even when the King and Richard both speak the name "*Philip*".

174

Scœna Secunda.

Allarums, Excurfions : Enter Baftard with Auftria's bead.

Baft. Now by my life,this day grows wondrous hot,
Some ayery Denill houers in the skie ,
And pou's downe mifchiefe.*Auftrias* head lye there,
     Enter Iobn, Arthur, Hubert.
While *Philp* breathes.
     Iohn. Hubert, keepe this boy: *Philip* make vp,
My Mother is affayied in our Tent,
And tane I feare.

Before we go mining what Shakespeare *meant* by all this, we might recall that the variation of speech-tag names, in fact, is found in *The Troublesome Raigne* (London, 1591) too, which is either a source play for Shakespere or derived from his work—either in performance or in manuscript. Either way this kind of naming rubs off. This role is tagged *"Philip"* for the first scene (even after he had been knighted as "Richard"), and *"Bastard"* thereafter. The indivi dual folio-Shakespeare who variously named his characters was perhaps inhabited in part by some other Person. In any case, it would have been practical in both plays to call our friend something other than *"Philip"* altogether, to avoid confusion; for the French King's speeches, beginning with his first appearance in the next scene, are always so tagged. Philip Faulconbridge was a fiction after all, and there was no need to name him in a way that collides with the names of historic characters.

All in all, the change from *"Philip"* to *"Bastard"* in Shakespear's play is overdetermined. It reflects the source play (if *The Troublesome Raigne* is a source play), this character's (and others') fervour that he cease to be a Faulconbridge, the author's proleptic preoccupation with the character's choice of parentage, and the freeing up of the tag *"Philip"* for another character. Among these various microscopic considerations are reflected the major conflicts of state—of legitimacy, of title and succession. As the themes on the macroscopic level do not admit philosophical or dramatic resolution, why should editors bully the little guys? Why should art be made safe for the unartistic?

Of course, the epithet *"Bastard"* in speech tags does not deny his identity as "Richard", and so one would think *"Richard"* must be a strong candidate for an editor's choice of tag for him when *"Philip"* is dropped (later than when Shakespeare dropped it, we may remember). But what editor does call him RICHARD? Only rarely can this tag be found in a modern edition. Usually the role is identified in modern editions as BASTARD in dramatis-personae list, in stage direction, and in speech tag all the way through, although this editorial consistency gives the reader the ironic edge (Do we dare call it an *inconsistency*?) of knowing the character's birth long before he himself does?

When Shakspower used five names for the Old Lady in *All's Well*, the dialogue was not affected. But in *King John* there is no way round Shakespoore's variation of *spoken* names. And that means that the variation is detectable by theatre audiences. We've *really* hit the jackpot now. It seems the Old Boy didn't care. But it bugs the hell out of the editors, who want to displace art in the direction of consiste*May I introduce to you*—excuse me, Randy—*Ladies and Gentlemen*, F. G. Fleay, M.A. *writing in 1878 for* Collins' School and College Classics *about this play of our great National Author*:

> . . . and when we consider that the celebrated passage alluding to the English fleet of 1596 . . . is also contained in I, ii, I feel little doubt that these subsequent insertions were made after Hamnet's death, and that the blunders of *Philip* for *Richard*, and *Lewis* for *Philip*, are to be attributed to the confusion caused by grief in Shakespeare's mind. None but those who have had to write compulsorily under similar bereavements, can tell how errors do creep in at such times.

What's the Bastard's Name? Random Cloud.

His words remain as apt today as they

> *Descend hastily* RONALD BRUNLESS M^CKERROW.
> *Reads aloud from "A Suggestion Regarding*
> *Shakespeare's Manuscripts".*

It may be noted that in *King John* the Bastard is in his
earlier speeches "Robert," but as soon as his bastardy is
established his name is altered.

Exit

Now, it is one thing for an *author* or a *scholar* to be confused, but such nonsense must stop at the stage doo

Re-enter RONALD BRUNLESS MCKERROW *through stage door.*

But in any case a copy intended for use in the theatre
would surely, of necessity, be accurate and unambiguous
in the matter of the character-names. A prompter of a
repertory theatre could hardly be expected to remember
that Bertram was the same person as Rossillion, or
Armado the same as Braggart. Such variations would be
an intolerable nuisance to him when he suddenly needed
to know what actors were on the stage in a particular
scene, or to follow the action and be ready to prompt while
thinking about something quite different, as one familiar
with his job would probably do! It is difficult to imagine a
theatrical scribe, at any rate, not attending to a point of
this kind.

> *To him* BOWERS *through stage door,*
> *silently reading footnote 4 from* SB *32, 1979, p. 61.*[14]

4. The significance of these variable prefixes as evidence
for foul-papers copy as against a transcript was first pointed out by R. B. McKerrow, "The Elizabethan Printer and
Dramatic Manuscripts," R. E. S.. 11, (1935), 459–465. His
interpretation has never seriously been challenged.

BVT

Exeunt to a confused noise, manet libri

██Opposite is an *intolerable nuance,* what with its diversely tagged speeches. But see clever Henry Irving's pen yoke them into one role![15]

And over the next leaf is clever David Garrick's partbook, a scribal manuscript dating from 1745 with alterations in the actor's hand.[16] Six lines from the bottom was originally King's John's closing line from 3.1—"No more than he that threats. To arms, let's hie."; it was altered to address the French king, "Philip I scorn thy Threats—To Arms. To Arms,!—ever living Soul!" The last three lines of dialogue on the page were cut, but not until Shakespeare's inconsistent "Phillip" was regularized to "Richard".

*Nota bene: Recipes get adapted in the kitchen
by those who do the cooking.*

Beginning in the next opening are eight photoquoted pages from an old *King John* promptbook.[17]

p. 181   —The first (see the next opening) shows the editorial DRAMATIS PERSONÆ, which, for the character we are interested in, uses the surname alone: "FALCONBRIDGE", Bastard Son to Richard the First." —Surprise, there's no surprise about his birth!—His brother however, has both a first name and a surname: "ROBERT FAULCONBRIDGE . . . .".

p. 182   —The second excerpt (signed "A 2") shows the opening of the first scene. The handwritten notation (numbered "/2./" in the lower right) anticipates the entrance on the Prompter's Side of three characters: "*Sheriff / Bastard / Phillip*"). (The only character with this last name in the *dramatis personae,* of course, is the King of France!)

p. 183   —In the third excerpt (p. 4) we see the two printed stage directions that the previous prompt call anticipated: the first direction (deleted then restored) is for the Sheriff; the second is unaltered, as if it were unproblematic, and reads "*Enter*

178

Or the reputed son of Cœur-de-Lion,
  Lord of thy presence, and no land beside ?
FAULCON. Madam, an' if my brother had my shape,
  And I had his, Sir Robert his, like him ;
  And if my legs were two such riding-rods,
  My arms such eel-skins stuffed ; my face so thin,
  And, to his shape, were heir to all this land,
  Would I might never stir from off this place,
  I'd give it every foot to have this face :
  I would not be Sir Rob in any case.
ELINOR. I like thee well. Wilt thou forsake thy fortune,
  Bequeath thy land to him, and follow me ?
  I am a soldier, and now bound to France.
FAULCON. Brother, take you my land, I'll take my chance.
  Your face hath got five hundred pounds a-year ;
  Yet sell your face for five-pence, and 'tis dear.—
  Madam, I'll follow you unto the death.
ELINOR. Nay, I would have you go before me thither.
FAULCON. (R.) Our country manners give our betters way.
K. JOHN. (advances, L. C.) What is thy name ?
FAULCON. Philip, my liege—so is my name begun :
  Philip, good old Sir Robert's wife's eldest son.
K. JOHN. From henceforth bear his name whose form thou
          bearest :
  Kneel thou down Philip, but arise more great.
      (FAULCONBRIDGE kneels in front of the KING, who
        strikes him on the right shoulder with his sword)
  Arise Sir Richard, and Plantagenet.
SIR RICHARD. (rises) Brother by my mother's side, give me
          your hand :
  My father gave me honor, yours gave land.
  Now blesséd be the hour, by night or day,
  When I was got, Sir Robert was away.
ELINOR. The very spirit of Plantagenet !—
  I am thy granddame, Richard : call me so. (goes up)
SIR RICH. Madam, by chance, but not by truth : what
          though ?
  Something about, a little from the right,
    In at the window, or else o'er the hatch ;
  Who dares not stir by day must walk by night,
    And have is have, however men do catch.

Phillip, what say'st thou to the Cardinal?
—— from heaven'd.
~~The thing is mov'd, & answer not to this?~~
—— French Inconstancy.
France, thou shalt rue this hour, within this
Hour
—— my Life dies.
Cousin, go draw our ~~Puissance~~ together.
France; I am burn'd up with inflaming wrath,
A Rage, whose heat hath this Condition;
That nothing can allay, nothing but Blood,
The Blood &dearest valued Blood of France.
—— in Jeopardy
~~Ho more than ...~~ To Arms, Kelebie.
Philip from thy threats —
[Alarms, Excursions, &c — ... Exit ...]
[Enter with Arthur.]
There
Hubert; keep this Boy. Phillip, make up.
My Mother is Assailed in our Tent
And ta'en, I fear.

DRAMATIS PERSONÆ.
MEN.

King JOHN.
Prince HENRY, Son to the King.
ARTHUR, Duke of Bretagne, and Nephew to the King.
PEMBROKE,
ESSEX,
SALISBURY,   } Englifh Lords.
HUBERT,
~~BIGOT,~~
FAULCONBRIDGE, Baftard Son to Richard the Firft.
ROBERT FAULCONBRIDGE, Half Brother to the Baftard.
~~JAMES GURNEY,~~ Servant to the Lady Faulconbridge.
~~PETER~~ OF POMFRET, a Prophet.
PHILIP, King of France.
LEWIS, the Dauphin.
Arch-Duke of Auftria.
Cardinal PANDULPHO, the Pope's Legate.
~~MELUN, a French Lord.~~
CHATILLON, Ambaffador from France to King John.

WOMEN.

ELINOR, Queen Mother of England.
CONSTANCE, Mother to Arthur.
BLANCH, Daughter to Alphonfo King of Caftile, and Niece to King John.
Lady FAULCONBRIDGE, Mother to the Baftard and Robert Faulconbridge.
Citizens of Angiers, Heralds, Executioners, Meffengers, Soldiers, and other Attendants.

The SCENE fometimes in England and fometimes in France.

1. B. Low
1. B. Paper with a Seal
1. B. Paper

KING JOHN.

Palace

ACT I. SCENE I.

Throne
States chair
Stool

Northampton. ~~A Room of State in the~~ Pálace.
Discovered
~~Enter~~ King JOHN, Queen ELINOR, PEMBROKE, ESSEX,
and SALISBURY, with CHATILLON. *×2 Flourish*
Gents 12.

King John. *Ladies 10.*

NOW fay, Chatillon, what would France with us?
  Chat. Thus, after greeting, fpeaks the king of France
In my behaviour to the majefty,
The borrow'd majefty of England here.
  Eli. A ftrange beginning;—borrow'd majefty!
  K. John. Silence, good mother; hear the embaffy.
  Chat. Philip of France, in right and true behalf
Of thy deceafed brother Geffrey's fon,
Arthur Plantagenet, lays moft lawful claim
To this fair Ifland and the territories;
To Ireland, Poictiers, Anjou, Touraine, Maine:
Defiring thee to lay afide the fword
Which fways ufurpingly thefe feveral titles;
And put the fame into young Arthur's hand,
Thy nephew, and right royal fovereign.
  K. John. What follows, if we difallow of this?
  Chat. The proud control of fierce and bloody war
To enforce thefe rights fo forcibly withheld.
  K. John. Here have we war for war, and blood for blood,
Controlment for controlment; fo anfwer France.
  Chat. Then take my king's defiance from my mouth,
The fartheft limit of my embaffy.
  K. John. Bear mine to him, and fo depart in peace:
Be thou as lightning in the eyes of France;
For ere thou canft report I will be there;
The thunder of my cannon fhall be heard:
So, hence! Be thou the trumpet of our wrath,
And fullen preffage of your own decay.—
An honourable conduct let him have;—
Pembroke, look to't:—Farewell, Chatillon.

OP [*Exeunt* CHAT. *and* PEM.

A 2

K John
Q Elinor
Pembroke
Essex
Salisbury
Chatillon
Gents
Ladies
Disc.
Drums
Trumpets

2.
Sheriff
Bastard
Phillip
PS.

4   KING JOHN.

Eli. What now, my fon? have I not ever faid,
How that ambitious Conftance would not ceafe,
'Till fhe had kindled France and all the world
Upon the right and party of her fon?
This might have been prevented, and made whole,
With very eafy arguments of love;
Which now the manage of two kingdoms muft
With fearful bloody iffue arbitrate. ✱

K. John. Our ftrong poffeffion and our right for us.
Eli. Your ftrong poffeffion much more than your right;
Or elfe it muft go wrong with you and me:
So much my confcience whifpers in your ear;
Which none but heaven and you, and I, fhall hear.

Enter the Sheriff of Northamptonfhire, who whifpers Essex. /PS

Essex. My liege, here is the ftrangeft controverfy
Come from the country to be judg'd by you
That e'er I heard: fhall I produce the men? [*Exit Sheriff.* PS
K. John. Let them approach.—
Our abbies and our priories fhall pay

✱ *Enter* ROBERT FAULCONBRIDGE, *and* PHILIP. PS
This expedition's charge. ✱ What men are you?

Phil. Your faithful fubject I, a gentleman,
Born in Northamptonfhire; and eldeft fon,
As I fuppofe, to Robert Faulconbridge;
A foldier, by the honour-giving hand
Of Cœur-de-lion knighted in the field.

K. John. What art thou?

Rob. The fon and heir to that fame Faulconbridge.

K. John. Is that the elder, and art thou the heir?
You came not of one mother then, it feems.

Phil. Moft certain of one mother, mighty king,
That is well known; and, as I think, one father:
But, for the certain knowledge of that truth,
I put you o'er to heaven and to my mother;
Of that I doubt, as all men's children may.

Eli. Out on thee, rude man! thou doft fhame thy mother,
And wound her honour with this diffidence.

Phil. I, madam? no, I have no reafon for it;
That is my brother's plea, and none of mine;
The which if he can prove, 'a pops me out
At leaft from fair five hundred pound a year:
Heaven guard my mother's honour and my land!

ROBERT FAULCONBRIDGE, *and* PHILIP". The prompter, therefore, seems not to have known that "Bastard" and "Philip" are the same character; like McKerrow, he must have thought—intolerable nuisance—that the Bastard's name was "Robert".

p. 185   —In his second speech in the fourth excerpt (p. 7) King John bids "Philip" kneel, but "Richard" arise. Elinor's address to this new Richard is cut, but John's survives, and so the audience does hear this scarce-minted Philip addressed as a Richard. In the last of his notations on this page the prompter indicated a flourish as opposite himself. It is written in beside the stage-direction name, "Philip", which is also, surprisingly, still in use as the speech tag. It is especially surprising, for this is the speech in which the character addresses himself conspicuously as "*Sir Richard*". It seems that the editor, prompter, audience—and even the author—all can have their own blithely uncoordinated and inconsistent nomenclatures.

p. 186   —The fifth excerpt (p. 9) shows the continuing editorial "*Phil.*" tag; it functions throughout the scene (though the folio used it only at the start of the scene). In his note, just above the rule that marks the end of the scene, the prompter has written a different name: "*Bastard Dresses.*" The prompter had thought Philip was Robert; but now that Philip is Richard, he calls him "Bastard". *You* figure it. You figure it in *your* reparto.

To the right of this notation by the prompter is his line-up for Scene 2, beginning with the name "Philip"—which name must refer no longer to the English character we have been discussing, but to that bastard, "PHILIP, *King of France*" (you'll see him so-designated in print in the stage direction to the left of the prompt notation).

p. 187   —On page 15, the sixth excerpt, the prompter has cancelled the printed text with a handwritten version. He is now calling What's-His-Name "*Faulc.*", which he no doubt derives from the editorial usage of his printed copy.

p. 188   —On page 32 we see such editorial designation of him, as "*Faulc.*"; but now the prompter's call is for "Bastard" again, who, when he appears—our eighth and last excerpt

KING JOHN. 7

K. John. What is thy name?

Phil. Philip, my liege; fo is my name begun;
Philip, good old Sir Robert's wife's eldeft fon.

K. John. From henceforth bear his name whofe form thou
    bear'ft:

Kneel thou down Philip, but rife more great;
Arife Sir Richard, and Plantagenet!—

Phil. Brother by the mother's fide, give me your hand;
My father gave me honour, your's gave land:
Now bleffed be the hour, by night or day,
When I was got, Sir Robert was away.

Eli. The very fpirit of Plantagenet!—
I am thy grandame, Richard; call me fo.

Phil. Madam, by chance, but not by truth; What though?
Something about, a little from the right,
In at the window, or elfe o'er the hatch:
Who dares not ftir by day muft walk by night;
And have is love, howe'er men do catch:
Near or far off well won is ftill well fhot;
And I am I, however I was begot.

K. John. Go Faulconbridge! now haft thou thy defire,
A landlefs knight makes thee a landed 'fquire.—
Come, madam, and come, Richard; we muft fpeed
For France for France; for it is more than need,

Phil. Brother, adieu; Good fortune come to thee
For thou waft got i' the way of honefty!
A foot of honour better than I was; *Exeunt all but* PHILIP.
But many a many foot of land the worfe.
Well, now can I make any Joan a lady:—
Good den, Sir Richard—*God-a-mercy, fellow* ;—
And if his name be George, I'll call him Peter:
For new-made honour doth forget men's names;
'Tis too refpective, and too fociable,
For your converfing. Now your traveller—
He and his tooth-pick at my worfhip's mefs;
And when my knightly ftomach is fuffic'd,
Why then I fuck my teeth, and catechife
My piked man of countries:——*My dear fir*
(Thus, leaning on my elbow, I begin)
I fhall befeech you—That is queftion now;
And then comes anfwer like an ABC-book:——
O, fir, fays anfwer, *at your beft command;*
At your employment; at your fervice, fir :——

A 4

185

KING JOHN. 9

Lady. Haſt thou conſpired with thy brother too,
That for thine own gain ſhould'ſt defend mine honour?
What means this ſcorn, thou moſt untoward knave?
  Phil. Knight, knight, good mother—Baſilifco like!
What! I am dub'd; I have it on my ſhoulder.
But, mother, I am not Sir Robert's ſon;
I have diſclaim'd Sir Robert, and my land;
Legitimation, name, and all is gone:
Then, good my mother, let me know my father;
Some proper man I hope; Who was it, mother?
  Lady. Haſt thou deny'd thyſelf a Faulconbridge?
  Phil. As faithfully as I deny the devil.
  Lady. King Richard Cœur-de-lion was thy father;
By long and vehement ſuit I was ſeduc'd
To make room for him in my huſband's bed:
Heaven lay not my tranſgreſſion to my charge!
Thou art the iſſue of my dear offence,
Which was ſo ſtrongly urg'd paſt my defence.
  Phil. Now, by this light, were I to get again,
Madam, I would not with a better father.
Some ſins do bear their privilege on earth,
And ſo doth your's; your fault was not your folly:
Needs muſt you lay your heart at his diſpoſe——
Subjected tribute to commanding love——
Againſt whoſe fury and unmatched force
The awleſs lion could not wage the fight,
Nor keep his princely heart from Richard's hand,
He that perforce robs lions of their hearts
May eaſily win a woman's Ay, my mother,
With all my heart I thank thee for my father!
Who lives and dares but ſay thou did'ſt not well
When I was got, I'll ſend his ſoul to hell.
Come, lady, I will ſhew thee to my kin;
  And they ſhall ſay when Richard me begot,
If thou hadſt ſaid him nay it had been ſin:
  Who ſays it was he lies; I ſay 'twas not. [*Exeunt.*

ACT. II. SCENE I.

Before the walls of Angiers in France.

Enter PHILIP *King of France,* LEWIS *the Dauphin, the
Arch-Duke of Auſtria,* CONSTANCE, *and* ARTHUR.

BEFORE Angiers well met, brave Auſtria.——
  Arthur, that great forerunner of thy blood,

Arth: - Good my Mother, peace!
I would that I were low laid in my Grave;
I am not worth this Coil that's made for me.
Elin: His mother shames him, poor Boy! he weeps.
Const: His Grandam's injuries, and not his mother's shames,
Draw those heaven-moving Pearls from his poor Eyes;
Which Heaven shall take in nature of a Fee,
Ay, with these chrystal Beads Heaven shall be bribed
To do him Justice, and Revenge on you.
Elin: - Thou monstrous Slanderer of Heav'n and Earth!—
Aust: - Peace.
Faulc: Hear the Crier.
Aust: - What the Devil art thou?
Faulc: One that will play the Devil, Sir, with you,
An a' may catch your Hide and you alone.
You are the Hare of whom the Proverb goes,
Whose Valour plucks dead Lions by the Beard;
I'll smoke your skin-coat, an I catch you right—
Sirrah, look to't— i'faith I will, i'faith.

K: Phil: - King John, this is the very sum of all.—
England and Ireland, Anjou, Touraine, Maine,
In right of Arthur I do claim of thee:
Wilt thou resign them, and lay down thy arms?

K: John: - My Life as soon— I do defy thee, France.
Arthur of Bretagne, yield thee to my Hand;
And out of my dear Love, I'll give thee more
Than e'er the coward Hand of France can win.

32   KING JOHN.

That need muſt needs infer this principle——
That faith will live again by death of need:
O, then, tread down my need and faith mounts up;
Keep my need up and faith is trodden down.

    K. John. The king is mov'd, and anſwers not to this.
    Conſt. O, be remov'd from him, and anſwer well.
    Auſt. Do, ſo king Philip, hang no more in doubt.
    Faulc. Hang nothing but a calf's-ſkin, moſt ſweet lout.
    K. Phil. I am perplex'd, and know not what to ſay.
    Pand. What canſt thou ſay but will perplex thee more,
If thou ſtand excommunicate and curſt?

    K. Phil. Good reverend father make my perſon yours,
And tell me how you would beſtow yourſelf.

This royal hand and mine are newly knit;
And the conjunction of our inward ſouls
Marry'd in league, coupled and link'd together
With all religious ſtrength of ſacred vows;
The lateſt breath that gave the ſound of words
Was deep ſworn-faith, peace, amity, true love,
Between our kingdoms and our royal ſelves;
And even before this truce, but new before—
No longer than we well could waſh our hands,
To clap this royal bargain up of peace ——
Heaven knows they were beſmear'd and over-ſtain'd
With ſlaughter's pencil; where revenge did paint
The fearful difference of incenſed kings:
And ſhall theſe hands, ſo lately purg'd of blood,
So newly join'd in love, ſo ſtrong in both,
Unyoke this ſeizure and this kind regreet?
Play faſt and looſe with faith? ſo jeſt with heaven;
Make ſuch unconſtant children of ourſelves,
As now again to ſnatch our palm from palm;
Unſwear faith ſworn; and on the marriage bed
Of ſmiling peace to march a bloody hoſt,
And make a riot on the gentle brow
Of true ſincerity? O, holy ſir,
My reverend father let it not be ſo:
Out of your grace deviſe, ordain, impoſe
Some gentle order; and then we ſhall be bleſt
To do your pleaſure, and continue friends.

    Pand. All form is formleſs, order orderleſs,
Save what is oppoſite to England's love.
Therefore to arms! be champion of our church!

KING JOHN. 35

K. John. Coufin, go draw our puiffance together.—
[*Exit* FAULCONBRIDGE.
France, I am burn'd up with inflaming wrath;
A rage, whofe heat hath this condition,
That nothing can allay, nothing but blood,
The blood, and deareft-valu'd blood of France.
K. Phil. Thy rage fhall burn thee up, and thou fhalt turn
To afhes ere our blood fhall quench that fire:
Look to thyfelf, thou art in jeopardy.
K. John. No more than he that threats.—To arms,
let's hie.
[*Exeunt.*

SCENE II. *A Field of Battle.*—
Alarums, Excurfions.

Enter FAULCONBRIDGE, with AUSTRIA's Head.

Faulc. Now, by my life, this day grows wondrous hot;
Some airy devil hovers in the fky,
And pours down mifchief. Auftria's head lie there;
While Philip breathes.

Enter King JOHN, ARTHUR, *and* HUBERT.

K. John. Hubert, keep this boy:—Philip, make up;
My mother is affailed in our tent,
And ta'en, I fear.
Faulc. My lord, I refcu'd her;
Her highnefs is in fafety, fear you not:
But on, my liege; for very little pains
Will bring this labour to an happy end.
[*Exeunt.*

SCENE III.
Alarums, Excurfions, Retreat.
Re-enter King JOHN, ELINOR, ARTHUR, FAULCONBRIDGE,
HUBERT,

K. John. So fhall it be; your grace fhall ftay behind,
[*To* ELINOR.

So ftrongly guarded.—Coufin, look not fad:
[*To* ARTHUR.

Thy grandam loves thee; and thy uncle will
As dear be to thee as thy father was.
Arth. O, this will make my mother die with grief.
K. John. Coufin, away for England; hafte before.
[*To* FAULCONBRIDGE.

D

189

p. 189

—page 35, exits and enters as "FAULCONBRIDGE" and also speaks under *Faulc.*; but he is addressed by his King and also refers to himself neither by that name nor by "Richard", but rather by "Philip".

All in all, we can say that the creation of the Renaissance art form and its consumption by readers in its own era, and its production centuries later (from arbitrarily edited texts) all bumbles along very well, thank you, with unstable nomencl
BAST▪▪▪▪▪▪ So *those* are the *Bastard's* name!

*

An annotated copy of the third-folio "A Midsummers nights DREAM" is the first extant promptbook for this play. It was used in Smock Alley, Dublin in the 1670's.[18] In the speech tags and stage directions one character is now *Duke*, now *Theseus*; another is now *Dutchess*, now *Hippolyta*; a third is now *Robin*, now *Puck*, and so on. The reviser or prompter, whoever he was, and whatever his precise functions, seems to have had little difficulty navigating, never altering the *intolerable nuance* of variant speech tags in the imprint. When he cancelled the opening lines of a speech—here it is Hippolyta's speech—and therefore needed to write a new speech tag, he used the abbreviation which was ready to hand—"*Hip*".

190

When he rewrote the speeches of the Duke and Dutchess, he again used the local names—"[*Du*]*t:*" and "[*D*]*uk*" (though I do see a scratched-out "*Hip*" in an earlier state of the cut, in the fifth of the seven lines now deleted).

*

It may be alright for authors and theatre people to name promiscuously, but the reader *surely* needs all the help she

Enter Editor

Oh, I see you're readiDid you know that that is our new MIS-SISSAUGA Shakespeare? made right here in Canadand just off thAnd what's thisLet me put on my reading glthe *First* FoliOoooh you *are* an ambitious young lady. *Both* the old and the new, the tired and the true. It's usually only graduate students who*Do* note the editorial care with which the original has*Right there!* Don't turn so fas*Go* back. Further bac*Yes*, that page. On *that* page, look where I'm pointing. (This play is a gem of the comic genre.)   Do you get it?

> *Moon.* This Lanthorne doth the horned Moone pre-
> fent.
> *De.* He fhould haue worne the hornes on his head.
> *Du.* Hee is no crefcent, and his hornes are inuifible,
> within the circumference.
> *Moon.* This lanthorne doth the horned Moone pre-
> fent: My felfe, the man i'th Moone doth feeme to be.
> *Du.* This is the greateft error of all the reft; the man
> fhould be put into the Lanthorne. How is it els the man
> i'th Moone?
> *Dem.* He dares not come there for the candle.
> For you fee, it is already in fnuffe.
> *Dut.* I am vvearie of this Moone ; vvould he would
> change.
> *Du.* It appeares by his fmal light of difcretion, that
> he is in the wane : but yet in courtefie, in all reafon, vve
> muft ftay the time.
> *Lyf.* Proceed ~~Moone.~~
> *Moon.* All that I haue to fay, is to tell you, that the
> Lanthorne is the Moone; I, the man in the Moone; this
> thorne bufh, my thorne bufh; and this dog, my dog.

No? Well, then, look here.[19]

STARVELING (*as Moonshine*)
    This lanthorn doth the hornèd moon present –
DEMETRIUS He should have worn the horns on his head.
THESEUS He is no crescent, and his horns are invisible within the   230
    circumference.
STARVELING (*as Moonshine*)
    This lanthorn doth the hornèd moon present;
      Myself the man i'th'moon do seem to be –
THESEUS This is the greatest error of all the rest; the man should be
    put into the lantern. How is it else the man i'th'moon?   235
DEMETRIUS He dares not come there, for the candle; for you see it is
    already in snuff.
HIPPOLYTA I am aweary of this moon. Would he would change!

127   *A Midsummer Night's Dream* 5.1.259

THESEUS It appears by his small light of discretion that he is in the
    wane; but yet in courtesy, in all reason, we must stay the time.   240
LYSANDER Proceed, Moon.
STARVELING All that I have to say is to tell you that the lanthorn is
    the moon, I the man i'th'moon, this thorn bush my thorn bush,
    and this dog my dog.

Give up? OK, I'll explain it to you. (You'll love it.) Now, Shakespeare assigned these three *Moon* speeches (We guess it wasWho else would assign speeches in a play by Shakespeare, right?) only to *Moon.*—you see that period? That means Moon*shine*. (He **meant** *Moonshine* but in drama you have to use your imagination, because the text doesn't rise off the page the way it does on the boards. Compositors don't give a tinker's damn what the poet meant. They are always changing the text. Nothing's sacred to them. So, remember, Imagination. The text by itself is not enough. Why, you could say that's the Editors' Credo:

THE EDITORS' CREDO: THE TEXT IS NOT ENOUGH.

But it's OK; I can *fix* it. I have a system. Obviously, "*Du.*" becomes "THESEUS" and "*Dut.*" becomes "HIPPOLYTA". That is not *too*but here is where it becomes really subtle. So I assigned the first two *Moon.* speeches to Starveling. That's not too hard, but now it gets *really* subtle: but not just to

STARVELING (*qua Starveling*)

—(if such a concept makes sense), but to

STARVELING (*as Moonshine*).

To make it clear to you (as it wasn't in the folio) that Moonshine is not a *new* character—to add to the dramatic-per-sonae list (which he wrote at the front ofbut just a *role* in the play—a role in the play *within* the play—so you don't confuse what *is* (the actor *is* Starving), and who the actor is *pretending* someone pretending to be someone. (Someone *else*, I mean, of course—our "Moon." For, that's theatre. You're not going to *pretend* to be yourself! In life we don't pretend to be ourself, do we?

Deborah:

ED: Do we in life? In life we don't *pretend* to be ourself? We just *are* ourselves. People pretend to be *other* people though, don't they?

Ed: Yes, they do. Well, voilà, that's Theatre. So, I assign the last speech simply to "Starveling"—but not *as* anyone this time, not "Starveling *as* Anyone Else". Just "Starveling". Because he's Because he's falling apart, really.

Deborah: Falling apart because is it that he is speaking—not poetry anymore?

Ed: Prose, you mean? The opposite of po

Deborah: Yes, prose.

Ed: What?

Deborah: I said, "Yes, prose." I was agreeing with you.

Ed: That's the ticket. No. It definitely has nothing to do wiThough it's good you knew the distinction between prose and what you called "not prose", because—well, because he's out of character, really. I'll show you. When he says—when he says above—W*Here* it is, line 233:

Myself *the man i'th'moon* do seem to be,

He is talking as Starveling *as* the Man in the Moon. But when Lysander says, "Proceed moon.", and Moonshine responds prosaically, "I"—later on on page 127 (after he's fallen apart), on line 242

All that *I* have to say is to tell you *etc.,*

he doesn't mean "I", as if Moonshine were talking ("*I* Moonshine . . .") self-consciously referring to his *ego*, you see, as, well, his *ego*,—as "I". He now means "I *Starveling*" not "I *Moon*." So, I don't call him "Starveling *as* the Man in thI mean I mean I don't call him "Starveling *as* Moonshine". The text is clear.

Deborah: How can you tell?

Ed: He is speaking prose for one thing. That's always a good indicator.

Deborah: Well . . . Now, sure I can see he may be sort of out of his *part* in the play before the Duke and everybody, but can't what he says still be sort of in character—in the character of the ManIt *surely* conveys everything the Man in the

Moon *needs* to say, and is not all that different in *style* (though it *is* prose) from the *way* the Man inThough it certainly doesn't *refer* to himself as Starveling, for example, thus *proving* that he is out of character. OK, so if he is out of character now, I wonder ifCan I ask you a question? Is this supposed to be a funny play?

ED: Do you mean the *play*? Or do you mean the play *within* the play?

Deborah: Yes, the play within the play.

ED: Well, *it* is a gem of the comic genre. So is the *play as a whole*. They are *both* gems of the comic genre.

Deborah: I just thought I'dSo the play as whole is too?

ED: Yes, on *both* counts.

Deborah: OK. So I just thought I'dOK. So if he is out of his character now, I wonder if he *ever* was fully in his role as Moonshine. Isn't he always *trying* to be "*as* the Man", but falling short? Isn't this play throughout the play about the discrepancy between identity and and the discrepancy between the mask? It *can* be funny sometimes, but it's very *painful* too. Falling short in all his speeches, always betraying that the Man in the Moon *is* Starveling despite himself? Or in his outburst in prose we could just as well call him "Man *as* Starveling", because the lunar *costume* (He is the Taylor isn't he?) establishes the Man, but the Starveling identity leaks through the costume whenever Starveling speaks or tries to act. Isn't that what is delicious about our watching an actor with a simultaneous consciousness of him as role and as actor? And if Aristotle says that spectacwell the spectators could have perceived the lunar costume as the *primary* identity, and the Starveling identity is like *secondary* and filters through the chinks?

ED: You're new at thi

Deborah: Also the *as*-Manshine speeches that you jus

ED: Wouldn't you like to look at a clearer example of editori

Deborah: Where isHere it is in my folio text:

My selfe, the man i'th Moone doth *seeme* to be.

Wouldn't the real Man in the Moon just say he *is*. We don't *pretend* to be ourselves. And isn't he saying not that he seems to be *the Man in the Moone*, but that Man in the Moone seems to be *him*. That's different from your text. The folio says 'The Man <u>doth</u> seem to be myself' and the MISSISSAUGA Shakespeare says 'Myself <u>do</u> seem to be the Man.' Like, it doesn't say that. I'm paraphrasing. There is like this whole crisis of identity. Now, there isn't a textual note in your edition, so I wonder if there is some probl

PROF: You're new at this. Don't worry, you'll get the bang of it, eventually. The important thing is not to be ruffled. Shakespeare once looked strange to me too, before I became the Editor of the MISSISSAUGA Shakespeare. It will come. Just don't get ruffled. So just let me try another example. Wouldn't you like to look at a clearer example of editorial practice? I know *this* one will make it really clear. (You'll love it.) If this were a Lecture Situation and you were my student under me, which you can be my student when you are a sophomore, I would lead with this that I'm going toYou need to enter this body of material with a fixed system, you know. And I'm really glad you raised this issue of referring to himself by his name. *Nomen est numen.* That's one of the more advanced themes in the course. You're learning, and that's good. Very good. And what's *your* name, by the way?

DEBORAH: Oh, it'sMy name? It's GloriaIt's Gloria Moon, sir, Gloria MooneBefore you go on, can I ask a couple of pages further on? I don't quite get it inWhy are they in these square brackets in your edition? These stage directions after lines 284, 289 and and 290?

HIPPOLYTA Beshrew my heart, but I pity the man.
BOTTOM (*as Pyramus*)
    O wherefore, Nature, didst thou lions frame,   275
      Since lion vile hath here deflowered my dear?
    Which is – no, no – which was the fairest dame
      That lived, that loved, that liked, that looked with cheer.
        Come tears, confound!
        Out sword, and wound   280
      The pap of Pyramus,
        Ay, that left pap,

> Where heart doth hop:
> Thus die I, thus, thus, thus! [*Stabs himself.*]
>   Now am I dead,   285
>   Now am I fled;
> My soul is in the sky.
>   Tongue, lose thy light;
>   Moon, take thy flight;
>   [*Exit Starveling*]
> Now die, die, die, die, die. [*He dies.*]   290

DEMETRIUS No die, but an ace for him; for he is but one.
LYSANDER Less than an ace, man; for he is dead, he is nothing.
THESEUS With the help of a surgeon he might yet recover, and yet prove
an ass.
HIPPOLYTA How chance Moonshine is gone before Thisbe comes back   295
and finds her lover?

Does the "*He*" in the last one mean that Bottom stabs himself
and dies, or Pyramus does? I don't thinkNo it doesn't, the folio
has no stage directions here.

> *Dut.* Beſhrew my heart, but I pittie the man.
> *Pir.* O wherefore Nature, did'ſt thou Lions frame?
> Since Lion vilde hath heere deflour'd my deere:
> Which is: no, no, which was the faireſt Dame
> That liu'd, that lou'd, that lik'd, that look'd with cheere.
> Come teares, confound: Out ſword, and wound
> The pap of *Piramus*:
> I, that left pap, where heart doth hop;
> Thus dye I, thus, thus, thus.
> Now am I dead, now am I fled, my ſoule is in the sky,
> Tongue loſe thy light, Moone take thy flight,
> Now dye, dye, dye, dye, dye.
>   *Dem.* No Die, but an ace for him; for he is but one.
>   *Liſ.* Leſſe then an ace man. For he is dead, he is no-
> thing.
>   *Du.* With the helpe of a Surgeon, he might yet reco-
> uer, and proue an Aſſe.
>   *Dut.* How chance Moone-ſhine is gone before?
> *Thiſby* comes backe, and findes her Louer.

ED: Well, I'm very pleased to meet you, Gloria. Gloria, I do so enjoy your fresh eagerness. You seem so   open   to the text. If you just read on, when you know the play better, you'll see that Bottom does speak later in the scene—so it's obviously not the *actor* of the play *within* the play, Bottom, but his *role*, Pyramus, that the stage direction refersHe is after all *in* the role (*within* the role, that is, the role *within* the role, I mean). And wouldn't it be ludicrous to think that the *actor* of the role "Bottom" was dying? Ha ha. *I* think so. Don't you? Why, you'd have to have a different partner to play Bottom every night!

DEBORAH: Well, that's what confuses me about the intervening stage direction, "[*Exit Starveling*]".

ED: What's the confusion, dear? I'll just

DEBORAH: Well I thougOh Professor I'd like my purse besideIt's *not* in the way, really.

ED: What?

DEBORAH: I'd I'd like to keep my purse beside me. I might want to use it.

ED: Gloria, you might want to   use your purse?

DEBORAH: YesThere may be there maysomething I need.

ED: While we're discussing *text*, you might want your purse?

DEBORAH: Yes. I, yes, I might need it. I   *definitely* might want to use it.

ED:

DEBORAH:

ED: Well, if that's your *desire*if that's your desire, then I'll I'll just *definitely* put your little purse   right   back   *here*. How's that, Miss Moon?

GLORIAH: Thank you, sir. What I wanted to show you, sirNo it's alright, I can read it upside down alright. What I wanted to ask you was Why should the stage directions to stab and die in the "Bottom-*as*-Pyramus" speech refer to the *role* in the interlude, whereas the direction to exit refers to the name of the *actor* of the role—or rather to the *non*-actor, I guess (because he's failing to stay in character, we figured it out), of the role? Is that it? I *think* I get it. You refer to him as actor because he's not very good at mastering his role? Or can we say categorically that *every* exit in Shakespeare is out of character, say, because when you get off stage you drop your role and become your real self, but if you stab yourself and die on stage you are still playing yourself? As a corpse, though?

ED: Yes, that's it. Very good. I reRemember, he *is* out of his role. Remember the prose. You did grasp that, didn't you. The prose?

DEBORAH: Well yes, I think I understood that a bit.

ED: Good, so he's silent now, but it's *prosaic* not poetic silence. People don't appreciate that there is a balance: Poetic license and *prosaic* license. Poetic silence and *prosaic* silence. There has to be this balance.

DEBORAH: Because he's out of character?

ED: Do you *do* see the point, don't you?

DEB: Buthen why does the dialogue that precedes his exit as "Starveling" say

> Moone, take thy flight.

—that's the actual folio speech? Bottom's. Does Bottom not see that Starveling is out of his role? Or does "Pyramus" (that's the actual folio speech tag for Bottom) know him only on the level of the play within the play, know him as Moonshine, and so he can't call him by any other name—without becoming out of character himself? In which case, his own speech tag would have to revert to "Bottom".

ED: Yes, well that's an intelligent way to put it. You seem to have the makings of an editor on you. I think women should be editors too nowadays. They have much to contribute nowadays.

Deborah: But then I didn't understand why the Dutchess reacts to his exit, by saying,

> *Moonshine* is gone.

—Surely *she* can see that he hadn't ever been in character, or, if he had for a moment, when we first saw him, that the Man in the Moon was now long gone. Or do you think that he was back in character when he took his flight—or that maybe he'd

SHAKESPEARE'S SPEECH-HEADINGS

never really left it?—and her mode of address combined with all of Shakespeare's *Moon.* tags is the subtle evidence that this is so? The Moon is changeable after all—

th'inconstant moon

—so maybe this vacillation ofmaybe he's *always* been in character, like metaphorically. Shouldn't the direction read *"Exit Moon-shine"*, like it does in the folio, I think? (Where has it got to?)—or we could edit it: *"Exit Starveling as Moon-shine"*. Isn't that more comprehensive, isn't that what Shakespeare *must* have written?

ED:

Deborah: Sir? Isn't that what Shakespeare must have written?

ED: Yes? *Yes.* Well this *is* yes this is *very* subtle, and scholarshit may not scholarship may not have made the final judgement on it, but Shakespeare is nothing if not subtle. It may take one years, Gloria, to fathom what this subtle mindHe *was* the greatest English-speaking artist, you know. But trust the editorial tradition—over time—to show theWe have been perfecting the text since the 18th century, and there is still room for new penetration with each fresh and eager generation. Like yourself. Now, this will have to be tentative, but as I read it, Bottom *as* Pyramus *wants* Starveling to play the part of Moonshine alright, even though he is failing at it. You see you must get into the bottom of thiinto the *character* of this Bottom. We know from his soliloquy that he is a very subtle, he can simultaneously maintain several states of mind at the same time (foolishly, I grant you, for he is just a mechanical), and it is hard for a single stage-direction name to give credit to them all. It's not as layered as dialogue, after all. It's only a speech heading. It's only one word (unless you chose to edit it longer). And besides, who reads speech headings? It's not the sort of thing anyone is going to write a book about face it, nobody is going to write a book about *Shakespeare's Speech-Headings*, because the dialogue is so redolent of character that if I had accidentally left the heading off, people could figure it out just who the speaker just from the idiosocratic stamp on the vocabulary. That's enough. These headings are reductive. (Redundancy, we call them in Information Theory.)

As for Hippolyta, since you raise her too, I'll say something about the Duchess of Athens. A woman like this is nothing if not polite. She is *pretending* that all is well; and it is the gracious power of sovereigns like her, that their pretence can make things *really* happen. Don't get me wrong, I'm not a royalist. WomeA duchess couldn't do that nowadays. But I know true coin when I bite it. They can *really* make things happen. Not here maybe, but in a more perfect world, like that of *The Winter's Tale*. (You'll come to that in graduate school.) Women *are* enabling after all, aren't they? We know that nowadays with the Women's Movement, to which I am very, veryI think you are a prime example of a young woman who has *arrived*, that women can make so much happen if they want—if they want to. Yes, if they want to. Nowadays it's the turn for women like yourself to make thingsYou can *make* things happen. *I* think so. Not all menBut *I* think so, Gloria. You see here how much Shakespeare can encode in a seemingly insignificant choice of words (like "Starveling")—and out of the dialogue too. When Shakespeare called him "Starueling" to exit in the stage direction, he reveals a wealth of subtlety. There is also the exigencies of metrical versification. Suppose he has said "Starueling take thy flight."?—well, it's got one syllable too many, hasn't it? The right reading "Moon" is "overdetermined".

Deborah: Oh, this is more complicated than I ever thought. In high school, I only ever remember reading dialogue, not speech tags and things. I wanted toWait, isn't it we *as* editors that call him this?

Ed: What do you mean?

Deborah: Well, I was wrong a moment ago. Look, the folio has no stage direction here at all. It doesn't say *"Exit Moonshine"*. Why did I even think it did?

> *Dut.* Befhrew my heart, but I pittie the man.
> *Pir.* O wherefore Nature, did'ft thou Lions frame?
> Since Lion vilde hath heere deflour'd my deere:

> Which is : no, no, which was the faireſt Dame
> That liu'd, that lou'd, that lik'd,that look'd with cheere.
> Come teares , confound : Out ſword,and wound
> The pap of *Piramus* :
> I , that left pap, where heart doth hop ;
> Thus dye I, thus, thus,thus.
> Now am I dead, now am I fled, my ſoule is in the sky,
> Tongue loſe thy light, Moone take thy flight,
> Now dye,dye,dye,dye,dye.
>   *Dem.* No Die, but an ace for him ; for he is but one.
>   *Liſ.* Leſſe then an ace man. For he is dead, he is no-
> thing.
>   *Du.* With the helpe of a Surgeon,he might yet reco-
> uer, and proue an Aſſe.
>   *Dut.* How chance Moone-ſhine is gone before?
> *Thisby* comes backe, and findes her Louer.

ED: The folio hasWell, yes. Yes, you have a point. There *is* no stage direction there. At least it has no *textual* basis in the evidence. It is quite another thing to say it lacks *editorial* basis in the evideBut this may not be the best example youwe could chose in an Academic Situation. I have an example that may be clearer. (You'll love it.) Now, Shakespeare assigns this speech to Wall.

>   *Wall.* In this ſame Interlude, it doth befall,
> That I,one *Snowt* (by name) preſent a wall :
> And ſuch a wall,as I vvould haue you thinke,
> That had in it a crannied hole or chinke :
> Through which the Louers, *Piramus* and *Thisbie*
> Did whiſper often, very ſecretly.
> This loame,this rough-caſt ,and this ſtone doth ſhew,
> That I am that ſame Wall ; the truth is ſo.
> And this the cranny is,right and ſiniſter,
> Through which the fearefull Louers are to whiſper.

But Wall isn't a *new* character—playing off the paradigm that Shakespeare set up as a dramatic-personae list, say, but just a role within the play within the play, right? Like Starveling/ Moonshine is one role. So, applying the principles of editing, we keep you from making that fatal mistake, and so *I* say

202

"SNOUT (*as Wall*)", so you'll not be confused as you are in the folio. That he's not Snout but *as* Wall.

> SNOUT (*as Wall*)
>> In this same interlude it doth befall
>> That I, one Snout by name, present a wall;

123   *A Midsummer Night's Dream* 5.1.179

>> And such a wall as I would have you think   155
>> That had in it a crannied hole or chink,
>> Through which the lovers, Pyramus and Thisbe,
>> Did whisper often, very secretly.
>> This loam, this rough-cast, and this stone doth show
>> That I am that same wall; the truth is so.   160
>> And this the cranny is, right and sinister,
>> Through which the fearful lovers are to whisper.

Deborah: But if Snout is *as* Wall, why does "*as* Wall" say his name is "Snout"? Are they both named Snout?

ED: Where's that?

Deborah: So, when he says "I" he is speaking as himself, Snout. So, the speech heading should say—what should it say? It should say "Snout" not *as* Anything; because *as* Wall would never refer to "In this same interlude" because Walls in interludes don't *know* they're on stage. That's the difference between the roles and the audience, which has a higher ironic knowledge. So you could say

> SNOUT (*as Wall as* SNOUT)

—though I could accept

> SNOUT (*as Snout, the Wall*).

ED: Well, no. You see his *name* is Snout, but the wall he is *playing* is not named Snout. It doesn't have a name. That's absurd. Walls aren't animate. What kind of play would Shakespeare be if walls could talk? Renaissance Drama isn't Mr Dress Up! But I can see that we are running into the usual

problems when you don't penetrate into the subject systematically with a rigid system the way I do if you will take my
English 212 or 332 or beyond in graduate study. You've got to
walk before you runtoo much textual imagination will tip you
upI mean it will trip you up. Face it, it's hard to see straight
after you have come out of the labiarynthine twists and turns
ofThose old facsimiles just cause more trouble than they are
worth. It's *unfortunate* since they constitute the evidence, but
that's just the way itThey will wreck you for reading editions,
because you keep remembering them instead of what was
Shakespeare's intent. Best to keep away from them, until
you've mastered the text. Anyway, some of these editorial decisions are not my but *team* decisions. You see how extensive the
text is? Could just one person all byAnd you can't even expect
unanimity at the Board, from an International Team, and
someone has to take the finalI agree with you *here,* though
they are, they have to   It was a *team* decision. I was overruled
on this one.   I see it just the way you do, Gloria.   Gloria, I
wish someone like *you* had been on my Editorial Board with
me. We'd have been Like Minds on the Editorial Board. In a
mutlicultural world of international publishing, a made-in-
Canada Shakespeare isn't totallyBut that's just the way it has
to get on with the job nowadays. But *do* read this earlier
speech by Bottom. I can show it to you in *your* book. Just let
me sit overIt's a gem. OK, OK. It consoles, Gloria. It consoles.
It consoles. You'll see that when an actor is playing someone,
being himself, it's different from someone playing at being an
actor acting someone different in a play (I mean a play *within*
a play). You see the fine line the editor must walk between a
Lion with a man's snout coming out if hisI mean with a man's
face coming out of his neck and between a man with a Lion's
neck around his head on the other hand. It's verry subtle, but
verrry Shakespearian.

> *Snout.* Therefore another Prologue muſt tell he is not
> a Lyon.
>   *Bot.* Nay, you muſt name his name, and halfe his face
> muſt be ſeene through the Lyons necke, and he himſelfe
> muſt ſpeake through, ſaying thus, or to the ſame defect;
> Ladies, or faire Ladies, I would wiſh you, or I would
>   requeſt

> ## 1ʃ2   *A Midʃom*
>
> requeſt you, or I would entreat you, not to feare, not to
> tremble: my life for yours. If you thinke **I** come hither
> as a Lyon, it were pitty of my life. **No**, I am no ſuch
> thing, **I** am a man as other men are ; and there indeed let
> him name his name, and tell him plainly hee is *Snug* the
> ioyner.

(Don't you love it?) I always think of this when some of the editorial decisions prove not *quite* as durable over time as—as, well, as some that do, you can always come back to a *gem* of a speech like this for consolation. This clown is so   well, see for yourself. Read it. Imagine this clown thinking the ladies would be frightened! and that some kind of Prologue has to interfear with the play between the play and the audience. Who needs this kind of mediation it's pathetic. But *funny*?! Our fixing of the speech tags is in all the editions. It's a *system*. It's for your own good. Learn it here, and it'll serve you everywhere, whether you are just an actor, a stage manager, a director, or an author. Or a teacher. Because art is about Order, not Chaos. Except where I've made a radical departure, it's very conservative. It makes the matter of Shakespearan identity absolutely clear to anyone, so they don't have to thinkhave to think of the question of whom someone is at any moment—whether himself, or someone else, or (in the case of Wall, for example) a thing. This is what motivates me as an Editoras a Man, really. In the end, to achieve such *finality*. You should feel free to come to me office during office hours, or any time, Gloria, do us one favour, though? Leave this folio right where you

Debbie: Well, thank you, sir, very much. But couldn't you just help me right now with just this one last question in this one other play I've been reading? It's *King John*. It's one of the history plays? (I know it's not assigned.) I'm confused about this Phili

OLD: Ohhh *that* Bastard!

NOTES

1. Pages 133 to the top of 145 of this essay have been published under the title "'The very names of the Persons': Editing and the Invention of Dramatick Character" in David Scott Kastan and Peter Stallybrass, eds., *Staging the Renaissance: Reinterpretations of Elizabethan and Jacobean Drama*, Routledge, New York and London, 1991, 88–96. The present essay extends work on speech tags begun in my "The Psychopathology of Everyday Art" in G. R. Hibbard, ed., The *Elizabethan Theatre IX, Papers Given at the Ninth International Conference on Elizabethan Theatre held at the University of Waterloo in July 1981*, P. D. Meany Company Inc., Port Credit, Ontario, [1986,] 100–68.

The picture of Mr. Sanders is from *WINNIE-THE-POOH* by A. A. Milne, illustrated by E. H. Shepard. Copyright 1926 by E. P. Dutton, renewed 1954 by A. A. Milne. Used by permission of Dutton Children's Books, a division of Penguin Books USA Inc.

I wish to thank the Fisher Library, University of Toronto for permission to reproduce from their copies of Shakespeare's first folio, of Pope's 1723 and Rowe's 1709 editions of Shakespeare, and of Jonson's *Works*.

I am indebted to the Social Sciences and Humanities Research Council of Canada and to the Gugenheim Foundation for their support during the writing of this essay.

2. D4v.

3. V3r, p. 233.

4. The English and French texts offer slightly different meanings in this matter. In my French text of *En attendant Godot* (*Les Editions de Minuit*, no place, no date: a paperback edition in which the last numbered page is 163) the *dramatis personae* list stipulates "Un jeune garçon . . . . . .Serge LECOINTE" (from the original Roger Blin production), p. [7]; his entry in the second act reads "*Entre à droite le garçon de la veille.*", p. 157. The corresponding direction of Beckett's English version (Grove Press, New York, 1954) says merely "Enter Boy right.", and thus does not define him as *yesterday's* Boy (even if the same actor should play the Boy role in Act II as played the Boy role in Act I). The English text of the direction is thus more consonant with the ambiguity of the dialogue (in either language) than is that of the French version. In other words, the French direction *interprets* the dialogue, whereas in the English version the direction and the dialogue participate in the same mystery.

What's the Bastard's Name? Random Cloud.

5. The play was published without the author's name in London, 1889.
6. My English text is in *Three Tragedies: Blood Wedding, Yerma, Bernard Alba*, James Graham-Lujan and Richard L. O'Connell, trans., New Directions, New York, 1941. My Spanish text is Mario Hernández, ed., *Bodas de Sangre*, Madrid, 1984.
I am indebted to Prof. Ermineo Neglia, Erindale College, University of Toronto, and Dr. Clive Griffin, Trinity College, Oxford University for their helpful comments on my Lorca research.
7. An example of such editing can be found in Michael Dewell and Carmen Zapata, trans., *The Rural Trilogy: Blood Wedding, Yerma, The House of Bernarda Alba*, Bantam Books, Toronto and New York, 1987. They reduce the name in the "Cast of Characters" to "BEGGAR WOMAN"; "*A very old* BEGGAR WOMAN" is directed to enter; and the tag reads "BEGGAR WOMAN". Stupidly, however, the phrase *"The character does not appear on the cast list."* is not struck, though it is now a flat contradiction.
In a University of Manchester Press Spanish text with English preliminaries published in 1980, editor Herbert Ramsden argues that "there are a few apparent minor errors . . . caused by the author or by a printer or publisher. Thus Beggar Death, we are told, 'no figura en el reparto'—a nice reminder that for Lorca death is present even when it is not named—but Beggar Death does appear in the cast-list" (xlv). Ramsden misses the point that it is irrelevant whether his own creation "Beggar Death" figures in the reparto; the matter is whether Lorca's "una anciana" whom he tagged "MENDIGA" figures there. It is the *Personajes* alone among these three points in the text that refers to Death, and its mention of a beggar is not to *name* the role, but to characterize it parenthetically.
8. *En España con Federico García Lorca: Paginas de un Diario Intimo*, 1928–1936, Madrid, 1958, 333.
For details of production see Hernández, *op. cit.*; and Ian Gibson, *Federico Garcia Lorca: A Life*, London, 1989, 347–48, 363–69.
9. Marguerite Duras, *Hiroshima mon amour* (scénario et dialogues), 94. My copy is a 1967 printing; the copyright is dated 1960. It has 140 numbered pages and includes photographic illustrations. (All the page numbers in parenthesis in the body are from this edition.)
The second of my Gallimard editions is from its paperback *Collection Folio*; it has 155 numbered pages and is unillustrated. My two

English translations are by Richard Seaver. One is published along with *Une aussi longue absence* by Calder and Boyars, London, seemingly in 1966. The other, truncated, version is included in the fifth edition of *The Norton Introduction to Literature*, eds. Carl E. Bain, *et al.*, New York, without date.

10. Calder and Boyars, London, 1971.
11. My copy of Robert M. Adams, ed., *Ben Jonson's Plays and Masques: Texts of the Plays and Masques; Jonson on his Work; Contemporary Readers on Jonson; Criticism* is the first edition, published in New York, London and Toronto, 1979. Why "Robert" is not "Bob", or "Ben" "Beniamin" (as he *is* called on the titlepage of the early editions) is anybody's guess.
12. L. A. Beaurline, ed., The Regents Renaissance Drama Series, University of Nebraska Press, 1965, xxii.
13. The Mermaid Series, Vol. 3, Brinsley Nicholson and C. H. Hereford, eds., Woking and London: The Gresham Press, Unwin Brothers, Ltd., [1903], 148.
14. "Foul Papers, Compositor B, and the Speech-Prefixes of *All's Well That Ends Well*".
15. Irving's marked-up copy is an undated edition, *King John. A Play in Five Acts* published by Thomas Hailes Lacy. The dramatis-personae list identifies this role comprehensively as Philip Faulconbridge, Robert's half-brother, bastard, afterwards Sir Richard, and son to King Richard I. This edition is not listed in Charles Shattuck, *The Shakespeare Promptbooks*, University of Illinois Press, Urbana and London, 1965. The illustration is from the collections of The Theatre Museum. By courtesy of the Victoria and Albert Museum. The call number is "Promptbook collection S500–1982".
16. Garrick's partbook (Shattuck promptbook # 2, dated Feb. 20, 1745) is reproduced by permission of the Folger Shakespeare Library (W. a. 172—note that Shattuck's shelfmark is wrong). In this ms every other recto is numbered at the top in the gutter. This photo is of the recto between 6 and 7.
17. The photos from *King John* (Shattuck promptbook #3) are reproduced by permission of the Folger Shakespeare Library. Shattuck tentatively assigns this promptbook to one of the Powells at Drury Lane. William Powell played King John in 1766 and his brother John played Pandulph in 1800.
18. The photos from the Smock Alley, Dublin promptbook of *A Midsummer Night's Dream* (Shattuck promptbook # 1) are re-

produced by permission of Edinburgh University Library (call number: promptbook JY 441).
19. The modern text of *A Midsummer Night's Dream* photoquoted on this and the following pages is R. A. Foakes' New Cambridge Shakespeare edition, Cambridge, 1984.

Index of Playwrights and Plays

Index of Critics and Editors

(Boldface page numbers indicate complete articles)

Index

Harari, Josue, 16
Henry, Aurelia, 165
Herford, C.H., 165–66
Hill, W. Speed, 42
Hinman, Charlton, 74
Honigmann, Ernst, 46, 51–56, 58, 65, 68
Howard-Hill, T.H., xxii, xxiii
Hudson, Henry, 70
Humphreys, A.F., xviii
Hunter, G.K., 94

Irving Henry, 178

Johnson, Samuel, 75, 136
Jones, Emrys, 58–59
Jowett, John, 57, 59, 69, 75, 95

Keightley, Thomas, 79
Kennedy, R.F., xxiv
Knight, C.A., 70, 75

LONG, W.B., xii, xvi, xxi, **21–44**, 62–63, 69
Lower, C.B., 58

Malone, Edmund, 70
Matchett, William, 46, 52
McKerrow, R.B., xi–xvi, xxii, 1–9, 11–15, 17–19, 21–22, 26–32, 37, 41, 62–63, 177
MCLEOD, RANDALL, xii, xv, xxi, 42, 118, **133–209**
McMillin, Scott, 118
Melchiori, Giorgio, 62–65, 68, 77
Moon, Gloria, 196
Mulryne, J.R., 62
Murry, John M., 65, 81, 82

Patrick, D.L., 102

Pope, Alexander, xxi, 134–43
Prosser, Eleanor, 77, 80
PROUDFOOT, RICHARD, xvi, xvii, xx, xxi, **121–31**

Reid, S.W., xxiii
Rossiter, A.P., 78
Rowe, Nicholas, 139, 141
Sanders, Wilbur, 64, 70–71, 82–83
Saunders, Claire, 118
Simpson, Percy, 43, 165–66
Sisson, C.J., 76, 79
Smallwood, Robert, 46, 52
Sprague, A.C., 59

Theobald, Lewis, 75
THOMAS, SIDNEY, xiv, xv, xvi, xxi, **17–20**
Turner, Robert Kean, xxiv

URKOWITZ, STEVEN, xix, xxiv, **101–20**

Warburton, William, 65, 75, 76, 78, 81
Warren, Michael, xxiv, 64
WERSTINE, PAUL, xii, xiv, xvii, xx, xxii, xxiii, xxiv, **11–16**, 77, 118
White, R.A., 70
WILLIAMS, G.W., **xi–xxiv**, 62, 84, 169
Wilson, J.D., 34, 45–46, 51, 54, 59, 75
Wright, W.A., 50

Zitner, S.P., 95